BARBARA OSHENSKA

Transformative Inner Child Healing

A Holistic Guide to

Releasing Trauma

Reprogramming Patterns &

Embodying Your Authentic Self

Cerulean Harbor Publishing

Copyright © 2025 by Barbara Oshenska

All rights reserved.

The content contained within this book may not be reproduced, duplicated or transmitted without direct written permission from the author or the publisher.

Under no circumstances will any blame or legal responsibility be held against the publisher or author for any damages, reparation, or monetary loss due to the information contained within this book, either directly or indirectly.

Legal Notice:

This book is copyright-protected. It is only for personal use. You cannot amend, distribute, sell, use, quote or paraphrase any part of the content within this book without the consent of the author or publisher.

Disclaimer Notice:

Please note the information contained within this document is for educational and entertainment purposes only. All effort has been executed to present accurate, up-to-date, reliable, and complete information. No warranties of any kind are declared or implied. Readers acknowledge that the author is not engaged in the rendering of legal, financial, medical or professional advice. The content within this book has been derived from various sources. Please consult a licensed professional before attempting any techniques outlined in this book.

By reading this document, the reader agrees that under no circumstances is the author responsible for any losses, direct or indirect, that are incurred as a result of the use of the information contained within this document, including, but not limited to, errors, omissions, or inaccuracies.

Contents

A Personal Request from the Author	VI
Introduction	VII
1. Understand Your Childhood	1
How Early Experiences Shape Our Lives	
How a Child Experiences Life	
Universal Emotional Wounds	
What Counts as Trauma	
Interactive Element	
2. The Inner Child	49
How Unhealed Wounds Affect Adult Choices	
Defining the Inner Child	
Myths About the Inner Child	
The Wounded Inner Child in Adulthood	
Emotional Reactivity and Triggers	
The Main Steps of Inner Child Work	
Interactive Element	
3. Creating Patterns	89
How Our Inner Child Shapes Repeated Patterns	
Fear-Based Patterns	
Patterns in Self-Worth	
Patterns in Romantic Relationships	

    Patterns in Everyday Relationships
    The Mindsets That Keep Us Stuck
    Interactive Element

4. Illuminating the Shadows — 139
    Bringing Wounds into the Light
        Why We Need to Make the Unconscious Conscious
        The Dangers of Recreating Old Memories
        Unpacking Your Past—How to Identify What You Don't Want to Repeat
        Identifying and Reprogramming Negative Thoughts
        Interactive Element

5. Emotions as Energy — 165
    Understanding and Transforming Your Inner World
        Building Emotional Awareness
        Managing Emotions
        Transforming Negative Emotions
        Cultivating Emotional Resilience
        Embracing Positive Emotions
        Interactive Element

6. Sacred Alignment — 199
    Integrating the Mind, Body, Spirit, and Heart
        The Physical Body and Emotional Memory
        The Spirit and Its Relationship to the Mental, Emotional, and Physical Bodies
        How the Chakra System Connects These Bodies
        Combining Therapeutic Approaches
        Interactive Element

7. Heal and Release — 237

    Alchemizing the Past Through Forgiveness
        Reparenting Yourself
        Understanding the Impact of Unforgiveness
        Interactive Element

8. Integration and Embodiment   261
    The Compass to Continued Healing
        Recognizing When Old Patterns Resurface
        Breaking Free from Cycles That No Longer Serve You
        Cultivating Self-Trust and Inner Guidance
        Nurturing Growth Through Conscious Daily Practices
        Staying Committed to Your Healing in the Long Run
        Interactive Element

Final Thoughts   285

Thank You & A Special Request   288

References   289
    References

About the Author   301

A Personal Request from the Author

Dear Reader,

Before you dive into this journey of healing and self-discovery, I want to take a moment to share something from my heart. Writing this book was not just an act of creativity—it was a labor of love, written with the hope that it would reach those who need it most.

If this book resonates with you, if it offers even a single insight that helps you along your healing path, I have a small but deeply meaningful request: **please consider leaving a review.**

Reviews are more than just feedback. They are the lifeblood of books like this, especially for an independent author like me. They help others—those who are searching, those who are struggling, those who may feel lost—discover this message and begin their own journey toward healing.

Your words, whether a few sentences or a thoughtful reflection, have the power to guide someone else toward the very book they might need. And for that, I would be profoundly grateful.

With love and gratitude,

Barbara Oshenska

Introduction

I've spent weeks wondering how to begin this book. The answer came not through forceful searching but in a quiet moment on my patio, coffee in one hand, pen and journal in the other. A single line emerged from the stillness:

Dear Inner Child,

I stared at those three simple words, feeling a surge of emotions rise within me. Memories poured in—snapshots of a simpler time when joy and wonder were constants, when the world felt like an endless playground of possibilities.

But life grew more complicated. Responsibilities, expectations, and societal norms started to shape and mold me into someone I no longer recognized. The carefree spirit of my inner child slowly faded away, buried beneath layers of self-doubt, fear, and insecurities. The world had taught me to conform, to suppress my true self, and to forget the dreams and desires that once burned brightly within me.

That quiet morning, however, something shifted. I made a choice: to reconnect with that part of myself, to heal the wounds of the past, and to reclaim the joy and authenticity that had been buried. It wasn't just a sentimental decision—it was transformative.

In embarking on this journey of inner child healing, I discovered that it is not just about revisiting the past or dwelling on painful memories. It is about uncovering the layers of conditioning and beliefs that have shaped our lives and learning to embrace our true selves with love and compassion.

Inner child healing is a holistic process that involves nurturing the wounded parts of ourselves, re-parenting our inner child, and integrating all aspects of who we are. It requires us to delve deep into our subconscious, to confront our fears and traumas, and to release the emotional baggage that has burdened us for far too long.

But this journey is not without its challenges. It requires courage, vulnerability, and a willingness to face the darkest corners of our souls. It demands that we confront our own shadows, acknowledge our pain, and take responsibility for our healing. It is not a quick fix or a magical solution but rather a lifelong commitment to ourselves and our well-being.

Deep within our hearts, a flame of longing flickers, urging us to seek emotional liberation, self-awareness, self-love, and acceptance. It is a journey akin to shedding old skin, like a caterpillar transforming into a vibrant butterfly, emerging from the cocoon of past wounds and traumas. Embarking on this transformative path of holistic inner child healing will allow us to unravel the layers of our being, peeling back the veil of self-awareness. It is a process similar to gazing into a mirror, where

INTRODUCTION

we confront our true selves, embracing the cracks and imperfections that make us beautifully human.

Now as I write this book, my intention is to guide you through the intricate labyrinth of inner child healing. I will share with you the tools, techniques, and insights that have helped me on my own journey in the hope that they may serve as signposts along your path. Ultimately, it is up to you to embark on this journey and to do the inner work required for healing and transformation.

So, take that leap of faith with me. Let us jump into the depths of our soul, reconnect with our inner child, and embrace the healing journey that awaits us. Together, let us embark on a transformative adventure that will awaken our spirits, ignite our passions, and lead us back home to ourselves.

But before we embark on this truly transformative and empowering journey, take a moment to grab a pen and a piece of paper. Allow yourself to connect with the tenderest depths of your being and unapologetically pour onto the page those words that your inner child has been yearning to hear all along. Remember, this isn't about crafting a perfect masterpiece; it's about embracing your truth and opening up the floodgates of self-love. So, go ahead and let your heart speak. I'll go first:

Dear Inner Child...

You are a radiant force of nature, an exquisite being who has always been and will forever be worthy of love, acceptance, and celebration. Your presence alone is a gift, overflowing with immeasurable significance. Nothing about you is flawed or lacking.

You radiate a unique essence enriched with boundless potential and breathtaking beauty. Within you resides a resilient spirit, capable of triumphing through any adversity that may cross your path.

Embrace your innate strength, for it is the very fabric that weaves the glorious tapestry of your existence. Trust in your capabilities, your dreams, and your wonderfully complex nature. Your light shines bright, effortlessly illuminating even the darkest of times. Accept the profound truth that you are deserving of happiness, joy, and fulfillment.

Never allow doubts or external voices to dull your inner light or question your incomparable worth. Embrace your imperfections for they are the precious jewels of authenticity. From this moment forward, hold space in your heart for self-compassion, self-care, and unyielding self-belief. Embrace the adventure ahead, knowing that you are your own greatest ally, protector, and champion. You are deserving of a love so mighty, it ignites the galaxies within you and sets your soul ablaze with infinite passion. So, my dear inner child, keep spreading your wings, soaring through life's magnificent tapestry, and always remember that you are loved, cherished, and whole just as you are.

And as I set the pen down, I breathe. I remember the power of release.

This is where healing begins—with a single step, a single word, a single breath.

Let's take this journey together.

Chapter One

Understand Your Childhood

How Early Experiences Shape Our Lives

There is always one moment in childhood when the door opens and lets the future in. –Graham Greene

The profound words by Graham Greene encapsulate the essence of our existence, acknowledging that our childhood experiences are what shape our adulthood. It underscores the principle that to navigate the maze of our present, we must first understand our past.

Childhood is a delicate phase of development that lays the foundation for our beliefs, values, attitudes, and overall worldview. It's where we first encounter joy, love, fear, disappointment, and a myriad of other emotions. Our experiences during this period are akin to the first brush strokes on a blank canvas. They are the initial impressions that ultimately form the intricate painting of our lives. Learning to relate to and understand those early life experiences is like unraveling the threads of our personal tapestry. It's about revisiting, not with the intention to dwell on the past, but to illuminate the factors that have shaped our identity; it's carefully excavating an ancient site, uncovering artifacts that hold the key to understanding a bygone era.

You see, the experiences that we encounter, both positive and negative, leave indelible marks on our psyche. They influence our self-perception, our relationships, our decision-making, and our response to life's challenges. As adults, we often find ourselves reacting in ways that seem irrational or self-sabotaging. These behaviors often stem from unresolved emotions or unprocessed experiences from our past.

The journey to understand your childhood is a vital step toward healing your inner child in a holistic manner. The "inner child" is a metaphorical representation of the childlike aspects of a person's psyche, encapsulating the capacity for innocence, wonder, joy, vulnerability, and playfulness, but it also carries the scars of childhood wounds, traumas, and disappointments.

Revisiting these challenging places helps us gain insight into why we behave the way we do. We begin to comprehend the root causes of our fears, insecurities, and emotional triggers. This understanding is a powerful tool for self-transformation. It empowers the process of release, drives healing, and cultivates healthier ways of being.

In the same way that a broken bone needs to be reset to heal correctly, we must realign our skewed childhood narratives to foster a healthier emotional and psychological state. It is about acknowledging the past, understanding its impact, and choosing to rewrite our story from a place of strength and resilience.

These words by Graham Greene remind us that every moment in our childhood had a role in shaping our future. By understanding our past, we can better navigate our present and steer our future toward a more fulfilling, authentic life. It's through this understanding that we can truly begin the process of healing our inner child, ultimately leading to a healthier, happier, and more balanced adulthood.

Time for a bit of storytelling. I want us to read the following stories, stories that will shed light on the importance of understanding the things that happen to us in childhood.

Lily's Story

In a small town nestled among rolling hills, there lived a young girl named Lily. She had curly brown hair that danced in the wind and eyes that sparkled like the stars. Lily's world was filled with laughter, love, and the comforting presence of her beloved grandmother, Grandma Rose.

One sunny day, as Lily skipped home from school, her heart felt light with excitement. She couldn't wait to share her day's adventures with Grandma Rose. But as she opened the front door, a heavy silence enveloped her. The house felt empty, devoid of Grandma Rose's warm embrace.

Confusion and worry clouded her young mind. Where was Grandma Rose? Why wasn't she there to greet her? Her heart raced as she searched every room, hoping to find her grandmother's familiar smile. But all she found were memories etched in every corner of the house.

Days turned into weeks, and Lily's world became a labyrinth of unanswered questions. The adults whispered words like "illness" and "passed away," but she struggled to grasp their meaning. She yearned for Grandma Rose's comforting presence, her gentle words of wisdom that always made everything better.

In the midst of her grief, she found solace in her imagination. She would sit by the window, gazing at the clouds, and imagine Grandma Rose's face among them, smiling down at her. She would recount their cherished moments together, the laughter, the stories, and the love they shared.

But as Lily grew older, the absence of Grandma Rose weighed heavily on her heart. She longed for guidance, for the wisdom only a grandmother could impart. She wondered how different her life would be if Grandma Rose were still by her side.

This story can end in a couple of ways.

Ending One: A Blossoming Legacy of Love

Within the depths of her sorrow, Lily navigated the labyrinth of grief and discovered a newfound strength, a transformative power within her own heart. She realized that the love and lessons Grandma Rose had bestowed upon her were forever ingrained in her heart. She carried Grandma Rose's spirit within her, guiding her through life's challenges.

Lily turned her pain into purpose, channeling the wisdom Grandma Rose imparted into every aspect of her adulthood. She learned to honor her grandmother's memory by embracing life with resilience and compassion. She vowed to spread kindness, just as Grandma Rose had taught her. And though the pain of loss would always linger, Lily found solace in knowing that love transcends time and space.

As the years passed, and fueled by the strength of healed sorrow, Lily forged deep connections with others, sharing the warmth and laughter Grandma Rose once gifted her. She became a beacon of light for others who had experienced loss. She shared her story, offering comfort and understanding to those who felt lost in their own grief. Through her words, she reminded them that they were not alone, and that healing was possible.

And so, Lily's adulthood was a testament to the resilience of the human spirit, her life a beautiful tapestry woven with the threads of love, wisdom, and the enduring legacy of Grandma Rose. In her heart, she knew that even though the door to her childhood had closed, the lessons learned, and the memories cherished would forever shape the person she had become.

Here's what I want you to take away from this: If Lily had suppressed her emotions and neglected to process her grief, the impact on her adulthood would have been profound. Unresolved grief can manifest in various ways, affecting your emotional well-being, relationships, and overall life satisfaction, which leads us to...

Ending Two: Shadows of Unprocessed Grief

In the other realm of possibility, Lily found herself ensnared in the shadows of unprocessed grief. The weight of Grandma Rose's absence became an anchor, dragging her into a sea of sorrow that seemed insurmountable. At the bottom of this sea, Lily did not become a beacon of empathy and light for others. Instead, unable to reconcile with her loss, Lily's adulthood unfolded as a series of missed connections and fractured relationships.

She struggled to trust and open up to people, fearing the pain of potential loss. This drove Lily deeper into the belly of isolation, breeding a sense of detachment from others, which prevented her from experiencing the deep connections and support that relationships can offer.

As the years passed, Lily began to internalize her grandmother's death, harboring guilt for not being able to prevent it. These negative beliefs started to undermine her confidence and prevented her from fully embracing her own potential and pursuing her dreams. At times, rather than criticizing herself, Lily would carry resentment toward the world for taking her grandmother away. This led Lily to a pessimistic outlook on life, hindering her ability to find joy and appreciate the present moment.

Haunted by the ghost of unhealed wounds, Lily struggled to find joy in life. The laughter that once echoed in her childhood home became a distant memory, drowned out by the echoes of unanswered questions and unspoken words. The absence of Grandma Rose's guidance left Lily adrift, unable to tap into the well of strength she so desperately needed.

In this version of the story, Lily's adulthood became a poignant reminder of the importance of confronting grief and finding healing. Without addressing her loss, Lily carried that heavy emotional burden throughout her life, hindering her personal growth, relationships, and overall happiness. The consequences of unprocessed grief can be far-reaching and deeply impactful. It serves as a gentle urging for all of us to embrace the pain, navigate the labyrinth of loss, and emerge on the other side with hearts open to the transformative power of healing.

Alex's Story

This is a story about a boy named Alex. With his bright blue eyes and a mischievous grin, he was full of curiosity and wonder. But beneath his cheerful exterior, he carried the weight of a painful secret.

Every day, as he walked to school, his heart would sink with a heavy thud. The schoolyard felt like a battlefield where the bullies lurked, ready to strike. Their hurtful words pierced his fragile heart, leaving him feeling small and invisible. When they called him names and made fun of his glasses, it felt like a punch to the gut. Alex tried to brush it off, to pretend it didn't bother him, but deep down, it hurt more than words could express. He wondered why he was the target of such cruelty, why they couldn't see the pain they were causing.

The bullies' words echoed in his mind, chipping away at his self-esteem. Alex started to question his worth, wondering if there was something inherently wrong with him. He felt like an outsider, longing to fit in but feeling like he would never belong.

As the days turned into weeks, his spirit grew weary. He became quieter, more withdrawn, afraid to show his true self for fear of further ridicule. The vibrant and curious boy he once was seemed to fade away, replaced by a shadow of his former self.

Again, this story can have some alternative endings.

Ending One: A Phoenix Rising from Adversity

One day, as Alex sat alone in the schoolyard, a classmate named Maya approached him. Maya had a gentle smile and kind eyes that seemed to understand his pain. She sat beside him and shared her own experiences of being bullied, assuring him that he was not alone.

In that moment, Alex felt a glimmer of hope. Maya's words touched his wounded heart, reminding him that he wasn't the only one facing this battle. Her empathy and understanding gave him the strength to believe in himself again. With Maya's support, Alex found the courage to confide in his parents. As he poured out his heart, their love and support wrapped around him like a warm embrace. They listened attentively, validating his feelings and assuring him that he was not to blame.

Supported by a network of an understanding friend and a loving family, Alex blossomed into a resilient and self-assured adult. The scars of his past, though still present, became a testament to his strength rather than sources of shame. Embracing his uniqueness, he channeled the pain into empathy, becoming a fierce advocate against bullying. Alex's adulthood was marked by confidence, meaningful connections, and a determination to stand tall in the face of adversity, proving that wounds can transform into sources of strength.

In this ending, Alex did not allow the bullies' words to define him. He discovered that his worth was not determined by their hurtful comments. With each passing day, he was able to grow stronger, more resilient, and more determined to create a better world. Without any of that support, Alex's story may have ended differently.

Ending Two: *Shadows of Unhealed Wounds*

In the alternate trajectory, Alex's cries for help went unheard, and the shadows of his past continued to cast a long, dark pall over his adulthood. Without the support he desperately needed, he carried the weight of unprocessed emotions into his later years.

As an adult, Alex struggled to form healthy relationships, as his negative beliefs about himself made it difficult for him to trust and connect with others. The vibrant spark that once defined him flickered, subdued by the lingering pain of his past. Without the tools to process his emotions, he found himself stuck in a cycle of self-doubt and isolation.

These waves of self-doubt and isolation led to an ocean of anxiety and depression within Alex, significantly impacting his ability to work and socialize. Under the pressure of trying to engage in everyday activities, Alex resorts to self-destructive behaviors, as a way of coping with his pain and feelings of inadequacy.

Haunted by the echoes of the bullies' hurtful words, the scars of his childhood remained raw, affecting his relationships, self-esteem, and overall well-being. This ending is a powerful reminder of the profound impact that support, understanding, and inner healing can have on a child's life. It underscores the importance of addressing the processing the emotional wounds inflicted in youth to pave the way for a healthier, more resilient adulthood.

How a Child Experiences Life

Life is a mosaic of experiences, and with each stage, a new vibrant tile is added, contributing to the beautiful, ever-evolving pattern. From the moment we first breathe, we embark on a remarkable journey of growth, discovery, and transformation.

In the early years of infancy, the world is, simply put, a big, mysterious place. We rely on our caregivers for everything, from nourishment to comfort. Our needs are as basic as the beat of our tiny hearts—a warm embrace, a soothing voice, and a tender touch. Like a delicate flower, we bloom under the nurturing care of our parents, our innocent eyes wide with wonder at the world unfolding before us.

As toddlers, we turn into little explorers, with our curiosity being ignited like a spark in the night. We toddle and stumble, chubby hands reaching out to touch, taste, and experience everything within reach. Our needs expand beyond the physical—we crave a sense of independence, a chance to assert our budding identities. We yearn for patient guidance, a gentle hand to hold as we navigate the vast landscape of our newfound abilities.

Then comes early childhood, when our imaginations take flight. We transform into pirates, princesses, and superheroes, minds painting vivid worlds where anything is possible. We seek companionship, forging friendships that are as strong as the roots of an ancient tree. Needs start to extend beyond the immediate; this is where we yearn for nurturing environments, where creativity can flourish, where dreams can take shape, and our hearts can find solace in the warmth of acceptance.

Middle childhood brings with it a sense of wonder and a thirst for knowledge. Children become explorers of the mind, our curiosity leading us down winding paths of discovery. We seek meaning, grappling with questions that dance on the tip of our tongues. Our needs transcend the tangible—we yearn for a supportive community where our ideas are valued, our passions are nurtured, and our voices are heard.

Then comes adolescence. Like a butterfly emerging from its chrysalis, we spread our wings and soar into the vast expanse of adulthood. We seek independence, our spirits craving freedom like a wild stallion yearning for the open plains. This is the stage where we learn how to navigate the stormy seas of emotions and forge our identities. Our needs at this point in life encompass emotional support, guidance in decision-making, opportunities for self-expression, and a sense of purpose that lights the path ahead of us.

In each stage, our needs evolve; these needs mirror the growth of a sapling into a mighty oak. From the tender care of infancy to the blossoming independence of adolescence, the journey of childhood truly is a symphony of experiences, each note playing a vital role in shaping the melody of life.

Emotional Development

Emotional development in childhood is a fascinating journey that shapes how we understand and express our feelings. From the earliest stages of infancy to the complexities of adolescence, they play a very big role in how we relate to ourselves and the world around us.

In infancy, it starts with the foundation of trust and attachment. As babies, we essentially rely on our caregivers to meet our needs, and through consistent and responsive care, it is how we develop a sense of security and learn to trust the world around us. This early emotional connection is what lays the groundwork for healthy emotional development in the years to come.

As we enter our early childhood years, our emotional experiences become more nuanced. It's the period in time where we learn to identify with and put a label on basic emotions such as happiness, sadness, anger, and fear. We learn to express feelings through words, gestures, and facial expressions. This stage is marked by a growing understanding of empathy and the ability to recognize and respond to the emotions of others.

Middle childhood takes things to a whole new level. It is when we become more aware of our own emotions and those of our peers. We start to understand the complex interplay of emotions and how they influence behavior and relationships. This is the stage where emotional regulation skills start to form, as we learn to manage and cope with a wider range of emotions.

During adolescence, our emotional development reaches its peak of intensity. We experience a surge of hormones and undergo significant cognitive and social changes. We grapple with a rollercoaster of emotions, from the exhilaration of newfound independence to the depths of self-doubt and identity exploration. This stage is marked by the development of emotional resilience and the ability to navigate the complexities of relationships and self-expression.

So, we've taken a look at and discussed the whole process of emotional development, but how exactly do our childhood experiences impact this? Well, there's a whole myriad of factors, including the quality of relationships, the environment, and the experiences we encounter.

Positive and nurturing early childhood experiences lay a strong foundation for healthy emotional development. When we are raised in love, nurtured in love, and receive it regularly, with responsive care, we learn to trust, we form secure attachments, and we develop a positive sense of self. These experiences provide a safe space for emotional exploration and expression, fostering emotional intelligence and a more resilient state of being.

On the other hand, negative or challenging experiences can have a lasting impact on us. Traumatic events, neglect, or inconsistent caregiving can disrupt the formation of secure attachments and hinder emotional regulation skills. We grow into the kind of adults who struggle with emotional dysregulation, difficulty in forming healthy relationships, and challenges in understanding, relating to, and expressing our emotions.

Cognitive Development

Cognitive development refers to how our thinking and understanding of the world evolve as we grow and mature. Like a baby learns to crawl before walking, our cognitive abilities also develop in stages during childhood.

Have you ever seen a baby playing with a toy and trying to grab it? At this stage, their cognitive development focuses on simple actions and sensory experiences. They learn through trial and error, like realizing that shaking a rattle produces sound. These early experiences are what help them grasp the whole concept of cause-and-effect relationships. As they progress into the toddler stage, their cognitive skills become more advanced. They start exploring the world around them and asking endless questions like, "Why is the sky blue?" They begin to use their imagination and engage in pretend play, which helps them develop problem-solving skills and creativity.

Now, let's jump to the preschool years. Picture this: a group of four-year-olds building a tower with blocks. One child tries to put a big block on top of a small one, but it keeps falling. Through trial and error, they learn that the big block provides a more stable base. This trial-and-error process is called *scaffolding*, where children gradually acquire new skills by building upon what they already know. As they enter elementary school, their cognitive abilities become more logical and systematic. They start to understand concepts like time, numbers, and cause and effect in a more structured way. For example, they can solve simple math problems and understand that if they don't finish their homework, they might get a lower grade.

No two children grow up in the same manner, which is widely why they grow up to have different viewpoints of the world; why they all learn to engage differently with the world around them. If one child grows up in a household with stimulating toys, books, and engaging conversations, while another has limited access to such resources, the first will likely have more opportunities for cognitive growth because they are exposed to a rich environment that encourages learning and exploration, while the other one may face challenges in their cognitive development due to a lack of stimulating experiences. It's like having a garden without water or sunlight. Early childhood experiences, such as interactions with caregivers, exposure to books, and access to educational toys, play a crucial role in shaping a child's cognitive abilities.

You may be reading all of this and asking yourself, but where does this all come into play in inner-child healing?

Well, when it comes to inner child healing, cognitive and emotional development intersect in several ways. Firstly, cognitive distortions or negative thought patterns that develop during childhood can impact our emotional well-being in adulthood. By identifying and challenging these distorted thoughts, we can reframe them and promote emotional healing.

Also, understanding cognitive and emotional development helps us recognize and validate the emotions that arise during the healing process. We can acknowledge and process the pain, anger, or sadness that our inner child may be experiencing, allowing for healing and growth.

It's all about the bigger picture, like building a puzzle. As we dive deeper into these various elements of childhood, we'll learn to match the pieces that belong with one another so that we can become our most integrated selves.

Negative Experiences in Childhood

Some form of stress or negative experience in childhood is inevitable. Childhood is often associated with carefree days, innocence, and joyful memories. But in reality, even the happiest of childhoods can harbor unseen wounds that impact us at a later stage in life. That is a truth that we may not always be ready to acknowledge. What we should remember when looking at this is that it is not about the event itself but the person's individual experience of it that determines the level of impact—this cannot be decided by anyone but the person experiencing it.

Example 1: The Unbearable Weight of Lofty Expectations

Consider a child growing up in a loving and nurturing household. The parents are there, present and deeply invested in their future success. While the parents' intentions are pure, aiming to provide the best opportunities for their child, their high expectations and relentless pressure can inadvertently lead to emotional distress and trauma.

The child may feel suffocated and constantly feel the weight of their parents' expectations bearing down on them. They might fear disappointing their parents, leading to a persistent sense of inadequacy and anxiety. The child's individual experience of this seemingly positive upbringing can shape their self-esteem, self-worth, and overall well-being well into adulthood, which will manifest in various ways. It might show up as perfectionistic tendencies, a constant striving for unattainable standards. Or there might be a struggle with chronic self-doubt, fearing failure and avoiding risks altogether. These patterns can persist, influencing personal relationships, career choices, and overall life satisfaction.

Example 2: The Silent Pain of Neglect

Here's another example that illustrates how even a seemingly idyllic childhood can conceal the trauma of neglect. In this example, we have a child growing up in a materially comfortable environment, surrounded by possessions and privileges that many could only dream about having. On the surface, everything seems perfect, but behind closed doors, their emotional needs are consistently overlooked or dismissed.

In this scenario, there is a profound sense of loneliness and emotional abandonment that surrounds this child. The absence of nurturing and support can leave lasting scars, impacting their ability to form healthy attachments and trust others in the future. As they grow older, they may struggle with issues such as low self-esteem, difficulties in establishing intimate relationships, and a pervasive sense of emptiness. The effects can also extend far beyond emotional well-being. They may also face challenges in regulating their emotions, resulting in impulsive behavior or difficulty managing stress. This can have far-reaching consequences, affecting academic and professional achievements, as well as overall mental and physical health.

Other Types of Childhood Trauma

Childhood trauma comes in so many overt and subtle experiences. Let's take a look at some other examples and forms of childhood trauma.

- **Physical Abuse.** This involves intentionally having had physical force used against you as a child, resulting in harm or injury. It might have entailed being hit, slapped, kicked, or any form of violent physical contact.

- **Emotional Abuse.** This, unlike physical abuse that leaves scars or results in physical pain, is a kind of abuse that leaves you wounded from within. This type of trauma involves persistent emotional mistreatment that shows up in constant criticism, humiliation, or rejection by caregivers.

- **Sexual Abuse.** This can include molestation, rape, or exposure to inappropriate sexual content. Sexual abuse often leads to long-lasting psychological and emotional consequences.

- **Witnessing Domestic Violence.** When elephants fight, it's the grass that suffers. Growing up in a turbulent environment and constantly witnessing aggression and conflict can cause significant distress and leads to difficulties in forming healthy relationships later in life.

- **Separation or Loss.** The only word that I can think of for this is grief. Traumatic experiences such as the death of a loved one, parental divorce, or forced separation from caregivers can deeply affect your emotional state in childhood. These events lead to feelings of abandonment, grief, and anxiety.

- **Bullying.** Being subjected to repeated physical, verbal, or psychological aggression from peers can be traumatic for children. Bullying is something that happens almost everywhere at school, online (cyberbullying), or within the community, and it often results in feelings of fear, helplessness, and social isolation.

- **Medical Trauma.** Serious medical procedures, hospitalizations, or chronic illnesses can be traumatic as a child. The pain, fear, and uncertainty associated with these experiences can have long-term effects on your emotional well-being and may even impact your views on healthcare.

When it comes to childhood trauma, it's important to recognize that every person is unique and possesses different levels of emotional resilience. The way you reacted as a child to a certain type of situation may not necessarily be how I would have responded to it.

Let's use another example with two brave boys, Eddy and Ben, who both experience the same traumatic event. Eddy, being naturally emotionally resilient, might show remarkable strength in dealing with the trauma. He will be proactive in seeking support from a trusted circle, he will express his emotions openly, and he will gradually find ways to heal and move forward.

On the other hand, Ben, despite experiencing the same trauma, may struggle to cope. He might withdraw, exhibit signs of anxiety or depression, or find it difficult to trust others. These reactions do not imply that he is weak, just that his emotional regulation skills are not on the same level as Eddy's.

Several factors contribute to these differences in resilience. Individual temperament is a huge factor. Some children are naturally more adaptable and have an easier time regulating their emotions, while others may be more sensitive or reactive to stressors. Support is also a big contributing factor as well. Those who have strong relationships with caring adults along with access to mental health resources and a stable environment are more likely to be better at navigating trauma with better outcomes.

Childhood trauma is not something that we should generalize. Approaching it from a place of empathy and of open-mindedness is what allows us to navigate these nuances with care and sensitivity. It's what allows us to show up for ourselves along our own inner-child work journeys with grace and compassion.

As we navigate the intricate landscape of childhood trauma, its impact reveals itself not just in isolated incidents but in the enduring emotional imprints it leaves behind. Transitioning from exploring types of childhood trauma, we now delve into the profound concept of universal emotional wounds. These wounds, rooted in shared human experiences, transcend the individual narratives of trauma. Understanding their pervasive nature offers a transformative perspective on the interconnectedness of our emotional landscapes and paves the way for comprehensive healing strategies.

Universal Emotional Wounds

Healing emotional wounds is something that we have to be prepared to do if we want to prepare for joy's arrival in our lives. The only problem, however, is that we're often not always aware of what those wounds are in the first place. So many of these experiences are universal, affecting people from all walks of life. Whether it's the pain of rejection, the trauma of loss, or the scars of betrayal, emotional wounds can linger and hinder our ability to experience true happiness. Teaching ourselves about these emotions and how they hide behind the façade of "normalcy" is how we start to heal and open ourselves up to the possibility of joy and fulfillment.

Betrayal

There is a certain kind of grief that comes from being betrayed, and it's not about a fleeting sadness but rather a deep-rooted wound that can leave us feeling shattered. It is often like a sharp knife piercing through the fabric of trust, leaving behind a trail of emotional wreckage. It is a metaphorical earthquake that shakes the foundation of our relationships, causing cracks to form in the once-solid ground we stood upon.

In the impressionable years of childhood, betrayal often takes root when the unwavering trust that children place in their caregivers is broken. It could be the parent who promises to show up but doesn't, leaving a child waiting by the window, the hours stretching into a heartbreak that feels infinite. It could be the sibling who whispers a cherished secret to others, turning an innocent moment of connection into a source of shame.

Imagine a child whose truths are doubted or dismissed by those they depend on. Perhaps they see a parent say one thing but do another, teaching them, albeit unintentionally, that trust is fragile, conditional, and easily shattered. These small ruptures accumulate, subtly instructing the child that the world is not as safe as they once believed.

As adults, we carry these early lessons into our relationships. Betrayal in adulthood might feel like déjà vu—a familiar pain echoing from those first breaches of trust, and it can take various forms, each with its own unique sting. It shows up when a friend reveals our secrets, where someone you trust divulges your most intimate confidences to others, leaving you feeling exposed and vulnerable. There is also a betrayal of loyalty, when a close friend or partner turns their back on you in times of need, leaving you feeling abandoned and alone.

It manifests itself in subtle ways as well. It can be the friend who constantly belittles our achievements, undermining our self-confidence. It can be the colleague who steals our ideas and takes credit for our hard work, eroding our sense of fairness and justice. It can even be the family member who manipulates and deceives, causing rifts in the very fabric of our kinship.

Regardless of the form it takes, it leaves a lasting impact on our emotional well-being. It breeds anger, sadness, and distrust, making it difficult to forge new connections and maintain healthy relationships. It takes time to heal, and requires introspection, forgiveness, and a willingness to rebuild trust.

Navigating the profound wound of betrayal can feel like an arduous journey, one that demands gentle introspection and deliberate steps towards healing. It's a path towards reclaiming your capacity for joy, love, and all the goodness life still holds. Here are some exercises to guide you on this transformative journey:

- **Embrace Self-Compassion.** Like a gentle embrace, be kind to yourself, acknowledging the pain and offering forgiveness, allowing healing to begin.

- **Seek Solace in Nature.** Find solace in the gentle rustle of leaves, the soothing rhythm of waves, and the vibrant colors of flowers, allowing nature's beauty to heal your wounded soul.

- **Embrace the Power of Vulnerability.** Like a fragile butterfly emerging from its cocoon, allow yourself to be vulnerable, opening up to trusted loved ones who can provide support and understanding.

- **Nurture Your Inner Child.** Tenderly reconnect with the innocent and joyful parts of yourself, engaging in activities that bring you pure delight, reminding you of the resilience within.

- **Rewrite Your Story of Strength.** With courage as your pen, rewrite your narrative, transforming the pain of betrayal into a tale of resilience, growth, and empowerment, inspiring others on their own healing journeys.

Injustice

Injustice—a single word, yet it stirs up a tempest within us, doesn't it? An emotional wound that seems to be a part of our collective human experience. It's a feeling that comes from being unheard, unseen, or misunderstood. It's feeling like we have been dealt an ugly hand that feels impossibly unfair. It's a shared wound that binds us, even in our deepest solitude.

In our formative moments, when fairness is withheld, we feel our needs and emotions are disregarded, overshadowed by the brilliance of others. It can manifest in the sting of parental favoritism, where one sibling is celebrated while we feel invisible, or in the deepening sense of injustice that arises from arbitrary punishments and inconsistent rules. As a child, our heart can be bruised by the quiet dismissal of our feelings, brushed aside with a harsh "Stop being dramatic," which casts a shadow of self-doubt and diminishes our emotional worth.

This wound deepens in us, as children, when we are held to impossible standards, our worth tethered to unattainable perfection, as if we are forever "never good enough." It swells when we witness the unfairness around us—gender biases, racial inequality, or seeing a parent endure unjust treatment. These moments ignite a quiet rebellion within our souls, a heightened sensitivity to injustice that lingers long after. It takes root when we are silenced or controlled, denied autonomy, leaving us feeling powerless, unheard, and can result in the cultivation of a slow-burning resentment toward authority.

As we reach adulthood, the ride isn't over. The fiery torrent of injustice arises in situations where there's an imbalance of power that can be social, economic, or personal. It shows up in our workspaces when we're overlooked for promotions we've earned or in our communities when the voices of the marginalized are drowned out. It can even make an appearance in our intimate relationships when the scales are tipped too heavily toward one side, leaving the other feeling unheard or unloved. The fear associated with injustice is often rooted in feelings of vulnerability and powerlessness. It's the fear of being perpetually stuck in a state of imbalance, of being forever unheard or unseen.

We also need to discuss the myriad of fears that it breeds within us—the fear of rejection, fear of being marginalized, fear of never being able to change our circumstances. These fears are deeply personal and can often feel insurmountable. They cause us to retreat into ourselves, to build walls around our hearts, to close off from the world in an attempt to protect ourselves. But in doing so, we often inadvertently deepen our wounds, allowing the fear to fester and breed resentment.

In our relationships, it shows up as a feeling of imbalance or unfairness. It causes strain and tension, and, if left unchecked, can sow seeds of discontentment and resentment. When we feel unheard or unappreciated in our relationships, it can lead to feelings of injustice. It can cause us to question our worth and value and can shake the very foundations of our relationships.

As challenging as it can be to navigate its turbulent waters, it's important for us to recognize our feelings as valid. They are a testament to our human capacity for empathy and for recognizing when something is amiss. So, what can we do when confronted with feelings of injustice? How do we put in the necessary work needed so that we can heal this universal emotional wound?

1. **Acknowledgment.** Healing can't happen where there is no awareness. We start by bringing all of these feelings into the light, so that we can see where all the scars reside. We question the systems and beliefs that have perpetuated these feelings of imbalance and start to imagine a world where fairness and equality are the norm.

2. **Begin to Understand the Things that Trigger You.** Take time to understand the kinds of people, situations, and events that trigger you. Are there tough times of the day where the effects of the wound seem to echo loudest? You can even go so far as to keep a journal to keep track of these as a point of reference.

3. **Take Action.** This doesn't necessarily mean grand gestures or radical changes, but rather small, intentional steps toward fairness and balance in our own lives. It could be as simple as speaking up when we feel unheard or standing up for someone who is being marginalized.

4. Lastly, **You Empower—You Teach Yourself—How to Cope with the Feelings of Powerlessness.** And you can do this

by engaging in activities that make you feel most empowered. These are things like talking to friends about the things that are happening, learning a new skill, or even physical exercise.

When there's been injustice against us, it's so easy to feel that there is something wrong with us. But the truth is that it is something that all of us deal with and the more we talk about these hard feelings and difficult experiences, the less alone we'll feel as we navigate our way through them.

Humiliation

I've had many encounters over the years with humiliation, but the single, most profound one happened in the summer of my first year in college. I'd applied for an internship at this company that I'd set my eyes on before I even decided what it was that I wanted to major in. It was an opportunity I had eagerly awaited, envisioning it as a stepping stone toward my bright future. Little did I know it would turn into an experience that would shape my understanding of humiliation and its universal emotional wounds.

As the interview day approached, I arrived at the company with confidence, brimming, dressed in my best professional attire. The moment I stepped through the imposing glass doors, my heart raced with anticipation. The ambiance was a mix of excitement, anxiety, and the scent of success. I had rehearsed answers to potential questions and prepared myself for any situation.

The interview room was nothing less than intimidating. Gleaming with polished wood and artwork adorning the walls, it all seemed like a different world altogether. The panel of interviewers sat at the other end of the long table, composed of intellectuals who seemed to radiate competence and authority. My palms began to sweat, but I made sure to maintain a calm facade.

The interview started, and for the first few minutes, everything seemed to go according to plan. I answered confidently, eloquently expressing my passion and skills. However, as the questions delved deeper into technical knowledge, I felt myself stumbling, my mind drawing blanks. Panic started to creep in, impairing my ability to articulate my thoughts.

In a matter of moments, my eloquence transformed into incoherence. My voice cracked, and my hands trembled. The pride I had felt in my accomplishments gradually turned into embarrassment and humiliation. Each passing second felt like an eternity as I stuttered through my responses, feeling the disappointment in the eyes of the interviewers.

With every rejection that came my way, I had always managed to find a silver lining or a valuable lesson. But this experience was truly humbling. It made me confront the reality that failure can be a part of even the most carefully planned journeys. From that moment on, I realized that humiliation doesn't discriminate; it affects everyone, irrespective of their accomplishments or aspirations.

That fateful internship interview became a catalyst for growth in my life. Instead of letting humiliation consume me, I channeled it into fuel for self-improvement. I delved deeper into my field, honing my skills and determinedly working toward my goals. It taught me that setbacks are an essential part of the learning process and fuel for personal development.

Since that summer, I've faced more encounters with humiliation, but each time, I remind myself that it's a testament to my courage for daring to pursue my dreams. It's in those moments that I find solace in the fact that even amidst humiliation, one can rise stronger than ever before.

So, humiliation? What is it, and what about it makes us feel so small and insignificant?

Well, to start, it is more than just a fleeting feeling of embarrassment; it is a profound emotional wound that reaches deep into the core of our being. It strips away our pride and exposes our vulnerabilities. It comes in to shake the stable foundations of our self-esteem and challenges our sense of self-worth.

When we encounter it, we are confronted with the stark realization that we have fallen short of the expectations placed upon us, whether by ourselves or others. It is an overwhelming sense of inadequacy that engulfs us, like a dark cloud obscuring the light of our accomplishments. We become acutely aware of our flaws, weaknesses, and limitations as if they are magnified to an unbearable degree.

But what is it about it that cuts so deep? It is the way it invades our psyche, gnawing at our confidence and leaving us feeling isolated and exposed. Our self-image becomes shattered, fragments scattered across the landscape of our wounded pride. It erodes the very foundation of our identity, chipping away at the carefully constructed facade we present to the world.

The roots of this wound often begin in the fragile years of childhood, where innocence meets the harsh reality of a world that doesn't always offer kindness or understanding. As a child, our sense of self is fragile, and when exposed to ridicule, rejection, or the sting of failure, it can carve deep into our sense of worth. Humiliation takes root in moments when our efforts, our vulnerabilities, or our very essence were belittled or dismissed. Perhaps it was a scolding in front of others, a moment of failure ridiculed in front of peers, or even being compared unfavorably to others in a way that magnified our perceived flaws. These moments of shame can define our perception of ourselves for years to come, layering over our spirit like invisible scars.

As adults, its effects echo through our thoughts, actions, and interactions. We retreat into ourselves, hiding from the prying eyes of judgment and ridicule. The fear of being seen as less than, as imperfect, becomes a relentless companion, a shadow that follows us wherever we go. Our once-vibrant self-assurance is replaced by a constant need for validation, a desperate attempt to regain the sense of worth that has been stripped away. It stings us with its potent cocktail of shame and powerlessness. We feel diminished—as if our existence has been reduced to a mere whisper in the crowd. It erodes our belief in our abilities, leaving us doubting our own potential. It creates an invisible barrier, separating us from the happiness and success we yearn for, as if we are forever banished to a realm of insignificance.

But amidst the depths of this emotional abyss, there is hope—because in that hollow pit of our humiliation lies an opportunity for growth and resilience. It is through facing our vulnerabilities head-on that we can rise from the ashes, stronger and more empathetic than before. It is through embracing our imperfections that we can truly understand and connect with others who have experienced similar wounds.

Here is a list of a final few things that I want you to remember:

- **Humiliation is Not a Reflection of Your Worth.** It is a temporary emotional experience that does not define who you are as a person. Your inherent value and worth remain unchanged despite any setbacks or moments of embarrassment.

- **It Takes Courage to Face Humiliation.** It takes a wealth of bravery to confront humiliation head-on rather than hiding from it. Your willingness to embrace the discomfort and grow from the experience is a testament to your strength.

- **Humiliation is a Universal Experience.** Understand that everyone, in some form or another, has faced an encounter with it at some point in their lives. You are not alone in this journey, and by sharing your vulnerabilities, you connect with the shared humanity of others.

- **It is an Opportunity for Growth.** See it as an opportunity for personal growth and self-improvement. By reflecting upon the experience and learning from it, you can develop resilience, empathy, and a deeper understanding of yourself and others.

- **True Strength Lies in Vulnerability.** Embrace the vulnerability that comes with humiliation. It is through that nakedness in expressing our emotions that we foster authentic connections, learn humility, and cultivate inner strength.

- **Your Self-Worth Cannot be Defined by External Validation.** Remind yourself that your self-worth should not be reliant on external validation or the opinions of others. Embrace self-acceptance and focus on your own intrinsic value.

- **Humiliation Can be a Humbling Experience that Brings Perspective.** It reminds us of our shared fallibility and teaches us to approach others with empathy and compassion.

- **Failure is a Stepping Stone to Success.** Setbacks and moments of humiliation often pave the way for future success. Embrace the lessons learned from these experiences and use them as stepping stones toward your goals.

- **Humor Can be a Healing Tool.** Allow yourself to find humor in the experience, as laughter can bring relief and help you regain a sense of lightness. Sometimes, laughter can be the best medicine for healing the wounds of humiliation.

- **You Have the Power to Define Your Narrative.** Remember that you have the power to shape your own narrative. Don't let one humiliating moment dictate your entire story. Choose to redefine yourself, focusing on your strengths, resilience, and personal growth.

Abandonment

The abandonment wound says:

- *I constantly worry that other people will leave me.*

- *I had a caregiver who was neglectful, abusive, distant, and inconsistent.*

- *I reject others before they reject me.*

- *I am incredibly sensitive to criticism or negative feedback.*

- *I get easily jealous, even when there is no reason to be.*

- *I stay in relationships, even when I know very well that they aren't healthy for me.*

Abandonment is a silent echo in the chambers of our hearts, a haunting melody that plays on repeat in the background of our existence. It makes an appearance in those situations where we feel left behind, deserted, or discarded. It can be as subtle as a friend not returning a call or text or as shattering as losing a loved one to death. It's the child waiting for a parent to pick them up from school, the teenager unseen in a crowd, the adult left to navigate the choppy waters of life alone.

Its roots often begin in the tender soil of childhood, where seeds of insecurity are sown in moments of neglect, inconsistency, or emotional unavailability. If we had a parent who was physically present but emotionally distant, they might have taught us, as children, to equate love with absence. A caregiver who disappeared without explanation, whether due to work, illness, or personal struggles, could have left us wondering if we were the cause of their departure. Even well-meaning but inconsistent attention—being showered with affection one moment and ignored the next—could create a sense of instability, as if love were conditional and fleeting.

As a child, each unmet need becomes a crack in the foundation of trust, a whisper in our developing hearts that we are not important enough to stay for. We internalize these experiences, often interpreting them as a reflection of our own inadequacy. "If I were better, they wouldn't have left," becomes the quiet refrain of a mind too young to understand the complexities of adult lives. Over time, these moments accumulate, and the wound deepens, shaping the way we connect with others in the future.

The fear that it is associated with is visceral, as if we're free-falling into the abyss of the unknown. It's the fear of being alone, the fear of being unlovable, the fear of not being enough. It's the fear that we'll be left to weather the storm by ourselves, unsheltered, unprotected, unanchored. In our relationships, it wears multiple disguises. It's the clinginess we can't seem to shake off, the walls we build to protect ourselves, the panic that sets in when we don't receive a text back within five minutes. It's the constant need for reassurance, the insatiable hunger for affirmation, and the irrational fear that everyone we love will eventually leave us.

It really does paint a bleak picture, but it's not the end of the story. Just like a wound needs to be acknowledged before it can be healed, our fear of abandonment needs to be seen, to be heard, to be understood. We need to lean into the discomfort, to hold space for our fear, to sit with it and listen to what it has to tell us.

We need to remind ourselves that we are not alone, that we are lovable, that we are enough. We need to learn to trust again, to let go of our need for control, to embrace vulnerability. We need to understand that people come and go, but their departure does not define our worth. We need to realize that we are not the deserted islands we often feel we are, but rather, we are part of a vast ocean of humanity, interconnected, interdependent, beautiful in our shared brokenness.

You are not alone. You are seen. You are loved. And most importantly, you are enough. Abandonment may have left a scar on your heart, but it does not define you. You are not defined by those who left, but by the strength you found in their absence. You are not your wounds. You are the resilience and courage with which you face them. Now, I want you to hold on to these final few reminders to help you heal; to help you find the light you need:

- Start to acknowledge the things from your past that have hurt you.

- Allow the pain and the darkness to arise without resistance.

- Feel your feelings.

- Practice forgiveness for yourself and those who have hurt you.

- Let love from the right people in.

- Practice self-compassion and give yourself the kind of love that you've never received.

Rejection

Someone once asked me a while ago: "But how do you deal with rejection?"

I thought about it for a fair bit of time, and then it came to me. I actually deal with rejection in a whole lot of different ways.

I thank them, first and foremost. I thank them for being brave enough to be honest with me. I thank them for knowing themselves well enough to know that I wasn't what was best for them at that time. I thank them for opening up the space for someone else. I allow myself my feelings, but I try not to turn their rejection into me rejecting myself. They rejected me, yes, but I really do not have to go about rejecting myself for that.

Rejection finds its roots in our most primal need for belonging. As social creatures, we yearn for acceptance and love, striving to create connections that validate our very existence. When our attempts at connection are met with rejection, the sting can cut deep, unraveling our self-worth and casting shadows of doubt on our souls.

While we all have experienced rejection at some point in our lives, for some, the wound of rejection begins in childhood, in moments that may seem small to an outsider but leave a lasting mark on the tender hearts of the young. A parent or caregiver who withheld praise or affection, focusing instead on faults, might have planted seeds of self-doubt. A harsh word, a dismissive glance, or favoritism shown to a sibling—all these moments teach a child to question their worth.

If you were ridiculed for your ideas, excluded from play, or told outright that you weren't enough, you might have learned to fear expressing yourself or to shrink your presence to avoid further rejection. Even the perception of rejection—such as a busy parent's unintentional inattention—can echo through your psyche, telling you that you must work harder to earn love and belonging. Over time, these messages weave themselves into your self-concept, creating a pattern of guarding your heart or chasing external validation to feel whole.

Whispering in the recesses of our hearts, rejection gives birth to a myriad of fears. Fear of not being enough, fear of being insignificant, and fear of being unlovable reverberate through our beings, amplifying the pain of rejection. These fears grip us tightly, convincing us that we are flawed and undeserving of love and acceptance.

In our relationships, it manifests in various ways, leaving lasting imprints on our connections with others. We may find ourselves building walls to protect our fragile hearts, fearing the vulnerability that comes with letting others in. At the same time, it can drive us to seek validation from others, perpetuating a cycle of codependency and disconnection.

In the face of rejection, shame often takes center stage, whispering poisonous words. It consumes us, painting a distorted picture of who we are. But within each rejection, there lies an opportunity for resilience. It is through our courageous embrace of vulnerability and a commitment to self-compassion that we can rise, rewriting the narrative shaped by rejection and discovering the strength to embrace our true selves.

As we navigate the intricacies of rejection, may we always remember that we are not alone. Our shared human experience encompasses both the joy of acceptance and the pain of rejection. By opening our hearts, extending compassion to ourselves and others, and fostering authentic connections, we can create a place where rejection bears less weight. The power of vulnerability, empathy, and love holds the key to bridging the gaps created by it.

Here are some tips for dealing with rejection—the mountain you think you cannot climb:

- **Hold Space for Your Pain.** Often, it makes us feel embarrassed or ashamed of what happened, and that often results in us suppressing our pain, but it doesn't have to be that way. Allow yourself to grieve your feelings; let your feelings exist and when you're ready, you'll see how much easier it becomes to move on.

- **Don't Blame Yourself.** There won't always be a clear reason for rejection, which quite frankly, can be quite frustrating. Remind yourself that it is a normal part of life and that it doesn't say anything about you.

- **Build your Resilience Muscles.** Resilience is all about how well we are capable of bouncing back after a major setback. Keep an open mind; remember all of the strengths that make you who you are and let those be the things that define you.

- **Don't Stop Putting Yourself Out There.** Just because that one relationship didn't work out, it does not mean that you have to give up entirely. Keep on working toward chasing your dreams. Keep on hoping and believing that a healthy, tender, and one-of-a-kind love will find you.

Other Common Emotional Wounds

We've discussed the main and most common emotional wounds that we often find ourselves grappling with, but there are a few others that we don't shed enough light on and can shape our inner world in profound ways, influencing how we connect with ourselves and others.

The Trust Wound

The trust wound is as delicate as porcelain, its fragility often concealed beneath layers of vulnerability and uncertainty. Trust serves as the foundation of relationships—whether personal, professional, or even the one we have with ourselves. When this foundation is damaged, it leaves scars that may take a lifetime to heal. Often, the trust wound originates in experiences of betrayal, yet it is distinct in its scope and impact. Betrayal is an event—a sharp, specific action or series of actions that shatter our expectations of another. It is the emotional equivalent of a knife, a sudden and painful rupture in a relationship. The trust wound, however, is the lingering aftermath. It extends far beyond the initial act, creating a deeper and more pervasive sense of insecurity and fear that infiltrates our lives.

While betrayal stems from the actions of others, the trust wound becomes an internal struggle. It erodes our ability to trust, not only in others but also in ourselves. It shakes our confidence, casting doubt on our judgment and leading to hesitation in forming new connections. Betrayal might feel acute—a rupture in the moment, an emotional earthquake. The trust wound, however, is chronic. It's the cracks left behind, the pervasive fear and hesitation that linger, affecting how we engage with others long after the betrayal has occurred. Where betrayal focuses on what someone has done to us, the trust wound shifts the focus inward, forcing us to grapple with vulnerability, self-doubt, and the fear of being hurt again.

This wound manifests in our lives in tangible ways. It fosters a fear of vulnerability, compelling us to build walls around our hearts to guard against further pain. It leads to self-doubt, as we question our ability to judge character and hesitate to rely on others. It creates a fear of intimacy, prompting us to keep an emotional distance even in relationships that hold promise. Betrayal might feel like a dagger, but the trust wound is more insidious—a quiet whisper that urges us to remain guarded, even when it's no longer necessary.

Healing the trust wound requires time, patience, and a deliberate effort to rebuild what was fractured. It begins with reclaiming your inner compass, learning to trust your instincts, and reflecting on moments when your intuition has served you well. Trust can be extended gradually—it doesn't need to be all or nothing. Allow others to earn your trust in small, consistent steps, rebuilding it one moment at a time. Finally, challenge the walls you've built around yourself. Recognize when fear of vulnerability or intimacy is holding you back and gently question whether those defenses are still necessary. By distinguishing betrayal as the event and the trust wound as the lasting effect, we can uncover the layers of healing needed to move forward. While betrayal may leave scars, addressing the trust wound allows us to reclaim our sense of security and connection, ultimately enabling us to trust ourselves and others again.

The Scarcity Wound

Living with the scarcity wound is constantly focusing on what you're lacking. *I am not smart enough. I am not beautiful enough. I am not rich enough.* When we walk around the world feeling like we are not enough, we build enough evidence to prove that belief.

It is a deeply ingrained mindset that continually directs our attention toward what we lack. It is like a lens through which we view the world, constantly reminding us of our perceived inadequacies. We find ourselves caught in this tangled web of self-doubt and self-criticism, seeking validation and reassurance from external sources. This mindset manifests itself in various aspects of our lives, affecting our sense of worthiness, abundance, and opportunities for growth.

One aspect in which the scarcity wound shows up is in our self-image. We might doubt our intelligence, constantly comparing ourselves to those that we perceive as smarter, more accomplished, or more talented than us. This self-doubt becomes a barrier that limits us from fully expressing our abilities and pursuing our aspirations. The scarcity wound whispers in our ears, telling us that we are not enough, leading to self-sabotaging behaviors that prevent us from reaching our true potential.

It influences our perception of beauty. We are bombarded by societal standards that often seem unattainable. We start believing that we are not beautiful enough, as we compare ourselves to heavily edited images in the media, molding our perceptions of how we should look. This internalized belief can lead to a perpetual dissatisfaction with our appearance, damaging our self-esteem and breeding a continuous longing for acceptance and validation. Financial scarcity is another area where the scarcity wound can take hold. We become overly focused on what we lack financially, constantly feeling like we are not rich enough. This fixation prevents us from appreciating the abundance that surrounds us and limits our ability to attract prosperity.

But where does this wound come from? It can be from childhood experiences, where we faced limited resources and witnessed a scarcity mentality in our caregivers. We internalized these early teachings, forming a belief system that perpetuates scarcity in our adult lives. Also, societal conditioning, expectations, and the constant comparison to others contribute to reinforcing the scarcity wound.

To heal, we need to consciously shift our focus toward abundance, gratitude, and self-compassion. Acknowledging and challenging our limiting beliefs, we can start rewiring our mindset to one that recognizes our inherent worthiness and the limitless possibilities available to us.

The Neglect Wound

The neglect wound is an abandoned garden where vital nourishment and attention are lacking. It represents the emotional void originating from childhood experiences of neglect, emotional unavailability, or prolonged absence of nurturing figures in our lives. This neglect deprives us of the essential emotional sustenance necessary for our growth and well-being.

Like the garden, our neglected emotional landscape withers and struggles to flourish. We develop a deep-rooted belief that we are unworthy of love, care, and support. This belief permeates our relationships and self-perception, leading to a distorted reality where we constantly feel overlooked, unheard, or disregarded.

The wound reveals itself through patterns of seeking external validation and attention. We may unconsciously recreate situations that reinforce our sense of neglect, attracting relationships or circumstances that echo our past experiences. This perpetuates a cycle of unmet needs, leaving us emotionally starved and yearning for the affection and recognition we missed out on. In our quest for constant validation, we may find ourselves constantly prioritizing others' needs while neglecting our own. We become accustomed to self-neglect, valuing the well-being of others over our own, as if fulfilling our own needs is an indulgence we don't deserve. This pattern only deepens the neglect wound, leaving us feeling depleted and resentful.

Healing this wound requires a compassionate return to the self, learning to tend to your own emotional garden with patience and care. Begin by acknowledging the hurt and recognizing that your needs are valid, no matter how long they've been ignored. Gently challenge the old belief that you are unworthy of love, replacing it with the understanding that you are deserving of kindness and attention—starting with your own. Reconnect with your desires and set boundaries that protect your well-being, learning to nourish your emotional landscape in ways that foster true growth. The path to healing lies in offering yourself the same compassion you longed for, transforming the neglect wound into an opportunity for self-empowerment.

If we aren't the ones addressing our old wounds, then our relationships are going to be the things that address them for us. The key is to discover our triggers and to be more self-aware of the "whys" behind the ways in which we behave. Once we become aware of those patterns, then and only then will we be able to gravitate toward the kinds of healthy relationships that we do fully deserve.

At the end of the day, the person that you need to have the most self-respect for is yourself. If you don't have that, then no one else is going to be able to give that to you.

What Counts as Trauma

Trauma refers to an emotional response to an extremely distressing or disturbing event that overwhelms an individual's ability to cope. It can result from various experiences such as accidents, abuse, violence, natural disasters, or the loss of a loved one. Traumatic events often leave a lasting impact on our mental, emotional, and physical well-being.

To understand the impact of different stressors on ourselves, we can use the Holmes and Rahe Stress Scale. This scale assigns a numerical value to various life events based on the potential stress they may cause. By adding up the scores of significant events experienced over a specific period, such as a year, we can estimate the level of stress we are experiencing.

The scale, however, is a general guideline and may not capture the full complexity of an individual's experience. Trauma is highly subjective and can vary from person to person. What may be traumatic for one person may not be for another, because individual resilience, coping mechanisms, and support systems play a crucial role in how trauma is experienced.

Empathy and compassion have to be at the forefront when we approach conversations like these. When someone shares their traumatic experiences, it is important to listen actively and validate their feelings. It's about creating safe spaces that don't minimize our pain, but rather spaces that make it feel safe enough for us to talk about the hard things.

How a Negative or Traumatic Experience Can Create Emotional Blockages and Adult Patterns

The things we want most desperately as adults are often the things we desperately needed as children but didn't receive. Just as a tree can grow crooked if it doesn't receive enough sunlight, our emotional growth can become stunted if our early needs for love, validation, and security are unmet. Our childhood experiences, especially the negative or traumatic ones, can leave indelible marks on our emotional landscape. These experiences are like emotional seeds that get planted deep within us. They take root in our internal world and, over time, grow into towering trees of thoughts, feelings, and behaviors that end up shaping our adult lives.

Imagine a little girl who was constantly criticized by her parents. The seed of *I'm not good enough* is planted. As she grows up, this seed turns into a tree of self-doubt and low self-esteem. She might overwork herself to prove her worth or shy away from opportunities because she doesn't believe she's capable. Also, a boy who was neglected might grow into a man who's always seeking attention and approval or conversely, one who isolates himself, deeming himself unworthy of love and connection.

These are emotional blockages, and they are born from our attempts to protect our tender hearts from further pain. They're like emotional scar tissues that become barriers to experiencing life fully. We build walls around our hearts and create unhealthy patterns to avoid feeling the discomfort of our unhealed wounds.

Yet, these walls and patterns also block us from experiencing the love, joy, and connection we yearn for. They keep us stuck in a repetitive cycle of the past, unable to move forward. We might find ourselves attracted to partners who replicate the same dynamics we experienced in our childhood, or we might repeatedly find ourselves in situations that trigger our deepest insecurities and fears. But here's the hopeful part—we're not doomed to live out these patterns forever. Just as a tree can be pruned and guided to grow in a different direction, we too can change our emotional patterns. It requires courage, self-awareness, and often, professional help, but it is possible. We can uproot the harmful seeds, plant new ones of self-love and worthiness, and cultivate a garden of emotional well-being because we are not the negative experiences that happened to us. We are not the unhealthy patterns we've adopted. Those are things that have happened to us, and things we've done, but they are not who we are. We are beings of boundless potential, capable of learning, growth, and transformation. We have the power to heal our wounds, rewrite our stories, and create the kind of life we desire and deserve.

Interactive Element

Unhealthy Behavior Patterns Checklist

Healing work is a sobering journey, but the rewards that come from it are incredibly sweet. To help you in this process, I have created an interactive and engaging checklist of red flags that can indicate unhelpful childhood patterns negatively affecting us. Take a moment to reflect on each item and honestly assess whether it resonates with your own experiences. Remember, this exercise is meant to promote self-awareness and growth.

How to Use This Checklist

Step 1: Reflect on each item.

Step 2: Place a checkmark (✔) in the box if it resonates with you.

Step 3: Take some time to really consider the reflection questions. Use a piece of paper or journal to explore your thoughts or experiences.

Difficulty Setting Boundaries

[ ] Do you struggle to assert your needs and say "no" when necessary?

[ ] Are you often taken advantage of or find it hard to prioritize your well-being?

Reflection Questions: What situations make it hard for me to say "no"? What small step can I take to set a boundary today?

Perfectionism

[ ] Do you constantly feel the need to be perfect, fearing failure or criticism?

[ ] Are you excessively self-critical and find it challenging to accept mistakes or imperfections?

Reflection Questions: What's one area where I can embrace imperfection? How does perfectionism hold me back?

People-Pleasing

[ ] Do you often prioritize others' needs over your own?

[ ] Are you afraid of disappointing others or being rejected if you don't meet their expectations?

Reflection Questions: How can I honor my needs today? What is one way I can say "no" with kindness?

Low Self-Esteem

[ ] Do you struggle with feelings of worthlessness or inadequacy?

[ ] Do you frequently compare yourself to others and feel inferior?

Reflection Questions: What's one strength I can celebrate today? How can I affirm my inherent worth?

Difficulty Expressing Emotions

[ ] Do you find it challenging to identify and express your emotions?

[ ] Are you prone to bottling up your feelings or avoiding conflicts?

Reflection Questions: How do I currently express emotions? What's one safe way to let my feelings out?

Fear of Abandonment

[ ] Do you have an intense fear of being left alone or rejected?

[ ] Are you overly clingy or dependent on others to feel secure?

Reflection Questions: What brings me security in relationships? How can I build trust in myself?

Trust Issues

[ ] Do you find it hard to trust others due to past experiences?

[ ] Are you constantly on guard, expecting to be betrayed or hurt?

Reflection Question: What's one small way I can open up to someone I trust?

Avoidance of Intimacy

[ ] Do you struggle to form deep and meaningful connections with others?

[ ] Are you afraid of getting too close or being vulnerable?

Reflection Questions: What is one personal thing that I could share with a loved one that makes me feel vulnerable? What would it feel like to share something personal with a loved one?

Overly Self-Reliant

[ ] Do you have difficulty relying on others or asking for help?

[ ] Are you used to handling everything on your own, even when it becomes overwhelming?

Reflection Questions: What's one task I can ask for help with today? How can I embrace community?

Repetition of Destructive Patterns

[ ] Do you notice a recurring cycle of unhealthy relationships or behaviors in your life?

[ ] Are you drawn to situations that mirror your past experiences, even if they are harmful?

Reflection Questions: What pattern do I see in my relationships or choices? What's one step I can take to break free?

Additional Prompts for Self-Evaluation

Emotional Numbness. Do you struggle to feel emotions or connect with them fully? What might this be protecting you from?

Overthinking. Do you frequently replay past events or worry excessively about the future? How can you ground yourself in the present moment?

Fear of Conflict. Do you avoid disagreements to keep the peace, even at your own expense? What's one way to express your perspective kindly but firmly?

Remember, this checklist is not meant to diagnose any specific condition but rather to help you identify potential areas of focus for personal growth and healing.

Childhood Stress Self-Analysis: Reflecting on Your Past

Understanding the impact of childhood stress is crucial for healing and growth. Use this self-analysis tool to reflect on your past and gain insights into the level of stress you experienced during your formative years. By acknowledging and addressing these wounds, you can begin the journey toward healing and transformation.

Rate each item on a scale of 0 to 10, with 0 being no stress and 10 being extreme stress.

Reflect on your childhood experiences and assign a rating to each item based on how much stress it caused you.

Total up the scores to get an overall assessment of your childhood stress level.

Childhood Stress Self-Analysis Tool

1. Divorce or separation of parents.

2. Physical or emotional abuse.

3. Neglect or abandonment.

4. Loss of a loved one.

5. Moving or changing schools.

6. Financial difficulties in the family.

7. Serious illness or injury.

8. Bullying or social rejection.

9. Witnessing domestic violence.

10. Substance abuse in the family.

Remember, this tool is meant for self-reflection and awareness. It can help you gauge your childhood stress levels, but it's important to seek professional help if needed.

So now that we've explored the intricacies of childhood development and the lasting impact of early experiences on our adult selves, it is imperative to shift our focus inward, delving into the realm of the inner child. Understanding the connection between childhood development and the inner child unveils a profound journey of self-discovery. This transition allows us to explore how these early imprints continue to influence our perceptions, relationships, and overall well-being as adults. By unraveling the layers of the inner child, we embark on a transformative path toward healing, reclaiming, and nurturing the essence of who we truly are. So what is this inner child and what does it mean for us? Well, we're about to find out in the next chapter, but before we dive right in, how about you go make yourself some coffee or tea? It's been a great first chapter and a little break won't do you any harm.

Chapter Two

The Inner Child

How Unhealed Wounds Affect Adult Choices

Caring for your inner child has a powerful and surprisingly quick result: Do it and the child heals. –Martha Beck

I magine for a moment a garden filled with vibrant flowers, lush greenery, and a gentle breeze that carries whispers of serenity. This garden represents the essence of your being, a place where your inner child resides. Just like a garden, your inner child needs careful tending and nurturing to flourish and heal.

In our fast-paced and demanding world, we often become disconnected from our childlike wonder, innocence, and joy. The weight of responsibilities, past traumas, and societal expectations can bury that inner child deep within us, leaving scars that manifest in various ways.

But what if there was a way to heal those wounds, to rediscover the magic and resilience of your inner child? This is where the power of understanding the inner child comes into play.

The words of Martha Beck echo with truth and wisdom, revealing the transformative potential of this profound healing process.

When we commit to caring for our inner child, we make a conscious choice to create a safe and nurturing space within ourselves. It is a journey of self-discovery, a deliberate effort to peel back the layers of adulthood and reconnect with the pure, unadulterated essence that resides within us all.

Healing the inner child is not an overnight process, but the results can be remarkably quick and powerful. It begins with acknowledging the wounds and pain that your inner child carries, recognizing the impact they have on your present experiences and emotional well-being.

Between these next few pages lie all the secrets you require to learn to tend to the needs, desires, and dreams of your inner child. Just as a gardener carefully tends to their plants, providing sunlight, water, and nourishment, you will provide your inner child with love, acceptance, and compassion.

The healing begins when you allow yourself to be receptive to joy and laughter, to explore the world with curious eyes, and to embrace the creativity and imagination that may have been stifled over time. By giving yourself permission to play, dream, and express your authentic self, you create space for healing and growth.

Throughout this chapter, we will not only learn what exactly the inner child is, but why it is important and how this inner child encapsulates the echoes of our past, embodying the emotions, needs, and vulnerabilities we have carried during our formative years. We will also explore various techniques that will help you dive deep into the reservoir of your inner child's emotions and experiences.

So, breathe and whisper to yourself, you are safe now. You are held. Loved. And deeply cherished.

Defining the Inner Child

The inner child is more than imagining you giving yourself a hug. It's a place of deep need, one that requires reparenting of the younger version of yourself that endured significant wounding or trauma.

I just want you to imagine, for a moment, that within you resides the younger, more vulnerable version of yourself. This isn't just a fanciful mental exercise or a whimsical throwback to your childhood. No, it's something much more profound and, dare I say, sacred. This is your inner child.

The inner child is not just an abstract concept or a psychological construct. It's the living, breathing heart of your past, a tiny time-traveler who has journeyed with you from the days of your youth, cradling all your early joys, fears, disappointments, and triumphs close to its little chest. This child within you holds the key to understanding many of your current struggles, reactions, and patterns that can often seem perplexing or out of sync with your adult self.

You see, our inner child is shaped by the experiences of our formative years. If that child received love, care, and nurturing, it blossoms into a source of creativity, joy, and compassion. But suppose that child experiences trauma, neglect, or emotional upheaval. In that case, it becomes a reservoir of unmet needs and unresolved pain because that place where the inner child resides is deeply sensitive, unguardedly honest, and ceaselessly seeking love and acceptance. It's the reason we crave the tiniest bit of validation, why we feel a sting when someone dismisses our ideas, or why we curl up into a ball when we feel unloved or neglected.

The journey to wholeness requires us to go back and "reparent" our inner child. This means meeting those unmet needs, soothing that unresolved pain, and offering the love and acceptance that the child within us has been yearning for. It requires courage, for this path will lead us through the shadowed valleys of our past. But it also carries the promise of liberation, the possibility of breaking free from old patterns that have kept our hearts shackled.

And so, this is where the beautiful intersection of psychology and spirituality comes in. You see, reparenting your inner child is not something you do alone. It's an intimate dance between you, your past, and the Divine Love that holds all things together. It's about learning to see yourself with the same compassion and tenderness that God/the Universe/Higher Consciousness sees you. And in doing so, you learn to extend that same compassion and tenderness to others.

So, yes, the inner child is much more than giving yourself a hug—although that's a lovely place to start. It's about diving deep, making peace with your past, and nurturing the most tender, vulnerable parts of yourself. It's about becoming the caregiver you needed when you were young. And in that journey, you'll find not just healing but a deeper connection to yourself and the world around you.

The Importance of the Inner Child

We've explored what the inner child is and where it comes from, but we also have to highlight the fact that it plays a crucial role in both the individual and society. At its core, the inner child represents our authentic self, untouched by societal conditioning or expectations. Nurturing and acknowledging this core aspect of ourselves is vital for personal growth and overall well-being.

On an individual level, the inner child holds our deepest desires, dreams, and emotions. By reconnecting with and healing our inner child, we can address unresolved traumas and emotional wounds, leading to greater self-awareness and emotional resilience. This allows us to make healthier choices, form more fulfilling relationships, and find true happiness.

Moreover, the health of our collective inner child directly impacts society. How we treat and nurture our inner child reflects in our interactions with others and the world around us. When society values and prioritizes the well-being of its members, it fosters a compassionate and empathetic environment. Conversely, neglecting the inner child can lead to societal issues such as violence, inequality, and disconnection.

By recognizing the importance of the inner child, we can create a society that values emotional well-being, empathy, and compassion. This involves providing safe spaces for emotional expression, promoting mental health awareness, and prioritizing the needs of children. When we prioritize the inner child, we lay the foundation for a healthier and more harmonious society.

Myths About the Inner Child

Before we trek too deep into inner child territory, let's discuss some common myths that may shroud this deeply profound process. In this section, we will unravel the misconceptions surrounding the inner child, illuminating the path to understanding and embracing this integral aspect of our psyche and spirit. Myths often arise from a lack of clarity and can impede the healing process. By delving into these misconceptions, we aim to provide clarity and pave the way for a more authentic connection with our inner child. Let's take a look at some of these myths.

Myth #1: The inner child is just imaginary.

Some people might dismiss the idea of an inner child as a figment of the imagination, a whimsical concept without any basis in reality. However, the inner child represents our truest self, our unfiltered emotions, needs, and desires. It's the part of us that retains the innocence, curiosity, and wonderment we experienced during childhood.

Myth #2: The inner child is all about immaturity.

Another common misconception is that connecting with the inner child means behaving childishly or refusing to grow up. This couldn't be further from the truth! Connecting with your inner child means nurturing your authentic self, understanding your emotional needs, and embracing the joy, creativity, and spontaneity that are often associated with childhood.

Myth #3: The inner child is irrelevant to adulthood.

Some may believe that the inner child only holds significance during childhood and loses relevance as we grow older. In reality, the inner child plays a crucial role in shaping our adult experiences. Unresolved childhood wounds, traumas, or unmet needs can manifest as emotional and psychological challenges in adulthood. By understanding and healing our inner child, we can foster personal growth and emotional well-being.

Myth #4: Inner child work is only for people with difficult childhoods.

While it's true that inner child work can be particularly beneficial for individuals who have experienced trauma or challenging childhoods, it is relevant for everyone. We all have an inner child within us, and regardless of the nature of our childhood experiences, tending to our inner child can enhance self-awareness, compassion, and self-acceptance.

Myth #5: Connecting with the inner child is complicated and time-consuming.

Some may shy away from exploring their inner child because they believe it requires lengthy therapy sessions or complicated techniques. However, connecting with your inner child can be as simple as allowing yourself to engage in activities that bring you joy and evoke a sense of wonder. Engaging in creative pursuits, spending time in nature, or simply indulging in nostalgic memories can all help you reconnect with your inner child.

The inner child is not a mere figment of imagination or a concept reserved for the immature. Connecting with this important aspect of ourselves is so very necessary to live a full and abundant life.

The Wounded Inner Child in Adulthood

As we debunk the myths surrounding the inner child, it becomes imperative to explore the tangible manifestations of its wounds in adulthood. Now, armed with clarity, we venture into the exploration of what the wounded inner child truly looks like in the landscape of our adult lives. By bridging the gap between myth and reality, we embark on a profound journey of self-discovery, unraveling the threads that connect our past to our present, and empowering ourselves with the knowledge needed for genuine healing.

So what does the wounded inner child look like in the adult self? How does it manifest?

You make a big deal out of seemingly insignificant and small things.

In adulthood, the wounded inner child will show themselves through an over-exaggeration of seemingly small things. These intense emotional reactions are often triggered by seemingly trivial events or interactions that remind the individual of past unresolved traumas or unmet needs from their childhood. For example, a simple disagreement with a friend may escalate into a full-blown emotional meltdown because the wounded inner child perceives the situation as a threat to their sense of safety or validation. These exaggerated emotional responses are a result of the wounded inner child wanting to protect itself and have its needs acknowledged and validated.

The wounded inner child may also project past hurts onto present situations, causing them to be disproportionately affected by minor setbacks or perceived slights. This can lead to patterns of overreacting, feeling overwhelmed, or experiencing intense anxiety or anger in response to everyday challenges. Recognizing and addressing these big feelings about small things is crucial for healing the wounded inner child. Through self-reflection, therapy, and inner work, you can learn to identify the triggers and underlying wounds that contribute to these intense emotional reactions, allowing you to respond in a more balanced and healthy manner.

You cause drama when there really doesn't need to be any.

Have you ever found yourself caught up in unnecessary drama, stirring up conflicts where there really doesn't need to be any? It's like a whirlwind of chaos that leaves you wondering, Why did I react that way? Well, it could also be the wounded inner child at play.

You see, drama is a way for our wounded inner child to be seen and heard. It's a cry for help, a plea for attention, albeit in a turbulent and tumultuous manner. The drama becomes a stage upon which they perform, demanding recognition and validation from others. In these moments, we may find ourselves embroiled in petty arguments, exaggerated emotions, and unnecessary conflicts, all in a bid to have our pain acknowledged.

But why does drama become our default response? Well, it's because drama, in all its chaotic glory, momentarily distracts us from the pain within. It provides a temporary escape, a momentary respite from the rawness of our wounded inner child. In creating a whirlwind of commotion, we can momentarily forget about the deep-seated hurt that simmers beneath the surface.

It also serves as a shield, protecting us from the vulnerability of facing our inner child's wounds head-on. It becomes a smokescreen that conceals our true pain and prevents us from delving into the depths of our emotions. By engaging in drama, we can avoid the momentary discomfort of self-reflection and the harsh realities about healing.

As we delve deeper into the intricate landscape of inner child healing, it becomes evident that recognizing the wounded inner child in adulthood is a pivotal step towards lasting transformation. We've explored how this wounded aspect may manifest through behaviors like making mountains out of molehills and inciting unnecessary drama. These are but the surface ripples, indicative of deeper currents.

Now let's navigate further into the heart of this process by shedding light on emotional reactivity and triggers. These phenomena are intricately connected to the wounded inner child, unveiling patterns that often lie dormant until stirred. Understanding these elements will grant us insight into the layers of healing that await, offering a pathway towards lasting inner peace and self-liberation. With this understanding, let's now turn our attention to the profound interplay of triggers, illuminating yet another facet of our path to health and wholeness.

Emotional Reactivity and Triggers

I read something a while ago that said that being triggered is not a choice. I cried at that line, because it was just what I needed to hear. It was so comforting to know that I wasn't overreacting or "being too much."

Emotional and sensory information from traumatic experiences is usually stored in the brain and in the body. Those memories of the past traumas not only include where, when, with whom, and what you say, but they also include what you heard, tasted, smelled, and felt. When you're reminded of those traumatic events that you experience through these internal or external cues, your fear structure gets activated. Even though what happened is in the past, your mind interprets these as current threats. That is because your emotional triggers are messengers; they are what unveil the depths of our unresolved experiences. Rooted in the realms of psychology and spirituality, they hold transformative potential, urging us to embark on a quest of self-discovery and healing.

Emotional triggers arise from unhealed wounds, unaddressed traumas, or suppressed emotions within our psychological makeup. These triggers have the remarkable ability to transport us back to the scenes of our past, stirring up powerful emotions and reactions. Examining where they come from is what can help us unravel the mysteries they hold.

Emotional triggers often come from unresolved experiences that have left imprints on our psyche. For instance, if you have experienced betrayal in the past, you may find yourself getting triggered by similar situations that evoke feelings of distrust and insecurity.

Our upbringing and societal conditioning shape our beliefs, values, and behavioral patterns. Emotional triggers can be rooted in learned behaviors or beliefs that were ingrained during our formative years. Being raised in a critical environment, for example, could be triggered by even the slightest hint of criticism, initiating a defensive response.

Beyond the psychological aspects, emotional triggers also hold deep spiritual significance because they offer us an opportunity for self-transcendence and spiritual growth; they are an invitation for self-reflection. Our emotional triggers serve as mirrors, reflecting aspects of ourselves that need attention and healing. They call us to embark on a journey of self-reflection and introspection, prompting us to explore our values, belief systems, and personal growth opportunities.

We develop a heightened sense of empathy and compassion toward others. Recognizing our own vulnerabilities and struggles allows us to extend understanding and support to those around us who may be experiencing similar triggers.

Remember that you are not alone, and each step you take brings you closer to inner harmony and healing.

Limiting Beliefs and Negative Self-Talk

Our inner children carry the imprints of past wounds, the echoes of pain reverberating through the chambers of our mind. Like fragile birds with a broken wing, they seek solace and healing, yearning to find respite from the shadows that haunt its tender heart.

Within the make-up of our psyche, the wounded inner child weaves its presence into the fabric of our beliefs. It whispers softly, sometimes imperceptibly, manifesting as limiting beliefs and negative self-talk. Hear its voice, laden with the weight of past experiences, echoing through the corridors of your mind. It murmurs tales of unworthiness, self-doubt, and fear—the remnants of earlier wounds that have left a painful bruise on your soul.

They show up in various forms and can affect different aspects of our lives. Some examples of limiting beliefs include:

- *I'm not good enough.*
- *I don't deserve success.*
- *I'm too old/young to achieve my goals.*
- *I'll never be able to change.*
- *I'm not smart/talented enough.*

These beliefs can show up in our thoughts, behaviors, and emotions, and can hold us back from reaching our full potential.

Fear is also often a significant factor in limiting beliefs. When we experience fear, it can trigger a cascade of negative thoughts and emotions, leading us to doubt ourselves and our abilities. This fear can manifest in different ways, such as a fear of failure, that fear of rejection, or a fear of the unknown.

It's important to recognize that fear is a natural and normal response to certain situations. But, it's also important to remember that fear does not have to control our actions or beliefs. By acknowledging our fears and working to confront them, we can begin to break free from the limitations they impose.

We can also teach ourselves to reframe our thoughts and beliefs. Instead of focusing on the potential negative outcomes of a situation, we can try to shift our mindset to focus on the positive possibilities. For example, instead of thinking, I'm going to fail, we can reframe the thought to, I'm going to do my best and learn from the experience, no matter the outcome.

Ultimately, overcoming our limiting beliefs will require patience, perseverance, and a willingness to confront our fears head-on. With time and effort, we can learn to let go of our limiting beliefs and tap into that well of potential that exists within us.

Defense Mechanisms and Coping Strategies

Our defense mechanisms are strategies that our minds use to help us deal with difficult situations, thoughts, or feelings.

If we were to imagine our minds as bustling cities, our defense mechanisms could be seen as the lineup of guardians waiting and ready to protect and help us when things get tough.

Denial is one of the most common types, and it's like an invisibility cloak. When we encounter something overwhelming or painful, denial swoops in and wraps us up in a shield, making it easier to avoid or ignore the difficult situation. At the root of all denial lies fear and resistance to accepting the truth, because if we're being honest with one another, sometimes, the consequences of accepting the truth are less than savory. Denial can take on many forms, each as insidious as the next:

- **Ignoring Evidence.** Ignoring overwhelming evidence or facts that contradict your beliefs. Turning a blind eye to clear signs of trouble, such as physical symptoms, financial struggles, or relationship issues.

- **Minimizing Problems.** Minimizing or downplaying the severity of a situation or problem, convincing oneself that "it's not that bad."

- **Blaming Others.** Redirecting responsibility onto external factors to avoid facing uncomfortable truths.

- **Rationalizing.** Crafting excuses that justify harmful behaviors or poor decisions.

- **Selective Perception.** Only acknowledging information that aligns with one's preferred narrative while dismissing contradictory evidence.

Denial whispers comforting lies into our ears, telling us that if we ignore the problem long enough, it might just disappear.

But denial is no gentle guardian; it is a quiet thief. It robs us of the opportunity to address issues head-on, leaving cracks in the foundation of our lives that widen over time. Denial can manifest in subtle, everyday moments. Let's explore how denial unfolds in the theater of our everyday lives:

The Overworked Parent

Lisa is a dedicated mother who juggles her career and family responsibilities with precision. Lately, however, she's been feeling a tightness in her chest and shortness of breath. Her doctor recommends further testing, but Lisa brushes it off, insisting it's just stress and nothing more. Her denial shields her from the terrifying possibility of discovering a more serious health condition, but it also delays the care she needs.

The Failing Relationship

Tom and Rachel have been together for years, but cracks have begun to form in their relationship. Late-night arguments, distant glances, and unanswered messages have become the norm. Tom refuses to acknowledge the growing distance, telling himself that every couple goes through rough patches. His denial allows him to avoid the discomfort of addressing their issues, but it also prevents them from finding a path to reconciliation—or closure.

The Struggling Student

Aaron is a college student who has fallen behind on his coursework. Instead of acknowledging his struggle and seeking help, he convinces himself that he works best under pressure and that he'll catch up closer to the deadline. His denial blinds him to the mounting stress and potential consequences of procrastination, keeping him locked in a cycle of avoidance.

The Substance Problem

Maria's friends have started noticing her reliance on alcohol to unwind after work. When they gently bring it up, she laughs it off, saying, "Everyone needs a little stress relief. It's not like I drink every day." Her denial keeps her from seeing the early warning signs of dependency, pushing the issue further into the shadows.

Awareness is the sharpest tool we have to disarm denial and reclaim our truth. Recognizing denial requires courage, for it means standing face-to-face with the very truths we've been avoiding. Begin by asking yourself:

- *Am I ignoring warning signs in any area of my life?*
- *Are there truths I'm afraid to confront, and why?*
- *How might facing reality open the door to healing and growth?*

Denial isn't inherently malicious—it's a survival mechanism, a way of protecting ourselves when the truth feels too heavy to bear. But like a wound left untreated, denial can fester, preventing us from living authentically. When we gently peel back the layers of denial, we create space for truth to flourish and for healing to take root. Facing the truths we've avoided may feel like stepping into the unknown, but it is in this vulnerability that we reclaim our strength. By stepping beyond denial, we not only heal—we grow into the fullest, most authentic version of ourselves.

Then there's **projection**, which creates illusions all around us. When we're feeling uncomfortable or threatened by our own thoughts or feelings, projection steps in and projects those thoughts and feelings onto someone else. It's like saying, "Hey look, that person over there is the one causing all my problems!" We try to shift the blame to them, instead of facing the uncomfortable truth within ourselves. This is what shields us from the discomfort of acknowledging our own shortcomings or vulnerabilities. We convince ourselves that the source of our troubles lies solely in the actions or qualities of others. In externalizing our internal struggles, we divert attention away from the introspection required for personal growth and healing.

Projection operates on both conscious and subconscious levels. Sometimes, we are aware of our projection and deliberately assign our insecurities to others. In doing so, we create a narrative that absolves us of responsibility, providing temporary relief from our own perceived flaws. But, more often than not, projection happens without our conscious awareness. It becomes an automatic response, deeply ingrained within our psyche, shielding us from the discomfort of self-reflection.

This kind of self-deception permeates our relationships, both personal and professional. We find ourselves caught in a toxic cycle of blame shifting, failing to recognize that the root of our discontent lies within. When we project, we inadvertently sabotage the connections we so desire. Our inability to confront our own emotions and experiences prevents us from truly understanding and empathizing with those around us.

Let's uncover how projection subtly weaves itself into the fabric of our daily lives:

The Perfectionist's Perspective

Sarah is a self-proclaimed perfectionist. She meticulously plans every detail of her life, striving for flawlessness in everything she does. One day her friend, Emily, excitedly shares her new business venture. Instead of celebrating Emily's success, Sarah finds herself nitpicking and criticizing every aspect of the venture. Unbeknownst to Sarah, her projection is at play.

In this scenario, Sarah's projection is manifesting as a deep-rooted fear of failure. When she projects her own insecurities onto Emily's business, she is attempting to shield herself from the vulnerability of taking risks. She masks her own fear of imperfection by finding faults in the efforts and endeavors of others.

The Envious Explorer

Shawn is an aspiring artist who has big dreams of showcasing his work in galleries. One day, he stumbles upon an art exhibition featuring a friend whom he has known for years, April. Instead of feeling inspired, he is overcome by pangs of envy and dismisses April's talent as mere luck. Little does he know, projection is at play, busy coloring his perception.

In this scenario, Shawn's projection is showing up as a reflection of his own self-doubt. In belittling April's achievements, he is being avoidant in confronting his own fears of not being good enough. He projects his own insecurities onto April, attributing her success to external factors rather than acknowledging the talent and hard work that contributed to her success.

The Defensive Partner

Meet Mark and Lisa, a couple deeply in love. When it comes to communication, they often find themselves in heated arguments. One evening, Mark innocently suggested they try a new restaurant. Lisa immediately becomes defensive and accuses Mark of never keeping her preferences in mind.

In this scenario, Lisa's projection manifests as her own fear of not being heard or valued. By projecting her own insecurities onto Mark's innocent suggestion, Lisa avoids addressing her deeper concerns about feeling overlooked in the relationship. She shifts the blame onto Mark, creating a narrative that shields her from vulnerability and the need for open communication.

In each of these scenarios, projection serves as a shield, deflecting attention away from personal vulnerabilities and insecurities. Yet, by recognizing projection for what it truly is—a natural but unhelpful defense mechanism—we open the door to greater self-awareness and the possibility of cultivating deeper, more authentic connections with others. And remember, projection doesn't define you as flawed or unworthy; it simply highlights areas within that are calling out for compassion, understanding, and growth. To be human is to have shadows, and to work on them is a testament to your strength.

When we make choices or behave in ways that don't align with our values or beliefs, **rationalization** jumps in and presents logical arguments to justify our actions. It's like convincing ourselves that eating a whole tub of ice cream is perfectly fine because we had a tough day, even though we might know deep down it's not the healthiest choice. Have a look at these three scenarios:

The Procrastinator's Justification

Mike is a chronic procrastinator. He consistently puts off important tasks until the very last minute, causing stress and missed deadlines. When confronted by his boss about a missed project, he usually quickly comes up with a rationalization. He blames external factors like a heavy workload or unexpected distractions, rather than acknowledging his own tendency to procrastinate.

In this scenario, his rationalization shields him from taking responsibility for his actions. By blaming external circumstances, he avoids facing the uncomfortable truth that his procrastination habits are the root cause. This is what allows him to preserve his self-image as a competent employee, despite his recurring pattern of delay.

The Shopaholic's Excuse

Joy, a self-proclaimed shopaholic, often finds herself making impulsive purchases, accumulating a mountain of credit card debt along the way. When confronted by her concerned friend about her spending habits, she is always quick to rationalize her behavior. She justifies her purchases as a form of self-care or retail therapy, claiming that she deserves to treat herself. Framing her purchases as self-care allows her to avoid confronting the underlying emotional issues that drive her impulsive behavior. This allows her to maintain a sense of control and avoid the discomfort of addressing the unhealthy relationship she has with shopping.

The Cheater's Alibi

Joshua is in a committed relationship but has recently engaged in an affair. When confronted by his partner about the suspicious behavior, he goes on to claim that his actions were a result of feeling neglected or unappreciated in the relationship, shifting the blame onto the partner for his infidelity.

Joshua's rationalization is a cowardly way to justify his betrayal. By attributing his actions to his partner's perceived shortcomings, he avoids taking responsibility for his own choices and the impact it has on the relationship.

By rationalizing, we try to make sense of our choices using logical explanations that align with our beliefs, experiences, or desires. It's as if we are constructing a bridge between the conflicting sides of our minds, creating a smoother path forward. It is also not inherently negative; in fact, it plays a big role in our everyday lives. It helps us maintain a sense of coherence and self-integrity, allowing us to navigate the complexities of the world around us. We do, however, need to be discerning enough to know that rationalization can also lead us astray. We must be cautious of falling into the trap of self-deception or using rationalizations to justify harmful actions or beliefs. It's essential to remain vigilant and open to self-reflection, ensuring we don't distort reality or blind ourselves to alternative viewpoints.

When something too painful to face enters our thoughts, **repression** locks it away deep in the recesses of our minds, protecting us from the full intensity of that memory. It's like throwing a dark, mysterious artifact into a secret treasure chest, hoping to never stumble upon it again. Let's take a look at a couple of scenarios to see what repression can look and show up like in our everyday lives:

Forgotten Trauma

Emily experienced a deeply traumatic event in her childhood. Yet, she has no recollection of it. Her days seem untroubled, and she lives as though the past left no mark. What Emily doesn't realize is that repression is silently at work, burying the memory so deeply that it never surfaces in her conscious mind. This defense mechanism shields her from the overwhelming distress tied to the event, allowing her to function. However, the unprocessed emotions linger like a shadow, subtly influencing her choices and emotional well-being.

Unexpressed Grief

Mark recently lost someone he loved dearly. Instead of allowing himself to grieve, he dons a brave facade, sidestepping the pain and refusing to speak about his loss. Repression helps Mark push his grief aside, creating the illusion that he's fine. While this may help him maintain composure in the short term, the emotions he suppresses do not disappear. Instead, they take root in his subconscious, waiting to manifest as unresolved grief—perhaps through emotional detachment, unexpected bursts of anger, or even physical symptoms in the years to come.

Ignored Desire

Irina has always dreamed of pursuing a creative career. But due to societal expectations and fear of failure, she suppresses her true aspirations and settles for a conventional job that brings little fulfillment. In repressing her creative ambitions, she avoids the potential risks and uncertainties that come with pursuing her true passion. Repression allows Irina to bury her yearning for a different path, convincing herself that this safer option is the right one. Yet, in doing so, she stifles her personal growth and silences the part of her soul that longs for self-expression and fulfillment.

We can see that in each of these scenarios, repression serves as a defense mechanism that allows individuals to push away or bury uncomfortable thoughts, memories, or desires. However, this temporary relief comes at a cost. The buried emotions and unacknowledged desires continue to influence behavior, often in subtle and unexpected ways. Repression may protect us in moments of crisis, but it can also hinder personal growth and prevent us from addressing the root of our struggles.

Lastly, there's **displacement**. When we're feeling angry or frustrated, but it's not socially acceptable or safe to direct those feelings at the source, displacement bounces us in a different direction. Instead of confronting the person or situation causing the anger, we might vent our frustration by snapping at a harmless bystander or taking it out on a household object. It's like that trampoline propels our anger somewhere else entirely. Let's have a look at what that might look like in our day to day:

Frustrated at Work

Jason spends his days under immense pressure at work. After enduring a particularly stressful meeting with his boss, he arrives home feeling like a storm cloud ready to burst. His partner leaves a cupboard door open, and Jason snaps at them, letting out a torrent of frustration over something insignificant. In truth, his anger isn't about the cupboard—it's the weight of work stress finding an outlet. By displacing his emotions onto his partner, Jason avoids confronting the true source of his tension, but at the cost of straining his relationship.

Road Rage

Amanda is running late for an important appointment when she hits a wall of traffic. Agitation bubbles within her, and before long, she's honking her horn, shouting at other drivers, and making angry gestures. The real source of her frustration is the ticking clock and her anxiety about being late. Yet, displacement shifts her anger onto the innocent motorists around her, momentarily easing her emotional buildup while sowing chaos in the process.

The Sibling Scapegoat

Carl, a teenager, gets reprimanded by his parents for a mistake he feels was blown out of proportion. Seething with anger but unable to lash out at his parents, Carl turns his frustration onto his younger sister, Carmen. He picks on her, exaggerates her faults, and blames her for unrelated issues. In this scenario, Carl displaces his feelings of injustice onto Carmen, channeling his unresolved anger into sibling conflict.

While displacement can provide a fleeting sense of relief, it often leaves behind a trail of tension, damaged relationships, and unaddressed emotions. It's like sweeping dirt under the rug—out of sight, but never truly gone.

The key to breaking free from displacement lies in recognizing its patterns and gently redirecting that emotional energy in healthier ways. Whether it's through journaling, physical activity, or honest communication with the source of your frustration, addressing emotions at their root paves the way for genuine relief and stronger, more authentic connections with others.

Self-Sabotage

Imagine standing at the threshold of a door that opens to everything you've ever wanted—peace, love, fulfillment, and joy. But instead of stepping through, you hesitate. Your hand hovers just above the doorknob, and something inside whispers, *You don't deserve this. It's safer to stay where you are.* This is the voice of self-sabotage, a subtle yet powerful force that keeps us bound to the familiar, even when the familiar is what holds us back.

Self-sabotage doesn't always announce itself loudly. It wears many disguises, blending seamlessly into the patterns of our daily lives. It can look like:

- not asking for help when you need it.

- rejecting praise or brushing off compliments.

- isolating yourself from people when you feel hurt or misunderstood.

- putting your dreams on hold for the sake of others.

- procrastinating, even when it matters most.

- over-complicating simple situations.

- being conditional with yourself—for example, *I can't do X unless I first accomplish Y.*

Why do we do this to ourselves? Why do we stand in our own way, stalling our growth and dimming our light? We self-sabotage for a lot of reasons.

At its core, self-sabotage is often an act of self-protection, born from experiences that taught us joy, peace, and contentment were dangerous or fleeting. Perhaps as a child, moments of happiness were met with ridicule or punishment. Or maybe the chaos of your upbringing made safety feel like an illusion, leaving joy to feel foreign and unsafe.

There's also the guilt. Joy arriving in our lives can feel like an undeserved gift, stirring shame for daring to think we might deserve it. It whispers that happiness is a luxury reserved for others, not for us, and the weight of this belief compels us to push it away. We question whether we've earned it, whether we've done enough to be worthy, and in doing so, we sabotage the very moments that could bring light into our lives.

Then there's the fear—that letting ourselves feel good means the universe might snatch it away, leaving us devastated. So, we sabotage ourselves before life can and avoid having to deal with the grief that comes from losing the things that we were looking forward to having.

We also self-sabotage because it gives us a false sense of control. When we feel uncertain or unsafe in the world, we crave control to anchor us, believing it's the only way to restore trust and stability. Self-sabotage gives the illusion of control—if we ruin things ourselves, at least we're the ones holding the reins. But control, as comforting as it seems, is an illusion, and the more tightly we grip it, the more elusive it becomes, slipping through our grasp like sand through our fingers.

As we've explored, the wounded inner child profoundly shapes our decision-making. Unresolved emotions, traumas, and fears write the scripts that dictate our behaviors. These self-sabotaging patterns become the armor our inner child wears to shield against pain, the strategies they've crafted to navigate a world that once felt unpredictable and unsafe.

But here's the paradox: these survival mechanisms, while born from wisdom and resilience, no longer serve us in adulthood. The very behaviors that once protected us now create barriers to our happiness and growth. Yet within these patterns lies an extraordinary opportunity—for they are the breadcrumbs leading us back to our truest selves.

Awareness is the first step to liberation. By shining a gentle light on these behaviors, we begin to loosen their grip. We can start to ask ourselves:

- *Why am I resisting this joy, this praise, or this opportunity?*

- *What am I afraid will happen if I embrace this fully?*

- *What might change in my life if I allow myself to feel safe, worthy, and deserving?*

It is through this compassionate self-inquiry that we can process the fear, guilt, and shame that underpin self-sabotage. We can rewrite the narrative that tells us joy is unsafe or fleeting, awakening to the truth that happiness is not something to fear but a divine right to claim.

Remember, these self-sabotaging tendencies are not signs of weakness but evidence of the inner child's remarkable ingenuity to survive in a world that once felt overwhelming. They are the stories we wrote to make sense of chaos, the shields we forged to weather life's storms. Now, as adults, we can choose to lay down that armor and rewrite the story.

The Main Steps of Inner Child Work

Inner child work involves the compassionate act of meeting your inner child exactly where they are, offering a warm greeting, attentive listening, and heartfelt validation. As you bring this once-neglected aspect of yourself into the luminosity of your consciousness, you wield the transformative power to provide the love and support your inner child has longed for but may have never received. In this section, we will explore a structured approach, offering practical steps that guide you through this poignant process of inner child work.

1. **Acknowledge.** Those early years are the foundations of your emotional reactions and relationship dynamics. To understand your inner child, you can start by recognizing and acknowledging what caused all the pain during your childhood years. Avoid any judgment on what comes up here. Simply create a space of non-judgment and self-compassion as you allow your inner child to step into your awareness.

2. **Validate**. To be validated is to be seen and heard. Once acknowledged, validate the emotions and experiences of your inner child. Listen to what they have to say to you in those moments of self-reflection. Understand that every emotion, no matter how intense or seemingly trivial, is valid. Offer compassion to your inner child, acknowledging that their feelings are real and deserve acknowledgement. I know that this is a difficult prairie, especially if you are used to pushing away emotions when they're uncomfortable. So, just remind yourself with these statements: You are safe now. Your emotions are welcome here. I see you. I feel you and, most importantly, I understand you.

3. **Identify**. With tenderness, turn your gaze inward. Listen closely to the language of your heart. Can you name the emotions that arise? The ability to identify and recognize our emotions is a cornerstone of emotional intelligence and an essential aspect of inner child healing and personal growth. When we can name and understand our emotions, we gain valuable insights into our inner world, allowing us to navigate life with greater clarity and intention. Identifying emotions provides a crucial link between our internal experiences and external responses, enabling us to communicate effectively with ourselves and others. It lays the foundation for self-awareness, allowing us to comprehend the root causes of our reactions and make informed choices in how we respond to various situations.

4. **Embrace the Emotions that Surface**. Not every emotion you experience will be pleasant, but true strength lies in allowing them all to surface without resistance. Pushing them away only breeds guilt and shame, creating barriers that slow your healing and keep you trapped in the very pain you seek to overcome.

Just remember that allowing yourself to fully experience and embrace the emotions that surface is a vital part of inner child healing. This might involve sitting with discomfort, allowing tears to flow, or expressing yourself in a way that feels authentic. By confronting challenging emotions, you cultivate a deeper understanding of yourself, build emotional resilience, and pave the way for transformative growth.

5. **See How Emotions Reflect in Your Current Choices**. It's important to take note of how your emotions are reflected in your choices and behaviors. By being mindful of how your emotions guide you, you can use them as signposts to help you navigate through life. When you encounter difficult emotions, try to avoid placing blame on yourself or others. Instead, view them as a natural part of the human experience and an opportunity to learn more about yourself. By doing so, you can identify areas in your life that may benefit from more tender care and understanding. Remember, the goal is not perfection but rather progress toward a more fulfilling life.

6. **Process and Release Emotions**. Once you have gathered the wisdom and compassion needed for your healing journey, it's time to begin the gentle process of releasing what no longer serves you. You may find comfort in journaling, artistic expression, or confiding in a trusted friend or therapist. However you choose to release, allow your emotions to flow freely, knowing that in letting go, you create space for deeper healing and transformation. The goal is not just to feel but to consciously navigate these emotions, freeing them from both your heart and body, so you can step forward with greater lightness and clarity.

7. **Make Different Decisions.** When we're on a healing journey,

it's important to remember that the choices we make can have a big impact on our progress. As we work to cultivate a loving and nurturing energy within ourselves, it's essential that we empower ourselves to make choices that align with that energy. Whether in relationships, career, or personal habits, consciously choose paths that align with your authentic self, steering away from patterns that no longer serve you. Think of each decision you make as a promise to your inner child that their well-being is cherished and safeguarded.

Perhaps it's choosing to eat a healthy meal instead of indulging in something that may make you feel sluggish and unwell. Maybe it's taking a break from work to go for a walk and get some fresh air, rather than pushing yourself to the brink of burnout. Whatever choices you make, remember that you have the power to make different ones. Even if it feels scary or uncomfortable at first, know that you're taking an important step toward healing and self-love. As you continue to make choices that align with your highest good, you'll find that the healing process becomes easier and more fulfilling.

It's essential to view the main steps outlined here as a foundational guide, offering a compass for the transformative path ahead. Throughout the course of this book, we will delve deeper into specific facets of inner child healing, providing a nuanced exploration of crucial topics. In the upcoming chapters, we'll navigate the intricate terrain of mindfulness, offering practical insights on how to cultivate awareness and presence. Additionally, we'll embark on a profound exploration of processing and releasing emotions, guiding you through practices that facilitate healing. Consider these main steps as signposts, promising a more comprehensive exploration of each aspect as we traverse the rich landscape of inner child healing, fostering a holistic understanding of your inner self. So, throughout the pages and chapters of this book, please feel free to refer back to these steps as memories, emotional triggers or patterns arise.

Balancing the Inner Child and the Adult Self

Balancing the adult self and the inner child is a delicate dance that allows us to harness the wisdom and responsibilities of adulthood while still nurturing and connecting with our playful, creative, and spontaneous inner child. So, let's explore how we can strike that harmonious balance.

Firstly, it's essential to recognize and acknowledge the needs and desires of both the adult self and the inner child. The adult self represents responsibility, rationality, and practicality, while the inner child embodies curiosity, joy, and creativity. Understanding and honoring these aspects of ourselves allows us to approach life with a balanced perspective.

One way to strike a balance is by creating designated time and space for both the adult self and the inner child. As adults, we often get caught up in the busyness of life and forget to prioritize our inner child. Carve out time for spontaneous play, engaging in hobbies or activities that bring you joy and invoke a sense of childlike wonder. Allow yourself the freedom to explore, create, and let go of inhibitions.

It is also important to cultivate self-compassion and practice meeting our own needs. As adults, we can nurture our inner child by providing a safe and supportive environment. This means acknowledging and comforting ourselves when we experience emotions or challenges. Treat yourself with kindness, just as you would comfort a child who's feeling upset or overwhelmed.

Communication between the adult self and the inner child is also essential. Develop a dialogue within yourself, where the adult self listens and responds to the needs of the inner child. Reflect on the desires and dreams that your inner child holds and find ways to manifest them realistically in your life.

It's important to remember that the adult self and the inner child are not opposing forces but rather complementary aspects of our being. They can work together to create a balanced and fulfilling life. As adults, we can tap into the wisdom and experience of our adult self while still embracing the innate joy and curiosity of our inner child.

Ultimately, finding a balance between the adult self and the inner child is a continuous process. Listen to your inner child, honor its needs, and integrate those needs into your adult life in a healthy and responsible way. Embrace the spontaneity, joy, and creativity of your inner child while navigating life with the wisdom and maturity of your adult self.

By nurturing and harmonizing both your inner child and adult self, you create a life that embraces both playfulness and responsibility. This balance allows you to move through the world with greater fulfillment, authenticity, and joy. So, step into the rhythm of this delicate dance—where wisdom meets wonder—and let the harmony of both guide you on your unique journey.

Interactive Element

Inner Child Evaluation

Developmental Stage	Healthy Adult Characteristics	Unhealthy Adult Characteristics
Infancy (0-2 years)	Emotional resilience, secure attachment in relationships, ability to trust and form healthy connections, self-soothing skills, a sense of security and confidence.	Excessive fear or anxiety, difficulty forming secure attachments, challenges in trusting others, struggles with emotional regulation, insecurities affecting relationships and self-esteem.
Early Childhood (2-6 years)	Playfulness and spontaneity, creative expression in daily life, a sense of wonder, healthy independence, positive social interactions, openness to new experiences.	Difficulty expressing creativity, struggles with independence, challenges in social interactions, limited openness to new experiences, inhibited self-expression.
Middle Childhood (6-12 years)	Confidence in abilities, social competence, a sense of mastery in various areas, healthy relationships with peers, continued engagement in creative activities.	Low self-esteem, poor social skills, lack of confidence, difficulties in forming and maintaining relationships, limited engagement in creative endeavors.
Adolescence (12-18 years)	Emotional intelligence, healthy exploration of identity and self-expression, adaptability to change, positive body image and self-worth.	Emotional volatility, identity crises, challenges in self-expression, resistance to change, negative body image, low self-worth, engagement in risky behaviors.

Table 2.1

Table 2.1 outlines both healthy and unhealthy inner child characteristics as they manifest in adulthood, organized according to the developmental stages of childhood. It is structured this way because, while these traits shape our adult selves, their roots can be traced back to our earliest years. This is why understanding your childhood—the focus of the first chapter—is essential to your healing journey.

As you observe this table, see what characteristics you identify with. Are they more healthy or unhealthy? A mix of both, perhaps? What developmental stage do you sense the most trauma? We can use this table as a sort of roadmap to figure out where things have gone right in our childhood and where things may have come off the rails a bit.

This table serves as a valuable guide for your inner child healing journey. By understanding these traits, you can gain insights into evaluating the health and vitality of your own inner child. The developmental stages outlined—infancy, early childhood, middle childhood, and adolescence—offer a framework to assess various aspects of adult well-being. For instance, emotional resilience, secure attachments, and self-soothing skills developed during infancy contribute to a healthy adult emotional landscape. Similarly, qualities like playfulness, independence, and creativity from early childhood continue to shape an individual's openness to experiences and self-expression in adulthood. To evaluate your own inner child, you can reflect on your current emotional responses, interpersonal dynamics, and self-perception, considering how these align with the characteristics indicative of a healthy inner child. This introspective process offers a nuanced understanding of your inner child and paving the way for intentional healing.

The Inner Child Trigger Checklist: Recognizing Emotional Reactivity and Behavioral Patterns

Use this checklist to become more aware of how your inner child wounds might be influencing your emotions, thoughts, and behaviors. Take a moment to reflect on each question and notice any patterns that resonate with you.

- **Emotional Reactivity.** Do you find yourself experiencing sudden and intense emotional reactions, such as anger, fear, sadness, or feeling overwhelmed, without an apparent cause? Strong emotional reactions may indicate unresolved wounds from childhood.

- **Physical Sensations.** How does your body respond when difficult emotions arise? Pay attention to physical cues like muscle tension, a tight chest, rapid heartbeat, or a sinking feeling in your stomach.

- **Changes in Behavior.** Do you ever notice yourself reacting in ways that feel disproportionate to a situation? For example, do you withdraw, become defensive, engage in people-pleasing, or act impulsively—only to later regret it?

- **Negative Self-Talk.** Listen to your inner voice. Do you find yourself engaging in self-criticism, feeling unworthy, or constantly seeking approval from others? These patterns can stem from childhood experiences that shaped your self-perception.

- **Triggering Situations.** Are there certain situations, interactions, or environments that consistently stir up strong emotions? These can be similar to events from your childhood or remind you of unresolved issues from your past.

- **Pattern Recognition.** Reflect on any recurring themes or patterns in your life that may be connected to your inner child wounds. This may include difficulties with setting boundaries, low self-esteem, or challenges in forming healthy relationships.

- **Inner Dialogue.** Pay attention to the thoughts and inner dialogue that arise when you feel triggered. Notice if these thoughts are rational or if they seem to stem from a younger, more vulnerable part of yourself.

- **Regression in Behavior.** Do you tend to revert to certain behaviors or coping mechanisms from your childhood when you feel triggered? These could be habits or reactions that were helpful in the past but no longer serve you as an adult.

- **Strong Emotional Attachments.** Are there certain people, places, or objects that evoke strong emotions within you, almost as if they have a magnetic pull? Recognize if you have overly strong attachments to these triggers, as they may be linked to unhealed inner child wounds.

- **Difficulty in Self-Soothing.** Notice if you struggle to regulate your emotions or comfort yourself when you feel triggered. This can manifest as difficulty calming down, seeking external validation or reassurance, or being self-critical.

Working With Our Triggers

Understanding the strong link between environment, emotion, and reaction makes it easier for us to forgive misbehavior in ourselves and others. Remember that recognizing our triggers doesn't justify any behavior; instead, it empowers us to take responsibility for our reactions and make conscious changes. Reflecting on the concept of what is triggering can lead us to make wiser choices in our thoughts and actions.

Here is an exercise I want you to try:

1. **Identify Your Triggers.** Take a moment to reflect on your

personal triggers. They can be certain smells, sights, sounds, or even specific situations. Grab a piece of paper and write them down.

2. **Explore Your Childhood Wounds.** Now, let's delve deeper into your childhood wounds. Think about the painful or traumatic experiences from your past that still affect you today. How do these experiences relate to your triggers? Take some time to journal or make notes about your reflections.

3. **Develop Self-Awareness.** Self-awareness is crucial for healing. Take a moment to cultivate self-compassion and non-judgment. Acknowledge that these wounds are a part of your journey, but they don't define you. Embrace your strength and resilience as you navigate this healing process.

4. **Create Your Safe Space.** Find a comfortable and quiet space where you feel at ease. Close your eyes, take a deep breath, and imagine yourself in a safe and peaceful environment. This space will serve as your refuge throughout the exercise.

5. **Choose One Trigger.** Select one trigger from your list to focus on for this exercise. It can be something that frequently affects you or one that holds significant emotional weight. With this trigger in mind, let's move forward.

6. **Explore Your Trigger.** Allow your mind to explore the chosen trigger. What emotions or memories does it bring up for you? Pay attention to how it makes you feel physically. Notice any thoughts or beliefs that arise. Take your time in writing down your observations.

7. **Use Emotional Regulation Techniques.** Breathe deeply and

ground yourself. Give yourself a hug or whisper comforting words to yourself. Experiment with different techniques and notice which ones resonate with you. Use them whenever this trigger arises. (See Chapter 5 where we dive deeper into emotional regulation techniques.)

8. **Journal and Reflect.** Reflection is an important part of the growth process; take a moment to reflect on your experience. Journal about any insights you gained, progress you made, or challenges you encountered. Make this a regular practice to track your healing journey. This is something that can help you determine whether progress is being made or if you need to make any adjustments to your process—it is what can help you find what is and isn't working.

As we unravel the layers of inner child healing, we now focus our journey towards understanding the profound impact of our childhood experiences on the patterns woven into our adult lives. The intricate tapestry of our past forms the backdrop for the recurring themes and behaviors that shape our present. In the upcoming chapter, we will explore how the echoes of our early experiences reverberate through time, influencing the choices we make, the relationships we form, and the narratives we live. By gaining insight into these patterns, we unlock the key to recognizing the threads connecting our past to our present. This exploration is an integral step in our quest for healing, offering a profound understanding of the intricate dance between our past selves and the adults we've become.

Chapter Three

Creating Patterns

How Our Inner Child Shapes Repeated Patterns

Creativity involves breaking out of established patterns in order to do things in a different way. —Edward de Bono

Childhood is a canvas upon which the colors of our experiences blend, forming intricate patterns that persist well into adulthood. The encounters we have during these formative years heavily influence the lens through which we perceive the world. Whether it's the nurturing or neglect we receive, the love or abandonment we feel, or the stability or chaos we encounter, these experiences create patterns that shape our adult selves. They also seep into our relationships as adults because our early interactions with family members, friends, and authority figures shape our understanding of trust, intimacy, and vulnerability.

Edward de Bono's insightful quote reminds us that growth necessitates breaking free from established patterns. Our childhood experiences act as the architects of these patterns, shaping our beliefs, relationships, and coping mechanisms. But, by recognizing the power of these early imprints, we can teach ourselves to sieve through the disconnect and open ourselves up to growth and transformation. Let's first start by taking a look at how some of these patterns emerge in adulthood:

- **Abandonment Patterns.** These patterns may manifest as fear of being left or rejected, difficulty forming deep connections, or a tendency to push people away to protect oneself from potential abandonment.

- **Codependency Patterns.** This can involve excessively relying on others for validation and self-worth, struggling with boundaries, and feeling responsible for others' emotions and actions.

- **Trust Issues.** Patterns of mistrust may arise from childhood experiences of betrayal or broken trust, leading to difficulties in fully trusting others, being vulnerable, and forming intimate relationships.

- **People-Pleasing Patterns.** These patterns involve constantly prioritizing others' needs over one's own, difficulty saying no, and feeling guilty when asserting personal boundaries.

- **Emotional Avoidance Patterns.** These patterns may involve suppressing or avoiding emotions, as a result of childhood experiences where emotions were invalidated or not properly addressed. This can lead to difficulties in expressing emotions, forming deep connections, and self-awareness.

These patterns are mere threads intricately woven into the fabric of our journey. Understanding how these patterns manifest and intertwine is pivotal to our healing. By shedding light on these intricacies, we unveil the power to reshape and redefine our responses, fostering a path towards greater self-awareness and transformative change. So let's take a deep dive into this multifaceted landscape of patterns.

Fear-Based Patterns

Lately, when I am feeling anxious, queasy, or unsafe, I take my hand and place it at the helm of my heart, and I gently remind myself that uncertainty is where great possibility lives. Uncertainty is where freedom lives; uncertainty is where hope lives.

The need to control as a mechanism for creating a sense of safety is a fear-based behavioral pattern deeply rooted in psychology. The fear underlying this pattern often stems from past experiences where a lack of control led to feelings of vulnerability, discomfort, or even harm. This can lead to a need for control, as a response to this childhood stress or trauma, serving as a way to manage overwhelming emotions and create a semblance of safety.

We're never really going to have everything under control or have it all as figured out as we would like because so much of our lives is inherently uncontrollable and uncertain. And there is a certain kind of grief that comes to us when we realize that we're actually never really going to have it all figured out. But when we allow ourselves to grieve that loss of our illusion of certainty and control, uncertainty begins to feel a lot like freedom.

Imagine you're standing at the edge of a pool, ready to take a leap into the unknown depths. Suddenly, a strange sensation engulfs you, a mix of excitement and fear. Your heart starts racing, and all you want to do is feel that control, that safety, before taking the plunge. It's human nature to crave security in an unpredictable world.

Our need for control can manifest itself in various ways. Some people cling to rigid routines or meticulously plan every aspect of their lives. They intensively analyze and micromanage situations, hoping to anticipate any potential risks or uncertainties. It's like they're trying to place the whole world into a perfectly shaped box, attempting to prevent anything from going awry.

But why do we feel this way? Well, one reason is that control provides a sense of empowerment. When we feel in control, we believe we have the power to influence outcomes. It cushions us from the discomfort of uncertainty and vulnerability, fooling us into thinking we can protect ourselves from harm. When we feel in control, it's like we've created a cozy little bubble of safety.

But here's the paradox: The more we seek to control, the more we may actually distance ourselves from genuine safety. Life is unpredictable by nature. No matter how meticulously we plan or how tightly we hold onto control, there will always be variables and circumstances beyond our grasp. So, by fixating on control, we may inadvertently close ourselves off from the beauty of life's spontaneity and serendipity.

Brené Brown, the queen of vulnerability and courage, once said, "Vulnerability is the birthplace of innovation, creativity, and change." In other words, true growth and transformation can only happen when we relinquish that grip on control and allow ourselves to be vulnerable.

Patterns in Self-Worth

Imagine a delicate, porcelain doll, one that was once vibrant and full of life, now hidden away in the depths of a dusty attic. Its once-radiant colors have faded, and tiny cracks mar its fragile surface. The wounded inner child, much like that forgotten doll, resides deep within us, silently influencing our patterns of self-worth. Inside the intricate maze of our psyche, this wounded inner child whispers, softly but persistently, weaving a tangled web of self-doubt and insecurity. Like a shadowy figure lurking in the dimly lit corners of our minds, it casts doubt on our abilities, coloring our perception of ourselves. Their voice, fragile yet powerful, echoes through the chambers of our hearts. It whispers tales of unworthiness, recounting every harsh word and every hurtful gesture they endured. They cling to these painful memories, brandishing them as evidence that we are flawed and undeserving of love and acceptance.

These perceptions are deeply rooted in our beliefs about our own value, often stemming from childhood experiences and the relationship with our inner child. We may develop adaptive or maladaptive coping mechanisms as a response to early interactions, shaping our self-perception and influencing how we navigate the world. These coping mechanisms or behavioral patterns become ingrained over time, forming automatic responses to situations that reinforce the our self-concept. For example, someone with low self-worth may consistently seek external validation, avoid asserting themselves, or struggle with setting boundaries. On the other hand, a person with inflated self-worth might exhibit behaviors of superiority, constant need for attention, or difficulties in accepting feedback.

Under the umbrella of self-worth patterns, we may see the manifestation of **locus of control** issues. Locus of control refers to our belief or perception regarding the degree to which we have control over the events and outcomes in our lives. While interconnected to the need to control to feel safe, which is a fear-based pattern that stems from the pervasive desire for control as a means of managing anxiety and maintaining a sense of safety, individuals with locus of control issues may feel that external factors dictate their life, impacting their self-worth.

Take a child, for instance, who witnessed a series of uncontrollable events. The wounded inner child may feel powerless, as if their actions have minimal impact on outcomes, leading them to adopt a belief that they are at the mercy of external forces. This perception often carries into adulthood, influencing decision-making and fostering patterns of learned helplessness.

Another behavioral pattern that we may see with self-worth issues is **comparison**. The need to constantly compare ourselves to others, deriving our self-worth from external factors. We can see this manifest as constantly evaluating our achievements, appearance, or success in relation to those around us.

Picture a tapestry woven from threads of self-criticism and comparison, each strand meticulously placed by the wounded inner child. With careful hands, they craft a masterpiece of insecurity, measuring our worth against an unattainable standard—one we are always destined to fall short of. And with every perceived failure, the threads tighten, slowly suffocating our self-esteem.

But where did these threads of comparison even come from? What events from our childhood could be responsible for this behavioral pattern? Growing up in an environment with intense sibling rivalry, where constant comparisons are made between siblings, or experiencing high parental expectations and constant comparisons to other children in terms of academic achievements, behavior, or talents can lead to a pattern of comparing ourselves to others in adulthood. As children, we may internalize the belief that our value is determined by how well we measure up to others. The same is true for children who experienced significant pressure from their social environment in order to conform to certain standards, such as societal expectations related to appearance, success, or popularity.

Seeking validation is another behavior often observed within patterns related to self-worth. Comparison and validation-seeking patterns share some similarities, but they differ in their underlying motivations. The motivation of validation revolves around seeking external validation and approval from others to affirm our self-worth and significance, whereas comparison involves evaluating ourselves based on perceived benchmarks set by others. Individuals exhibiting validation-seeking behaviors often crave acknowledgment and positive feedback from friends, family, or peers.

The development of validation-seeking behavioral patterns in the adult can be linked to various childhood circumstances. For instance, if we did not receive consistent emotional validation or acknowledgment as children for our feelings and experiences, we may develop a heightened need for external validation in adulthood. Growing up in an environment where we learn to associate external validation with love and acceptance, where love and approval were conditional upon meeting certain expectations or achievements, may also lead to a persistent need for validation.

It is not just a lack of nurturing, love, or approval that can lead to validation-seeking patterns. An overemphasis on external achievements as a child can also lead to seeking validation as a pattern in adulthood. If the primary source of validation in childhood was tied to external achievements rather than intrinsic qualities, we may carry this pattern into adulthood. The belief that our worth is solely determined by external accomplishments can drive the need for ongoing validation.

But hope exists because we have the power to heal our wounded inner child, to mend the cracks in our self-worth. Through compassion and self-acceptance, we can gently cradle that fragile porcelain doll, restoring its vibrancy and strength. As we tend to our wounded inner child, showering them with love and understanding, their wounds begin to heal.

Slowly, they release their grip on self-doubt, allowing us to embrace our true value and potential.

In the end, it is through acknowledging and nurturing our wounded inner child that we can rewrite the narrative of our self-worth. With each step taken toward healing, we inch closer to liberation from the shackles of past pain. And as we embrace our inherent worthiness, we inspire others to do the same, creating lives where we are not defined by the past, but rather the potential of what lies ahead.

Patterns in Romantic Relationships

In the theater of our hearts, love is often the most enthralling act. But, amid the euphoria and enchantment, there's an enigmatic character lurking in the shadows—our wounded inner child. This subterranean sprite, though invisible, often takes center stage in our romantic relationships, playing out scenes of drama and discord that leave us questioning why love so often invites chaos into our lives.

When the curtain rises on a new relationship, we're filled with hope and anticipation. Our hearts are ripe with the promise of love. But, beneath this veneer of desire lies our wounded inner child, starved for attention and healing. It is this unattended part of us that can often hijack our relationships.

You can see this wounded inner child in the eyes of the lover who is hypersensitive to criticism, perceiving every feedback as a personal affront. There, in the depths of those wounded eyes, the old script of rejection is being replayed. The lover isn't just responding to a perceived slight in the present but to a chorus of past hurts that echo loudly in their heart.

The wounded inner child shows up in the insecurity that clings too tightly, smothering love in a desperate attempt to avoid abandonment.

It's as if a small, scared child within is pulling at the hem of their partner's clothes, pleading not to be left alone.

It is also the puppeteer behind the scenes of a fiery argument, where words serve as weapons and love is temporarily forgotten. In these moments, the adult facade crumbles, revealing the raw, unhealed wounds of a child who once felt powerless and unheard. Our romantic relationships, with their raw intimacy, have a way of scraping against these old wounds. In response, our wounded inner child throws tantrums, cries in silence, or erects walls. It's a defense mechanism, a desperate attempt to protect ourselves from reliving past traumas.

But the one thing that I want you to remember is that our wounded inner child isn't the villain of our love stories. It's just a vulnerable part of us, crying out for attention and healing. When it acts out, it's not to ruin our relationships but to signal that there are parts within us still longing for acceptance, understanding, and love.

The Attachment Theory

At its core, the attachment theory explores the deep-seated emotional bonds that we form with our primary caregivers, typically our parents or guardians, during our early years of life. Like a tender seedling seeking the nurturing warmth of sunlight, we instinctively seek love, care, and support from these trusted figures, creating an emotional foundation that molds our future relationships. Like a moon pulling a tide, this theory reminds us of the invisible forces that shape our emotional landscape.

Picture a newborn baby, fragile and utterly dependent on their caregiver for survival. In those first precious moments, a dance of connection begins to unfold. Through the caregiver's tender touch, soothing voice, and loving gaze, the baby's brain begins to wire itself, forging the pathways of attachment that will shape their emotional experiences throughout life.

The attachment theory posits that there are four primary attachment styles that we develop based on the quality of our early interactions with our caregivers. These styles, like different hues on the canvas of human connection, color our perceptions, expectations, and behaviors in our relationships.

We must also remember that attachment theory is not a life sentence but a framework to understand our early experiences and their impact on our lives. Through it, we see that our inner child—wounded or not—shapes our adult selves. Healing this inner child, therefore, involves revisiting these early attachment experiences, understanding them, and working to develop a more secure attachment style through self-awareness, therapy, and nurturing relationships.

The Avoidant Attachment Style

Avoidant attachment wears many faces, each shaped by past experiences and learned survival mechanisms. Here are some of the inner voices that often emerge from this attachment style:

- *I grew up in a daily life where I did not seek proximity physically or emotionally. My emotions were discouraged, and so therefore, I learned to deal with them all alone, or even to go so far as to ignore them altogether.*

- *I spend a lot of time alone and have learned to take care of myself. People always seemed to want my attention for their own needs, never for me. That's why I'm sensitive to feeling intruded upon or like someone is trying to take advantage of me.*

- *I have learned to think a lot before I speak because I always got into trouble for the way I was feeling. I tread lightly, and I don't trust that much. I harbor shame and wear a shield to look out for myself because no one else looks out for me.*

- *I feel the freest when I am by myself, without demands, because I have always felt like there was a demand from others, and the only way I felt safe was on my own.*

- *When people approach me, I assume they want something—my time, my energy, my skills. I don't feel wanted for who I am, only for what I can provide.*

The avoidant attachment style comes from a deep-rooted fear of intimacy, often from past experiences or a learned coping mechanism. With this attachment style, you have a strong desire for independence and self-reliance, often prioritizing your own needs and emotions over the needs of your partner.

In relationships, you can often appear aloof, emotionally distant, and fearful of vulnerability. You may struggle to express your feelings openly or may even keep your partner at arm's length to avoid the perceived risk of emotional intimacy.

Imagine being caught in the spellbinding embrace of love, only to find yourself slipping away in these moments of emotional intensity. This kind of inconsistency creates a push-pull dynamic, where you, the avoidant individual, shifts between periods of closeness and emotional detachment. You become uneasy or uncomfortable when your partner expresses strong emotions or a desire for closeness.

To fully understand and to be able to work with this attachment style, we must remind ourselves that this behavior comes from a deep-rooted fear of being engulfed or dependent on another person. When you have an avoidant attachment style, you often still carry a belief that you must rely solely on yourself, inherently devaluing the importance of emotional connection. Sometimes, this desire for independence can manifest as a strong need for personal space and alone time. You prioritize your own hobbies, goals, and interests over shared activities, sacrificing the opportunity to intimately connect with your partner. This doesn't necessarily mean you are incapable of love, but rather that your approach to love and intimacy requires a delicate understanding and patience from your partner.

How to Heal an Avoidant Attachment Style

Changing your attachment style is not an easy task—it requires patience, effort, and self-awareness. However, healing is absolutely possible. The key is to take small, intentional steps toward emotional openness and connection. Here are a few powerful strategies to help you on this journey:

- **Practice Communicating Your Needs.** When someone asks an intimate question, resist the urge to deflect or withdraw. Instead, challenge yourself to respond in a way that feels safe at the moment. You don't have to share everything, but practicing small moments of openness helps build trust over time.

- **Start an Emotions Journal.** Avoidant individuals often struggle with identifying and processing their emotions. Journaling can help you develop self-awareness and create a habit of acknowledging your feelings rather than suppressing them.

- **Expand Your Circle of Emotional Connection.** Spend time with people other than your partner to strengthen your ability to be open and vulnerable. Having multiple sources of emotional support can make intimacy feel less overwhelming.

- **Take Small Steps Toward Intimacy.** Learning to be emotionally present in a relationship may feel unnatural at first, but consistency is key. Experiment with different ways to express affection, and once you find a method that feels comfortable, keep practicing it until it becomes second nature. (See *Table 3.1*, on next page, for ideas on how to express affection).

The Anxious Attachment Style

It is absolute chaos when anxious attachment wounds are running the show in a relationship. This is what it looks like when an anxious attachment wound is at the wheel:

- Being preoccupied with what a partner is or is not doing and pursuing them to change or to behave in the way you want them to.

- Making a partner responsible for your big feelings and anxiety while neglecting the role that you are playing in creating the pattern.

- Self-abandonment and betrayal of your own inner voice, needs, and desires.

- Urgently attaching to new people without actually having gotten to know them all that well.

- Shutting down parts of yourself because you're afraid that people will leave.

Action	Why It Helps
Offer physical affection in small doses. A brief hug, holding hands, or resting your hand on their shoulder can gradually build comfort with physical closeness.	Helps bridge the gap between emotional and physical connection.
Share a meaningful experience together. Try an activity that requires teamwork, like cooking a meal, taking a dance class, or playing a cooperative game.	Encourages bonding in a low-pressure way.
Practice active listening. The next time your partner shares something personal, focus on being fully present instead of mentally preparing a response.	Builds trust and helps you engage emotionally.
Schedule intentional quality time. Plan small moments of connection, like a daily 10-minute check-in, a weekly date night, or a morning coffee together.	Creates consistency, which feels safer than spontaneous emotional demands.
Express appreciation verbally. Even if big emotional statements feel unnatural, a simple "I really appreciate you" or "I love spending time with you" can go a long way.	Helps normalize verbal intimacy in a low-stakes way.
Open up in writing. If verbal vulnerability feels intimidating, try writing a heartfelt note, text, or letter expressing something you appreciate about them.	Allows you to process and express emotions at your own pace.
Set small personal intimacy goals. Challenge yourself with one small act of connection each day, like making eye contact during a conversation or initiating a hug.	Makes emotional closeness feel more approachable and less overwhelming.

Table 3.1 Methods of Expressing Affection for Avoidant Attachment Style.

- Trying to control a partner or trying to psychoanalyze them with the conviction that they are the sole problem in the relationship.

- Obsessing over lost love and all the ways in which they have wronged you.

The not-so-talked-about part of anxious attachment is the inability or the capacity to recognize and to receive love. There's generally this whole narrative around avoidants being cold and dismissive, which makes them seem like the bad guys in the picture, but in reality, both the anxious and the avoidant are experiencing the same thing, but one is internal with their process and the other is external.

The anxious attachment wound creates obsession, dysregulation, and self-righteousness. It can be really challenging in the thick of it to see it, in all of its sinister ways, but that wound may actually also be perpetuating the pattern too.

Sometimes, anxiety isn't just an overreaction—it's a signal that something in the relationship truly isn't right. But when we haven't done the deeper inner work to separate our past wounds from present reality, it becomes nearly impossible to trust our own instincts. If we can't distinguish between what belongs to us and what belongs to our partner, our intuition loses its reliability.

For those with an anxious attachment style, it's essential to step back from the constant need to fix, manage, or control the relationship. Give yourself permission to breathe. If the relationship is meant to last, it will—without you having to hold it together single-handedly. And if it doesn't, trust that you will be okay. In fact, your anxious heart might just thank you for the freedom.

How to Heal an Anxious Attachment Style

Healing an anxious attachment style begins with building a sense of inner security. It's about creating a safe space within, so love and connection no longer feel like a source of anxiety, but a place of mutual respect and reassurance. Here are some key steps to help you move toward a more secure way of relating:

- **Learn to Self-Soothe.** When anxiety takes hold, grounding yourself in the present moment can help regulate your emotions. Try these calming techniques:
  - Practice deep, conscious breathing—inhale slowly, hold, and exhale with intention.
  - Allow yourself to cry if you need to. Release is healing.
  - Wrap yourself in layers of blankets, creating a cocoon of comfort.
  - Sip a warm, soothing drink to relax your nervous system.
  - Take a long shower or soak in a warm bath to ease tension.
  - Give yourself a tight, reassuring hug—your own embrace is powerful.
  - Place your hands on your chest, feeling the steady rhythm of your heart. With each beat, remind yourself: *I am here. I am alive. I am safe.*

- **Reframe Your Fears.** When you notice signs that your partner might be pulling away, don't automatically assume the worst. Instead of reacting with blame, control, or demands, express your concerns with calmness and vulnerability.

- **Stop Self-Abandoning.** Put your own needs first instead of exhausting yourself for approval. You deserve care and consideration—especially from yourself.

- **Detach from External Validation.** Other people's behavior is rarely personal. Often, their actions reflect their own struggles. Rejection isn't a reflection of your worth—it's simply a misalignment of energies.

- **Shift Your Perspective on Love.** For example:
  - Take your romantic partners off a pedestal—see them as equals, not saviors.
  - Choose emotional availability over chemistry alone.
  - Be honest about your feelings from the start. The wrong people will leave, and the right ones will stay.

The Fearful-Avoidant Attachment Style

Imagine wanting love and connection more than anything—yet feeling paralyzed by the fear of getting too close. One moment, you crave intimacy, and the next, you feel the urge to withdraw. You want to trust, but deep down, you question everyone's intentions, including your own. This emotional push-pull isn't just frustrating; it's exhausting.

Fearful-avoidant attachment says:

- *I generally hold negative views of myself and negative views of others.*

- *Relationships are often very confusing for me. I struggle to differentiate between who is safe and who isn't.*

- *I don't know who I can and cannot trust.*

- *I crave closeness in relationships, but I also fear abandonment deeply.*

- *I sometimes struggle with managing the mixture of emotions that I feel in relationships.*

- *I may sometimes tell people too much and then not want to share anything at all.*

- *Acting hot and cold makes it very difficult for me to maintain healthy relationships.*

Also known as anxious-avoidant or disorganized attachment, this style is marked by a deep internal conflict: the desire for connection battling against the fear of rejection or engulfment. If you identify with this, you may have grown up in an environment where caregiving was inconsistent—sometimes loving, sometimes neglectful, or even harmful. This unpredictability wired you to be hyper-aware of emotional shifts, leaving you unsure of who to trust and making relationships feel like a constant game of emotional tug-of-war.

As a result, you develop a deep fear of both intimacy and rejection. On one hand, you crave that comfort that comes from closeness and connection, but on the other hand, you fear being hurt or engulfed by others. Trusting others feels risky, as though betrayal or abandonment is inevitable. You've likely learned to be highly self-reliant, suppressing emotional needs because, in childhood, vulnerability may have felt unsafe. Expressing emotions openly feels foreign, and maintaining balance between connection and self-protection can seem impossible.

But healing is possible. Moving toward a secure attachment style requires stepping into discomfort—learning to stay present rather than running at the first sign of vulnerability. It means challenging the old beliefs formed in childhood and allowing yourself to experiment with new, healthier ways of relating. Over time, you may realize that your deepest fears aren't actually coming true, and that real intimacy doesn't have to feel like a trap.

How to Heal a Fearful-Avoidant Style

Healing from a fearful-avoidant attachment style takes patience, self-awareness, and a willingness to step into discomfort. Here are some key steps to help you move toward a more secure way of relating:

- **Acknowledge Your Past.** Recognize the experiences that shaped your attachment style. Understanding where your fears and patterns stem from is the first step toward healing.

- **Reconnect with Yourself.** Identify the parts of yourself that you've had to shut down in order to feel loved and accepted. True connection starts with embracing your authentic self.

- **Observe Your Triggers.** Pay attention to the core beliefs that surface when you feel triggered. (We'll explore core beliefs in more detail in the next chapter.)

- **Sit with Your Emotions.** Allow yourself to notice, name, and sit with all of your emotions, even if they are uncomfortable. The more you practice this, the less overwhelming they become.

- **Express Instead of Withdrawing.** Instead of shutting down, practice communicating your feelings, even if it feels unnatural at first. Small steps toward vulnerability build trust over time.

- **Take Small Steps Toward Openness.** Gradually practice emotional intimacy by sharing small, meaningful parts of yourself with others. It's okay to go at your own pace.

- **Set and Maintain Boundaries.** Healthy relationships require balance. Learn to identify, communicate, and uphold your boundaries so that you do not feel or become too burdened by the emotions and feelings of others.

- **Trust in Support.** Allow yourself to believe that others can and will be there for you. Trust is built through experience, but it begins with giving people the chance to show up for you.

- **Embrace Love Without Earning It.** Understand that love is not something you have to earn or prove yourself worthy of. Real love exists without conditions—allow yourself to receive it.

Bonus Tips: Staying Connected and Loving While Maintaining Boundaries

Maintaining boundaries in a relationship can feel challenging, especially when you deeply care for someone. You might fear that standing firm in your limits will create distance or conflict, but in reality, healthy boundaries foster deeper connection and mutual respect. When you honor your own needs, you show up more authentically in your relationships—able to give and receive love without resentment or self-sacrifice. Here are some practical strategies to help you stay connected and loving while standing firm in your personal limits:

- **Give Yourself Permission to Hold Your Boundaries.** Resist the impulse to cave in or run. Remind yourself that you have the freedom to adjust your boundaries later if needed. For now, choose to stand by them and trust your decision.

- **Stay Present in Your Body.** When emotions become overwhelming, it's easy to dissociate. Instead of disconnecting, focus on your breath and feel your feet planted firmly on the ground. This is your moment to ground yourself rather than retreat.

- **Reaffirm Your Personal Agency.** You are safe. You have the power to decide what your limits are, and no one can take that away from you.

- **Use a Grounding Mantra.** Repeat to yourself: *I can listen to you safely because you do not threaten my immutable safety.* This simple affirmation helps you stay engaged in conversations without feeling pressured to compromise your boundaries.

By practicing self-soothing in these moments, you give yourself the ability to remain present and connected in your relationships—without sacrificing your sense of self. Always remember, your right to decide what is best for you is yours alone.

The Secure Attachment Style

Secure attachment in a relationship is knowing that you deserve love and respect. It's setting boundaries when people don't treat you as well as they should. It is being comfortable with sharing how you feel and being able to clearly and confidently express your needs. It is trusting that you will survive even the most stressful of life events. It's trusting yourself enough with the decisions that you have to make. Secure attachment is being rooted. Think of a majestic oak tree standing tall and strong amidst a vast forest. Its roots delve deep into the earth, anchoring it firmly in place. Just as this tree thrives, so does a person with a secure attachment style. Secure attachment is like the nourishing soil that enables individuals to grow and flourish, providing a solid foundation for their emotional well-being.

In this metaphor, the oak tree represents a person with a secure attachment style. They have developed a strong sense of trust, safety, and connection with their caregivers, much like the roots of the tree that firmly hold it in place. Just as the tree draws sustenance from the soil, individuals with secure attachments draw comfort and support from their relationships.

Like the branches and leaves that reach toward the sky, secure attachment allows you to explore the world with confidence, knowing that you have a secure base to return to. It's the ability to form healthy and meaningful connections with others, just like the tree provides shelter and nourishment for various creatures in the forest.

How a Secure Person Shows Up in a Relationship

First off, individuals with a secure attachment style are less likely to take things personally. Because these individuals carry fewer emotional wounds, they are less prone to being triggered. As a result, they tend to interpret situations more objectively rather than overanalyzing or assigning negative meaning, as someone with an insecure attachment might.

Secure individuals also feel much safer when being vulnerable. During childhood, they were encouraged to express themselves openly, leading to positive subconscious associations with vulnerability. As adults, this foundation allows them to share their thoughts and emotions without fear or hesitation.

They are comfortable setting and maintaining boundaries. Having learned early on that their voices were heard and respected, they received the message that it is not only safe but also healthy to communicate their needs. Because of this, they can assert their boundaries with confidence and without guilt.

Unlike those with insecure attachment styles, secure individuals do not rely on repression as a coping mechanism. They are incredibly good at owning what they feel and need in real time. This ability also helps them remain in the moment without needing to hyper-focus on others.

Habits to Practice if You Want to Be More Secure in Your Relationships

Security in relationships isn't built overnight—it's cultivated through conscious effort, patience, and a willingness to grow. A secure relationship is not one without conflict, but one where both partners feel safe enough to navigate challenges with honesty, respect, and resilience. If you long to foster a deeper sense of stability and trust, these habits will serve as your foundation, allowing love to thrive without fear or uncertainty.

Trust and Transparency. No relationship can flourish without these two pillars. Trust is built through consistency—by showing up when we say we will, by following through on promises, and by respecting our partner's emotional safety. Transparency means being open about our thoughts, feelings, and intentions, ensuring that we never leave room for unnecessary doubt or fear. Secure relationships thrive in an environment where both people feel confident in each other's integrity and commitment.

Forgiveness and Repairs. Every relationship will face moments of disappointment or misunderstanding. The difference between a fragile bond and a resilient one lies in how we handle those moments. Owning our mistakes, offering sincere apologies, and making meaningful efforts to repair the damage are essential. Equally important is the practice of forgiveness—not to excuse harmful behavior, but to release resentment that erodes connection. However, forgiveness should never mean tolerating repeated disrespect or unhealthy patterns. True repair happens when accountability and change go hand in hand.

Personal and Relational Growth. Relationships are living, evolving entities that require care and adaptation. Secure individuals understand that growth is an ongoing process—both personally and within the relationship. This means embracing change rather than resisting it, committing to self-improvement, and nurturing the bond with curiosity and intention. It also means not shutting down, stonewalling, or withdrawing when challenges arise, but rather leaning into the discomfort of necessary conversations, knowing that growth often lies on the other side.

Understanding Love Languages

Imagine sailing through a vast ocean of love with your partner by your side. Suddenly, something gets lost in translation—you're expressing your affection in French, while your partner is trying to understand you in Italian. This is where the concept of love languages becomes your compass, guiding you through the complexities of love and ensuring that your expressions of affection are truly heard.

Dr. Gary Chapman introduced the idea of love languages, identifying five distinct ways people express and receive love: Words of Affirmation, Acts of Service, Receiving Gifts, Quality Time, and Physical Touch. Just as a child finds comfort in speaking their native tongue, each of us has a love language that feels most natural, a way of giving and receiving love that resonates deeply with who we are. It is through this language that our inner child expresses its needs, longings, and vulnerabilities. When our love language is spoken and understood, our inner child feels seen, nurtured, and valued.

Love isn't just about feeling—it's about communication. Like a symphony, a relationship requires harmony between both partners. If one person expresses love through words of affirmation, but the other only understands acts of service, they may feel unappreciated or even unloved. This is why learning your partner's love language and teaching them yours is essential—it builds a bridge of understanding and mutual care.

Every relationship is a dance of love languages, a rhythm of give-and-take where partners learn to express love in ways the other can receive. It's about speaking their language while also inviting them to learn yours. In doing so, you cultivate a relationship where both of you feel secure, cherished, and deeply understood. Embracing love languages isn't just about improving communication—it's about honoring the emotional needs that took root in childhood and continue to shape us today. When a relationship acknowledges and nurtures these needs, it becomes a sanctuary of love, safety, and mutual respect.

As Lysa TerKeurst writes, "The best kind of love is the kind that awakens the soul and makes us reach for more." Understanding and expressing our love languages awaken not only our souls but also the deepest parts of our being. It is an invitation to love more fully, to connect more deeply, and to create a relationship where love flows as effortlessly as the waves in the vast ocean we sail together.

What Your Love Language Says About You

Words of Affirmation. You feel most loved when your partner expresses their feelings through words. Simple phrases like "I love you," "I appreciate you," or "You mean so much to me" hold deep significance. Verbal validation reassures you, offering the recognition and connection you may have lacked in childhood. Whether you grew up in a home where praise was scarce or simply long for open communication, affirming words serve as a powerful anchor of love for you.

Gifts. You prefer to give and receive love through meaningful and thoughtful gifts. You see gifts as a visual symbol of love and that makes you feel seen, validated, and appreciated. It's not really about the gift but the meaning behind the gift. You value the effort that went into choosing it. A handwritten note, a carefully chosen book, or even a small token given "just because" makes you feel valued. It is a reflection, a representation of your partner's love for you. This love language often stems from childhood experiences where gifts represented love, acknowledgment, or consistency in an otherwise unpredictable environment.

Physical Touch. Holding hands, a warm embrace, or a reassuring touch on the shoulder—these are the ways you feel most connected. Physical affection makes you feel safe, grounded, and deeply loved; it is how you experience intimacy and reassurance. Perhaps you were raised in an affectionate household where hugs were freely given, or maybe you lacked that warmth and now long for it as an adult.

Acts of Service. You truly do believe that actions speak louder than words. When your partner shares the load—whether it's making your morning coffee, filling up your gas tank, or cooking you a meal—it makes you feel appreciated and cared for. You likely learned early on that love is best expressed through action. Maybe in childhood, love was conditional on achievement, or perhaps acts of service were the primary way affection was shown in your home. Either way, you now associate care with the willingness to help and support.

Quality Time. Presence means everything to you. Undistracted, meaningful time with your partner makes you feel valued and loved. You crave deep conversations, shared experiences, and one-on-one moments where you know you're their priority. If quality time is your primary love language, you may have grown up in an environment where people were always too busy, leaving you longing for attention, connection, and a sense of being truly seen.

A Few Things to Remember About Love Languages

Love languages are as unique as fingerprints—what speaks to one person may not resonate with another. Understanding your partner's love language is just as important as knowing your own. When you take the time to understand how they feel most loved, you create a stronger foundation for connection and intimacy.

Love languages can also evolve over time. What once felt essential to you may shift as your needs, experiences, and relationships grow. Stay open to change, both in yourself and in your partner, and be willing to adapt.

It's not about the quantity of love you show but the quality of it. Instead of overwhelming your partner with excessive gestures, focus on meaningful acts that align with their love language. A small, genuine act of love can often have a more significant impact than grand gestures.

Deciphering love languages isn't always easy. Open, honest communication is key—talk to your partner about what makes you feel loved, listen to their needs, and find ways to meet in the middle. Love languages aren't meant to be a guessing game; they thrive when both people make an effort to express and receive love in ways that feel fulfilling.

And lastly, love languages go beyond romantic relationships. They influence how we connect with family, friends, and even colleagues. When we understand how others give and receive love, we create stronger, more meaningful relationships in every area of life.

Patterns in Everyday Relationships

The way we relate to others in adulthood is often a reflection of the emotional patterns we learned in childhood. These patterns don't just appear in romantic relationships—they shape how we engage with family, friends, and even coworkers. Some patterns serve us well, fostering connection and trust, while others keep us trapped in cycles of misunderstanding, conflict, or emotional pain. By identifying these recurring dynamics, we can begin to break free from unhealthy behaviors and create more fulfilling relationships.

Below, we'll explore some of the most common relational patterns, how they manifest in different areas of life, and how they often stem from childhood experiences.

Toxic Family Patterns

As children, we are like sponges, absorbing our parents' values, behaviors, and emotional coping mechanisms. If we grew up witnessing unhealthy dynamics—such as verbal or physical abuse, substance abuse, manipulation, neglect, or codependency—we may internalize these patterns as normal or acceptable and unknowingly replicate them in our adult lives.

Let's take a look at some of the most common cycles that quietly take root in adulthood, waiting to be seen, understood, and rewritten:

- **The Cycle of Abuse.** If we witnessed or experienced physical, emotional, or verbal abuse as children, we may unconsciously perpetuate it in our adult relationships—either as the abuser or the abused, by tolerating harmful behavior or by struggling with anger and control issues ourselves.

- **The Cycle of Addiction.** Growing up with substance abuse can lead to a higher risk of developing addiction or being attracted to partners with addiction issues.

- **The Cycle of Neglect.** If we experience neglect as children, we may struggle with forming healthy attachments and may inadvertently neglect our own emotional needs or the needs of our loved ones.

- **The Cycle of Codependency.** Codependency is the repeated neglect of yourself in order to gain love and affection in relationships. It is a learned pattern of relating that often develops due to early emotional trauma. It teaches us that love is earned through self-sacrifice. If we were conditioned to ignore our own needs for the sake of keeping the peace or pleasing others, we may carry this dynamic into our friendships and romantic relationships.

- **The Cycle of Poor Communication.** If we witness unhealthy communication patterns, such as yelling, avoidance, or passive-aggressiveness we may struggle with effective, healthy communication in our adult relationships, leading to misunderstandings and conflicts.

As you begin to recognize these cycles, you may also feel the weight of invisible chains—binding you to the roles you played in childhood, tethering you to patterns that persist into adulthood. Whether the dysfunction in your family was extreme or not, you may still find yourself stuck in the role you were assigned as a child, such as:

- **The Fixer or Caretaker.** You feel responsible for managing others' emotions, solving their problems, and keeping the peace—even at your own expense.

- **The Scapegoat.** You were blamed for family issues, and now, you either rebel against authority or struggle with deep-seated guilt, shame, and self-blame.

- **The Overachiever or Golden Child.** You learned that love had to be earned through perfection, and now, your worth is tied to achievement rather than your intrinsic self.

- **The Invisible One.** You learned to stay quiet, small, and out of the way—and now, you may struggle with self-expression or believing that your voice matters.

These roles often shape our friendships, workplace dynamics, and romantic relationships, influencing how we navigate conflict, boundaries, and self-worth. The good news? Awareness allows you to step out of the role you were given and reclaim the one you choose. You are not bound to the dysfunction of your past—you have the power to break the cycle. Begin by:

- **Releasing Assigned Roles.** You are more than "the fixer," "the caretaker," or "the problem child." Give yourself permission to redefine who you are outside of family expectations.

- **Setting and Upholding Boundaries.** Your needs, emotions, and space matter. Saying "no" is not selfish—it's self-respect.

- **Letting Go of Guilt and Obligation.** Love should not be built on guilt. You are not responsible for fixing others or carrying their emotional burdens.

- **Reparenting Yourself.** If your family couldn't provide the nurturing you needed, start giving it to yourself. Offer yourself the kindness, validation, and love you once craved.

- **Choosing Relationships that Align with Your Healing.** Surround yourself with people who respect and uplift you. Family is not just blood—family is anyone who loves you in a way that feels safe and reciprocal.

Remember, breaking these cycles requires awareness, conscious effort, and self-compassion. Just as trauma can be passed down through generations, so can healing. By doing the inner work, you give yourself—and future generations—the gift of healthier, more fulfilling relationships.

Unhealthy Patterns in Friendships

Friendships should be a sanctuary—a place of trust, reciprocity, and emotional safety. Yet, for many of us, the friendships we build in adulthood unknowingly reflect the wounds of our childhood. The way we relate to others is shaped by the emotional blueprints we developed early on, and when those blueprints were drawn in dysfunction, we may find ourselves repeating unhealthy dynamics in our friendships.

Below are some of the most common friendship patterns that stem from childhood wounds:

- **The One-Sided Friendship.** You over-give, over-extend, and over-accommodate, yet your efforts are rarely reciprocated. This may stem from childhood experiences where love felt conditional—where being useful, self-sacrificing, or constantly earning affection was the only way to feel valued.

- **The Fear-Based Friendship.** You hold onto friendships out of obligation, guilt, or fear of being alone rather than genuine connection. If, as a child, you learned that rejection was painful and approval had to be earned, you may find yourself clinging to relationships that no longer serve you, simply to avoid the discomfort of being alone.

- **Over-Giving and People-Pleasing.** If you were taught that love must be earned through self-sacrifice, you may become the friend who always gives but struggles to receive. While generosity is beautiful, a friendship built on one person constantly overextending themselves is not sustainable—it leads to burnout, resentment, and emotional exhaustion.

- **Emotional Dumping vs. Emotional Support.** Some friendships take on a therapist-client dynamic, where one person constantly unloads their problems but offers little emotional support in return. If you were raised to prioritize others' emotions over your own, this dynamic may feel familiar—even if it's draining.

- **Lack of Boundaries.** You say yes when you want to say no, avoid confrontation at all costs, or tolerate disrespect because setting boundaries feels like abandonment. If you were made to feel guilty for expressing your needs as a child, enforcing boundaries in friendships may feel deeply uncomfortable—even though they are necessary for healthy relationships.

- **Fear of Abandonment.** If you experienced emotional neglect or frequent disappointment in childhood, you may find yourself walking on eggshells in friendships, afraid of being "too much" or pushing people away. You may overanalyze interactions, seek constant reassurance, or suppress your true feelings to avoid losing people.

- **Attracting Toxic Friendships.** If chaos, inconsistency, or conditional love were the norm in your childhood, you may unconsciously gravitate toward friends who are emotionally unavailable, manipulative, or unreliable. The familiarity of dysfunction can feel oddly comfortable, making it difficult to recognize when a friendship is actually harmful.

- **Keeping Emotional Distance.** If vulnerability wasn't safe in childhood, you may struggle to open up to friends, maintaining a surface-level connection while secretly craving something deeper. Trusting others with your true emotions may feel risky, leading to a pattern of self-isolation or emotional avoidance.

Healing begins with awareness. Are your friendships reciprocal? Do you feel safe expressing your needs? Are you drawn to people who mirror old wounds? By recognizing these patterns, you can begin consciously choosing relationships that are safe, balanced, supportive, fulfilling, and built on mutual respect. True friendships are not about obligation or emotional labor; they are about being seen, valued, and loved—not for what you can offer, but simply for who you are.

Unhealthy Patterns in the Workplace

Our childhood conditioning doesn't just impact personal relationships—it also shapes our behavior in professional environments. It has an astonishing influence over the way we interact with authority figures, handle criticism, set boundaries, and define succuss. If we were raised in homes where criticism was harsh, expectations were unrealistic, or our self-worth was tied to performance, we may carry those anxieties into our work life, unconsciously recreating cycles of seeking validation, fear of failure, or tolerating mistreatment.

Here are some signs of unhealthy workplace patterns that, sadly enough, many of us can relate to all too well:

- **Overworking for Validation.** If your worth was tied to achievement in childhood—if praise and love were only given when you excelled—you may find yourself pushing to the brink of exhaustion at work. Promotions, titles, and external recognition can feel like the only proof of your value, making it hard to rest without guilt.

- **Fear of Saying No.** If setting boundaries wasn't safe growing up, you may struggle to assert yourself in professional settings. You take on too much responsibility, hesitate to ask for help, and feel uneasy prioritizing your own well-being, fearing that saying "no" will lead to disappointment or rejection.

- **People-Pleasing with Authority Figure.** If you craved approval from caregivers who were distant, critical, or hard to please, you may unconsciously transfer that dynamic onto your boss or colleagues. You might go above and beyond to gain their favor, tolerate unfair treatment, or feel deeply wounded by even constructive feedback.

- **Perfectionism and Fear of Failure.** If love and praise were conditional on success in your early years, you may hold yourself to impossible standards at work. Mistakes feel catastrophic rather than part of growth, and the fear of failure can lead to anxiety, burnout, or paralysis in decision-making.

- **Conflict Avoidance or Defensiveness.** If disagreements in your childhood home were unpredictable, volatile, or emotionally unsafe, you may struggle with workplace conflict. You either avoid confrontation altogether, walking on eggshells to keep the peace, or react defensively, interpreting feedback as a personal attack.

- **Attracting Controlling or Dismissive Bosses.** If you grew up with emotionally unavailable, critical, or authoritarian parents, you may unconsciously find yourself working under similar authority figures. The familiarity of these power struggles can keep you trapped in cycles of seeking approval from those who withhold it.

- **Tolerating Toxic Work Environments.** If chaos, instability, or high stress were normalized in your home life, you may unknowingly gravitate toward workplaces that mirror that dysfunction. Constant pressure and emotional upheaval may feel familiar—even motivating—making it harder to recognize when a job is unhealthy or unsustainable.

By becoming aware of these workplace patterns, you can begin to shift them. You are not your productivity. Your value is not determined by the approval of a boss or the number of tasks you complete. To begin breaking free from these patterns, start by:

- Practicing self-validation rather than seeking it externally.

- Setting healthy boundaries around work-life balance.

- Advocating for yourself in conversations about workload, compensation, and expectations.

- Noticing when fear is driving your decisions—and gently challenging it.

Healing means learning to define success on your own terms and creating a professional life that aligns with your well-being, not just your output. Work is meant to support your life, not consume it.

The Mindsets That Keep Us Stuck

Recognizing toxic patterns is essential, but awareness alone isn't enough to break free from them. True transformation requires us to go deeper—to examine the mindsets that keep us tethered to these cycles, even when we long for change.

Many of the patterns we carry were once survival strategies, formed in response to difficult or painful experiences. They protected us. But what once kept us safe can become the very thing that holds us back. When we view ourselves as powerless, when we blame others for our struggles, or when we become defensive at the slightest discomfort, we unknowingly reinforce the very wounds we are trying to heal.

To move forward, we must confront these limiting mindsets with honesty and compassion. Victimhood, blame, and defensiveness may feel automatic, but they are not permanent. They are learned responses—and anything learned can be unlearned. By shifting our perspective and reclaiming our personal power, we can step into a life that is no longer dictated by past wounds but shaped by conscious choices.

Helplessness and Victim Mode

Place yourself in an imaginary situation where things don't go according to plan. Perhaps you're facing a challenging problem, experiencing a setback, or dealing with an unexpected turn of events. In these moments, it's natural for us to seek explanations or reasons for why things went wrong. And sometimes, the most readily available explanation is to place ourselves in the position of a victim. Now, entering "victim mode" isn't necessarily a conscious choice; it often happens when we feel overwhelmed or helpless in the face of adversity. It's a way our psyche copes with the discomfort and disappointment that comes with setbacks—it is how we temporarily shift responsibility away from ourselves to external factors or individuals.

In this mode, we may find ourselves ruminating on the unfairness of our circumstances, feeling a sense of powerlessness, and even seeking sympathy or validation from others. It's as if we put on a pair of victim-tinted glasses, through which every interaction and experience seems to reinforce our belief that we are the unfortunate target of life's obstacles.

But why do we do this? Well, for one, "victim mode" provides a certain level of emotional relief. When blaming external factors or others, we temporarily absolve ourselves of any personal responsibility for what went wrong. This can offer a soothing sense of reassurance that we're not at fault, and it allows us to bypass the uncomfortable task of introspection or self-evaluation. It also allows us to connect with others who might empathize with our struggles. As social beings, we naturally seek support and understanding from those around us when faced with adversity. Identifying as a victim can elicit sympathy and compassion from others, offering a form of emotional comfort and validation.

Victim mode doesn't mean that the challenges we face aren't valid or difficult, or that we should completely dismiss the pain we feel. Life can be truly challenging, and it's natural to experience periods of vulnerability. However, it's essential to acknowledge the pitfalls of staying in this mindset for too long because it can trap us in a cycle of repeated negativity and disempowerment. It can prevent us from taking proactive steps to overcome obstacles and limit our ability to find solutions or alternative perspectives. We have the agency and resilience to navigate and transcend difficult situations.

Here are some tips to help you change your mindset when victim mode kicks in:

- The first step in overcoming victim mentality is to acknowledge when you're falling into that pattern of thinking. Pay attention to the language you use and the stories you tell yourself. Are you constantly blaming others or circumstances for your problems? Awareness is key to initiating change.

- Instead of blaming others, take ownership of your life. Understand that you have the power to make choices and decisions that can impact your circumstances. Recognize that you are not powerless and that you can actively participate in creating a better future for yourself.

- Often, victim mentality stems from distorted thinking patterns and negative assumptions. Question your beliefs and challenge the validity of your thoughts. Ask yourself if there might be alternative explanations or perspectives that you haven't considered.

- Cultivating a mindset of gratitude can help shift your focus from what's wrong in your life to what's going well. Take time each day to reflect on the things you're grateful for, no matter how small. This practice can help rewire your brain to see the positive aspects of your life.

- Be kind to yourself and practice self-compassion. Understand that everyone makes mistakes and experiences setbacks. Treat yourself with the same kindness and understanding you would extend to a dear friend. By practicing self-compassion, you can build resilience and develop a healthier outlook on life.

- Rather than dwelling on problems, shift your focus to finding solutions. When faced with challenges, ask yourself, "What can I do to improve this situation?" By focusing on solutions, you'll develop a problem-solving mindset and become more empowered to effect change.

Blaming and Defensiveness

Blame shifting and defensiveness are our brain's way of protecting itself from potential harm. When we find ourselves in a situation where we might be at fault or face negative consequences, our instinctual response is to protect our ego and avoid taking responsibility. It's self-preservation at its best.

Think about it this way: You were working on something at work and things didn't go as planned. So, when someone points out a mistake or criticizes your contribution, you raise your walls and do everything you can to protect your dignity. You might immediately come up with excuses to protect yourself from feeling inadequate or facing potential consequences.

But where does this come from? Well, it often stems from our fear of judgment, rejection, or failure. It's a way to shield ourselves from uncomfortable emotions and maintain a positive self-image. Nobody wants to be seen as incompetent or at fault, right?

While blame shifting and defensiveness might provide temporary relief to our ego, they aren't sustainable. By avoiding responsibility, we deny ourselves the opportunity to reflect, improve, and take ownership of our actions. It takes self-awareness and humility to break this cycle. It takes courage to create a space for honest self-reflection; to ask yourself, *Is there any truth to what this person is saying? Could I have done something differently?* It's hard work, but certainly worth its weight in gold.

Let's take a look at some real-world examples of what blame shifting can look like in relationships:

The "It's Not My Fault" Defense

A couple is arguing about household chores. One partner says, "You never help with the cleaning!" Instead of taking accountability, the other partner immediately deflects: "Well, it's not my fault! I've been busy with work all day!" Rather than addressing the concern, they shift the focus to external circumstances, avoiding responsibility.

The "You Started It" Blame Shift

Two friends are in a disagreement over a last-minute cancellation. One friend expresses hurt: "You really upset me when you canceled our plans without notice." Instead of offering an apology or explanation, the other responds defensively: "Well, if you weren't so sensitive, this wouldn't even be an issue!" By shifting the blame onto their friend's reaction, they dismiss the original concern entirely.

The "But You Do It Too" Diversion

A parent reminds their child to complete their homework. Feeling cornered, the child fires back: "Well, my brother never finishes his homework either! Why are you always picking on me?" By pointing out someone else's shortcomings, they divert attention away from their own accountability.

The "I'm Always Right" Defense

During a group discussion, differing opinions are being shared. When someone challenges their perspective, one person becomes defensive and shuts down the conversation: "I'm always right! You just don't understand what I'm saying!" Instead of engaging in open dialogue, they assert dominance, making it difficult for others to express their viewpoints.

The "You're Just Trying to Hurt Me" Reaction

One friend offers constructive criticism to another, hoping to help them grow. Instead of considering the feedback, the recipient lashes out: "You're just trying to hurt me! I can't believe you would say something like that!" Here, they shift the focus to their perceived victimization rather than the message itself.

Blame-shifting keeps conflicts unresolved and creates barriers to healthy communication. Recognizing these patterns is the first step toward breaking them—allowing for more open, honest, and accountable relationships.

How to Stop Getting Defensive

1. Reconnect with Your Values

Remind yourself of the values that you hold dearly. Our values are what keep us grounded and make us feel less defensive when it feels like we are under attack. So, for example, if something happens at work and you receive not-so-stellar feedback, consciously redirect your focus to the areas where you excel. This doesn't mean dismissing criticism—it means balancing your perspective, reminding yourself of your worth, and approaching challenges with confidence.

2. Shift Your Perspective on Criticism

Instead of seeing criticism as a personal attack, reframe it as a gesture of investment in your potential. People who don't care about your growth are unlikely to offer feedback at all. When someone shares constructive criticism, it often reflects their belief in your ability to improve.

Ask yourself, *What can I learn from this?* By approaching feedback with curiosity, you shift from a defensive mindset to a growth mindset. This shift transforms criticism into an opportunity to grow and build stronger relationships.

3. Practice the Power of the Pause

In moments of criticism or conflict, our first instinct is often to defend ourselves or retaliate. Instead, pause. Take a deep breath and give yourself the gift of silence. Silence is not weakness; it's a powerful tool for reflection and emotional regulation.

Use this moment to ask yourself:

- *Why am I feeling defensive?*

- *Is there truth in what's being said?*

- *What response aligns with my best self?*

This pause allows you to step back from the situation, regulate your emotions, and choose a response that reflects thoughtfulness rather than reactivity.

4. Understand the Root of Your Defensiveness

Defensiveness often stems from deeper insecurities or fears of rejection. If you've consistently felt unsafe or criticized in the past, your mind may default to protecting itself through deflection, blame, or avoidance. Recognizing this pattern is the first step toward breaking it.

Instead of running from discomfort, lean into self-reflection. Ask yourself:

- *What am I afraid of in this moment?*

- *Am I reacting to this specific situation or to something unresolved from my past?*

When you identify these underlying emotions, you can address them with self-compassion rather than defensiveness.

5. Embrace Accountability as Strength

Accountability is not only attractive in others but also liberating in ourselves. When you acknowledge your mistakes or shortcomings, you take control of your narrative. You're no longer at the mercy of external criticism—you own your growth.

This doesn't mean agreeing with every piece of feedback. Instead, it's about being open enough to consider what's valid and taking responsibility for what's yours. A response like, "I see where I went wrong, and I'll work on it," can be incredibly empowering for you and disarming for others.

6. Build Self-Compassion

Defensiveness often arises from harsh self-criticism. The kinder you are to yourself, the less you'll feel the need to guard against external criticism. Practice speaking to yourself as you would to a friend:

- Replace thoughts like, *I'm such a failure,* with *I'm learning and improving.*

- Remind yourself that making mistakes doesn't diminish your worth—it highlights your humanity.

Developing self-compassion creates a foundation of inner safety, making it easier to listen to feedback without feeling attacked.

7. Shift From Reaction to Connection

When defensiveness arises in a conversation, it's easy to focus on proving your point or protecting your ego. Instead, focus on connection. Ask clarifying questions like:

- "Can you help me understand what you mean by that?"

- "What would you suggest I do differently?"

This approach shows openness and curiosity, fostering trust and collaboration rather than conflict.

8. Celebrate Progress, Not Perfection

Finally, remind yourself that unlearning defensiveness is a process. There will be moments when your old habits resurface, and that's okay. Each time you pause, listen, or respond thoughtfully, you're making progress. Celebrate those small victories—they're signs of your growth.

By integrating these practices into your life, you'll find that criticism no longer feels like a threat but an invitation to evolve. With time and commitment, you can transform defensiveness into resilience, and resistance into connection.

Interactive Element

Journaling Yourself to a Better Place

Journaling is how we teach ourselves to connect to and open up to the innermost parts of ourselves. It is a sacred space where we can explore our thoughts, emotions, and experiences with a gentle curiosity. Through the act of putting pen to paper, we create a bridge between our conscious and subconscious minds, gaining insights and awareness that can lead to profound healing. So now, using these journaling prompts, I want you to invite healing into your life. Take your time and be as honest as possible with yourself as you journal. Remind yourself often: *These pages of my journal are a safe space. They are a place for healing.*

1. Reflect on a recurring situation or circumstance in your life that leaves you feeling stuck or frustrated. What emotions or thoughts come up for you when you think about it?

2. Think about a relationship pattern that you tend to repeat. What are some similarities you notice in the people you attract or the dynamics that unfold?

3. Consider a habit or behavior that you find difficult to break. What triggers this behavior, and what feelings or needs does it fulfill?

4. Recall a decision or choice you made in the past that didn't align with your true desires or values. What factors influenced your decision, and what did you learn from it?

5. Explore a belief or negative self-talk that frequently arises within you. Where do you think this belief originated, and how does it impact your life?

6. Identify a pattern of self-sabotage or procrastination that hinders your progress. What fears or underlying beliefs might be driving this pattern?

7. Reflect on a recurring theme in your dreams or recurring symbols that appear. What do you think they might be trying to communicate to you?

8. Consider a specific area of your life where you often feel overwhelmed or stressed. What patterns of behavior or thought contribute to this feeling?

9. Think about the ways in which you seek validation or approval from others. How does this pattern affect your self-worth and decision-making?

10. Recall a pattern of avoiding vulnerability or suppressing your emotions. What might have led you to develop this pattern in the first place? How has this tendency influenced your relationships, your ability to connect with others, and the way you express your true feelings?

11. Reflect on a pattern of perfectionism or high self-imposed expectations. How does this pattern affect your sense of self-worth and ability to enjoy the present moment?

12. Identify a recurring fear or limiting belief that holds you back from pursuing your goals or dreams. How does this pattern prevent you from reaching your full potential?

13. Consider a pattern of self-neglect or putting others' needs before your own. How does this pattern impact your overall well-being and ability to practice self-care?

14. Reflect on a pattern of seeking external validation or relying on external circumstances for your happiness. How does this pattern limit your sense of inner joy and fulfillment?

15. Think about a pattern of negative or self-critical self-talk. What strategies can you implement to challenge and reframe these thoughts?

To heal our inner child wounds, we must first bring them out of the shadows and into the light of awareness. Much of what holds us back—our fears, patterns, and limiting beliefs—operates beneath the surface, hidden within the depths of our subconscious. We cannot heal what we do not acknowledge, and we cannot change what remains buried.

In the next chapter, we begin the courageous journey of uncovering these wounds with clarity and compassion. We will explore the unconscious patterns that shape our present, the dangers of recreating painful memories, and the emotional baggage we unknowingly carry. Through this process, we will learn how to identify and challenge the negative thoughts and beliefs that keep us stuck, allowing us to take the first real steps toward transformation. Healing begins with awareness, and as we illuminate the shadows, we reclaim the power to rewrite our story.

Chapter Four

Illuminating the Shadows

Bringing Wounds into the Light

No problem can be solved from the same level of consciousness that created it. –Albert Einstein

In the journey of inner child healing, there comes a pivotal moment when we must confront our deepest wounds and unveil the hidden layers of our being. It is during this process of awakening that we begin to realize an immutable truth: No problem can be solved from the same level of consciousness that created it.

Imagine standing in a dark room, surrounded by the remnants of your past, the echoes of pain and unresolved emotions reverberating through the very fabric of your existence. You yearn for healing, for solace, but somehow, the answers seem elusive, just beyond your grasp. It is at this crossroads that the power of awakening reveals itself—a beacon of light illuminating the path toward profound transformation.

Over the course of this chapter, we embark on a sacred exploration, delving into the depths of our consciousness to bring our wounds to light. We will unravel the intricate web of our past, gently untangling the threads that have kept us bound and empowering ourselves to rewrite the narrative of our lives. We'll learn together that the key to healing lies not in denial or evasion but in the courageous act of facing our shadows head-on. We will learn to embrace vulnerability, to shed the layers of self-protection, and to stand boldly in the face of our own truths. We will emerge stronger, wiser, and filled with a renewed sense of purpose.

So, before we continue, I want you to breathe and summon up the courage to face your wounds, knowing that the light of awakening awaits us on the other side. It is in this sacred space that we will find the strength to heal and the wisdom to transcend and reclaim our authentic selves—to embrace the infinite possibilities that lie before us.

Why We Need to Make the Unconscious Conscious

Just beneath the surface of our conscious awareness, there lives a silent conductor, orchestrating the symphony of our thoughts, emotions, and actions. This silent conductor is our subconscious mind, a realm of our psyche that is as powerful as it is elusive. It's the canvas upon which our dreams are painted, the stage where our fears perform, and the quiet whisper that guides our decisions.

Imagine the subconscious mind as an enormous, complex, and intelligent iceberg. The part of the iceberg that we see above the water, the conscious mind, comprises only about ten percent of our mental capacity.

The rest, the ninety percent that lies beneath the water's surface, is our subconscious mind, silently and steadily steering our lives. Learning to understand our subconscious mind is akin to learning a new language. It communicates not through words, but through symbols, feelings, and intuition. Its vocabulary is the language of dreams, emotions, and gut feelings. It's like the whispering wind that rustles the leaves, the gentle nudge that sways the grass. It's subtle, but when we are quiet and attentive, its messages can be heard loud and clear.

Now, let's talk about the rules that govern this mysterious entity:

1. The first rule of the subconscious mind is that it is always active. Even when we are asleep or not consciously focused, it continually processes information and maintains the body's functions. It's the tireless worker diligently making sure the heart beats, the lungs breathe, and the body heals.

2. The second rule is that the subconscious mind is extraordinarily literal. It does not understand sarcasm, humor, or false statements. It accepts what we tell it as the absolute truth. This is why negative self-talk can be so damaging and why positive affirmations can be transformative.

3. The third rule is that the subconscious mind operates in the present moment. It does not distinguish between past, present, or future. This is why our bodies respond to a distressing memory or a fearful future scenario as if it were happening right now. It's also why visualization is a powerful tool for change: Our subconscious mind cannot distinguish between a vividly imagined experience and a real one.

4. And the fourth and final rule is that the subconscious mind is a creature of habit and patterns. It learns through repetition

and reinforces behaviors that have been frequently repeated, regardless of whether these behaviors are beneficial or harmful. This is why we can find ourselves stuck in unhealthy patterns or behaviors, despite our best conscious efforts to change.

So, how does all of this impact our day-to-day lives? Well, it's our subconscious mind that shapes our beliefs, influences our emotions, and determines much of our behavior. It's the silent conductor that dictates the music our lives dance to. And just like a symphony, if we want to change the music, we need to engage with the conductor. Understanding and working with our subconscious mind is not about gaining control or mastery over it, but rather learning to dance in harmony with it. It's about fostering a relationship of respect, curiosity, and compassion with this silent conductor. It's about learning to listen to its subtle whispers and understand its symbolic language.

Embracing our subconscious mind is like inviting a powerful ally into our lives. It's the first step toward making the unconscious conscious. It's the beginning of a journey of self-discovery and healing.

The Dangers of Recreating Old Memories

Our mind is a fascinating and powerful tool that holds a vast collection of memories. Within the depths of our subconscious lies a treasure trove of experiences, emotions, and thoughts that shape who we are. But there's one peculiar aspect of the subconscious and it's the tendency to occasionally bring forth old memories, sometimes in unexpected and vivid ways.

The subconscious mind, you see, acts as a reservoir, storing memories that we may not even be aware of on a conscious level. These memories can be triggered by various stimuli, such as sights, sounds, smells, or even certain words. When we encounter these triggers, our subconscious mind retrieves associated memories, often without our conscious control.

It's important to understand that memories retrieved from the subconscious mind may not always be entirely accurate. Over time, memories can become distorted or embellished, influenced by our emotions, beliefs, and perceptions. This is known as memory reconstruction. Our mind fills in the gaps and alters details based on our current state of mind, making it challenging to distinguish between what is real and what is a product of our subconscious.

To avoid the overwhelm of these old memories or the potential inaccuracies they bring, there are a few strategies we can employ. Mindfulness, for example, is a powerful tool that can help us stay grounded in the present moment. By focusing our attention on the here and now, we can reduce the influence of past memories and prevent them from dominating our thoughts.

Engaging in activities that promote positive thinking and emotional well-being can also be beneficial. Maintaining a positive mindset and nurturing our emotional health can help in the creation of a mental environment that is less susceptible to being swayed by negative or distorted memories. Practices such as meditation, journaling, or talking to a trusted friend or therapist can help us process and release any lingering negative emotions tied to old memories.

Additionally, consciously choosing to create new and positive memories can help overwrite the impact of old ones. Here are some examples of what that can look like:

Revisiting a Childhood Location with a Loved One

Suppose you have a painful memory associated with a specific park where you experienced a traumatic event during childhood. Instead of avoiding the park altogether, you could choose to revisit it with a supportive loved one, such as a close friend or family member. By creating new memories in that familiar space, such as having a picnic, playing games, or simply enjoying nature, you can gradually replace the negative associations with positive ones. This process allows you to reclaim the space and reshape your narrative around it.

Engaging in Therapeutic Activities

Another approach could involve engaging in therapeutic activities or hobbies that evoke positive emotions and foster a sense of empowerment. For instance, if you have negative memories associated with a particular skill or activity from childhood, such as painting or playing a musical instrument, you can choose to revisit that activity in a safe and supportive environment. Attending art therapy sessions, joining a community choir, or participating in group classes can provide opportunities to create new, positive memories associated with the previously challenging activity. Over time, you can develop a newfound sense of mastery and confidence, effectively rewriting the narrative surrounding that skill or hobby.

Creating Rituals or Traditions

Another approach involves creating new rituals or traditions that hold personal significance and foster positive emotions. For example, if you have negative associations with a specific time of year due to past traumatic events, you can choose to establish new traditions during that period. This could involve engaging in activities that promote self-care, such as meditation retreats, nature walks, or volunteer work, which are deliberately planned and repeated annually. By imbuing these rituals with personal meaning and intention, you can cultivate positive associations with the previously challenging time of year, gradually replacing negative memories with new, empowering ones.

By actively engaging in enjoyable experiences, learning new skills, or pursuing hobbies, we can shift our focus toward the present and future, allowing old memories to fade into the background.

Unpacking Your Past—How to Identify What You Don't Want to Repeat

It's much easier to pretend that the suitcases that carry our emotional baggage simply do not exist, but it's a far greater challenge to unpack them—to lay everything bare, strip away the unnecessary weight, and shine a light on the shadows we've been avoiding. In the landscape of our inner world, these suitcases are not mere luggage; they're the heavy trunks of our past, filled to the brim with experiences, memories, and emotions that have shaped us into who we are today. They're symbolic of the unresolved past, the unspoken words, the unleashed tears, the unexpressed emotions, and the unforgiven deeds. They are our emotional baggage.

Emotional baggage is an amalgamation of past experiences that have left an indelible mark on our psyche. It's a collection of feelings, thoughts, and reactions, all woven together into a complex tapestry that spans the entire course of our lives. They are the silent echoes of past hurts, the quiet whispers of unresolved conflicts, the hidden scars of painful memories. It is the burden we carry in our hearts and minds, invisible to the world but all too real for us.

Each piece of emotional baggage is unique, just like the person carrying it. It is shaped by our personal history, the relationships we've had, the situations we've experienced, and the choices we've made. It is the pain from a childhood trauma, the bitterness from a broken relationship, the guilt from a perceived failure, the insecurity from constant criticism, and so much more. These experiences, which often lie dormant deep within us, are the foundation of our emotional baggage. Imagine these experiences as a series of layers. Each layer represents a different event or period in our life. Some layers are thick and heavy, laden with intense emotions and painful memories. Others are thin and faint, carrying only the remnants of feelings that once were. And then there are the layers that are hidden so deep, they're often overlooked, ignored, or forgotten. But regardless of their size or intensity, each layer contributes to the weight of our emotional baggage.

But why do we carry this emotional baggage? Why don't we just leave it behind? Because it's part of who we are. It's a testament to our resilience, our strength, and our capacity to endure. It's a reflection of our journey, our growth, and our evolution as human beings. But it's also a prison that holds us back, a chain that keeps us bound to the past, a shadow that obscures our true potential.

Holding onto our emotional baggage is like holding onto a piece of our past. It's a way for us to remember, to learn, and to grow. But it's also a way for us to hurt, to regret, and to fear. Because as long as we carry this baggage, we allow the past to dictate our future. We let our old wounds influence our present actions. We let our past pains color our current perceptions.

Unpacking this emotional baggage requires courage, patience, and understanding. It's not about discarding our past, but about acknowledging it, exploring it, and learning from it. It's about taking each piece of baggage, examining it closely, and understanding its impact on our lives. It's about uncovering the layers of our past, one by one, and understanding the emotions, thoughts, and experiences that lie beneath.

And in the same way, identifying it begins with a deep and compassionate introspection. It is a process of looking back, peeling away the layers of experiences, and recognizing recurring themes. Instances of fear, shame, or abandonment are often signposts, pointing toward areas where old wounds may still linger. As you delve deeper into your emotional landscape, pay attention to recurring relationship dynamics. Patterns in how we relate to others often mirror our early experiences. This awareness allows us to discern which patterns no longer serve our growth.

We must also will ourselves to be kind to ourselves and understand that we are all imperfect beings. Additionally, we can practice mindfulness, which involves paying attention to our thoughts, feelings, and physical sensations without judgment. That way, we can identify when we are engaging in patterns that no longer serve us and make a conscious effort to change our behavior.

Having a community of supportive people is so important. Talking to someone about our experiences can also provide us with a fresh perspective and help us identify patterns that we may not have noticed before. It's important to remember that seeking help is a sign of strength, not weakness.

Lastly, we must be patient with ourselves. Letting go of patterns that no longer serve us is a process that takes time and effort. We must be willing to put in the work and understand that setbacks are a natural part of the process. Patience and persistence will allow us to create lasting change in our lives and move forward with greater clarity and purpose.

Letting Go of the Excesses

Not everything is meant to be carried through to the next chapter. Give yourself permission to let go of what you need to, the things that are holding you back. Unclip your wings and allow them to spread so that you can fly and go to where you need to in order to become the very best version of yourself. Below are some tips to help you let go of the baggage that no longer serves you:

- **Understand the Impact of Emotional Baggage.** Imagine carrying around a heavy backpack filled with unnecessary items. Just like physical baggage, emotional baggage weighs you down and prevents you from living fully. It can affect your relationships, self-esteem, and overall well-being.

- **Reflect on Your Emotional Baggage.** Take some time to sit with your emotions and identify the baggage you're carrying. Recognize any patterns or recurring themes that keep you stuck in the past. By acknowledging and accepting the emotional baggage, you're already taking the first step toward letting go.

- **Practice Self-Compassion.** Be kind to yourself throughout this process. Emotionally, we tend to hold on to past experiences as a way of protecting ourselves from future pain. Remind yourself that it's okay to let go and that you deserve emotional freedom. Treat yourself with love and understanding.

- **Identify the Root Cause.** Dive deep into understanding why you're holding on to certain emotional baggage. Is it fear, guilt, or a sense of injustice? Identifying the root cause allows you to address any underlying issues and find appropriate ways to heal.

- **Challenge Your Beliefs.** Our beliefs shape our perceptions and reactions. Examine any limiting beliefs that are keeping you stuck in the past. Replace them with more empowering thoughts, such as *I am worthy of happiness* or *I choose to focus on the present moment.*

- **Practice Forgiveness.** One significant step in the process of letting go is forgiveness. This involves forgiving yourself and others who may have contributed to your emotional baggage. Remember that forgiveness doesn't mean condoning or forgetting the past; it is a way of freeing yourself from the negative emotions associated with it.

- **Release Through Rituals.** Engage in symbolic acts to release emotional baggage. Write a letter expressing your emotions and then burn or bury it, symbolizing a release of the past. You can also visualize yourself letting go of the baggage as you meditate or practice deep breathing.

Identifying and Reprogramming Negative Thoughts

I sit in silence, grappling with the storm of thoughts swirling inside me. They are relentless—echoing doubts, insecurities, and fears, playing on repeat like a broken record. It's so easy to mistake them for truth, to believe that their weight defines me.

But they are not facts. They are not me.

I remind myself that negative thoughts have power only because they feed on insecurity and fear. They creep in when I'm vulnerable, when my confidence wavers, when stress and pressure bear down on me. They attack my self-worth, whispering lies that try to take root.

Still, I have a choice. I can recognize them for what they are—just thoughts, not reality.

We've all experienced negative thoughts, but the types of negative thoughts can vary depending on the situation and the individual. They can be categorized into various forms:

- **Catastrophic Thinking.** This is when we imagine the worst possible outcome. For example, if we make a small mistake, we might think that it will lead to a complete disaster.

- **Overgeneralization.** This occurs when we make a general conclusion based on a single event or piece of evidence. For example, if we fail at a task, we might think that we are complete failures.

- **Personalization.** This is when we blame ourselves for everything that goes wrong, even if we are not responsible. For example, if a friend is upset, we might think it's because of something we did.

- **Filtering.** This happens when we focus on the negative and ignore the positive. For example, if we receive feedback, we might only focus on the criticism and ignore the praise.

- **Mind Reading.** This is when we assume we know what others are thinking without any evidence. For example, if someone doesn't reply to our text, we might think they are ignoring us.

Thoughts are just thoughts; we are not them and they are not us. We do not have to believe them or let them define us. We are powerful beyond measure and the power to control them lies in our hands not in theirs.

Watching Your Thoughts: Using Mindfulness to Reshape Negative Thought Patterns

We will always be gifted with the ability to choose, and that gift also applies to the thoughts that we think and choose to invite into our heads. Embrace this gift with consciousness and intention.

For this exercise, we are going to use the metaphor of clouds to help us observe and reshape our negative thought patterns. This mindful awareness of our thoughts that we'll be working on is what is going to help us let go of those self-defeating patterns and cultivate a more positive mindset. So, find your sanctuary, a quiet and comfortable space to practice this exercise, and let's begin.

1. Settle into a comfortable position, either sitting or lying down. Close your eyes gently if that feels comfortable for you.

2. Take a few moments to focus on your breath, noticing each inhale and exhale. Feel the rhythm of your breath, letting it serve as an anchor for your attention.

3. Visualize a clear blue sky in your mind. Imagine that your thoughts are like clouds passing through this expansive sky.

4. As thoughts arise, notice them with a sense of curiosity. Imagine each thought as a cloud drifting by.

5. Observe the shape, color, and texture of each thought-cloud without judgment. Notice if any negative or self-limiting thoughts appear, and acknowledge their presence.

6. As you continue observing your thoughts, remember that you are separate from them. You are the witness, watching the

clouds in the sky of your mind.

7. Whenever you notice a negative thought-cloud passing by, gently label it as "negative" or "self-defeating." Recognize that these thoughts are not the essence of who you are, but rather passing phenomena.

8. Now, imagine a gentle breeze sweeping across the sky, gradually dispersing the negative thought-clouds. Feel the release and sense of lightness as they fade away.

9. As you let go of negative thoughts, intentionally shift your attention to positive and uplifting thoughts. Visualize these thoughts as bright, radiant clouds emerging in the clear blue sky.

10. Breathe in deeply and envision yourself absorbing the positive energy from these uplifting thought-clouds. Allow their positivity to replenish your mind and reshape your thought patterns.

11. Take a few more moments to simply observe the clear blue sky of your mind, free from negative thought-clouds. Embrace the peace and clarity that arises when you are mindful and aware.

With continued practice, you can develop greater mindfulness. So, whenever you find yourself entangled in negative thoughts throughout the day, remember to observe them and let them pass, just like the clouds in the sky.

Identifying Unhelpful Core Beliefs

First, what exactly are core beliefs? Core beliefs reside in our subconscious. They are deeply ingrained beliefs about ourselves, others, and the world, which have developed early in life based on experiences, interactions, and messages received from caregivers and society. These beliefs ultimately shape how we perceive ourselves, interpret events, and navigate relationships.

Core beliefs are closely intertwined with our universal wounds, which we discussed in Chapter One. These wounds often arise from unmet emotional needs or traumatic events during childhood and can manifest as persistent emotional pain or dysfunctional patterns in adulthood. Core beliefs emerge as adaptive responses to these wounds, serving as internalized narratives that explain one's experiences and shape self-perception.

For example, a person who experienced abandonment as a child may develop a core belief that they are unlovable or unworthy of love, leading to feelings of inadequacy and difficulty forming healthy relationships. Similarly, someone who experienced rejection may develop a core belief that they are inherently flawed or undesirable, impacting their self-esteem and interpersonal interactions.

Here is a process you can follow to help you identify and change your unhelpful core beliefs:

1. Find a quiet and comfortable space where you can reflect without distractions.

2. Take a few deep breaths to center yourself and bring your attention to the present moment.

3. Notice patterns. Pay attention to recurring thoughts, emotions, and behaviors. Negative core beliefs often manifest as repetitive patterns in our lives. For example, if you find yourself constantly feeling unworthy or undeserving, it could be a sign of a deeper negative belief about yourself.

4. Write down three unhelpful core beliefs that you think may be holding you back. For example, *I'm not worthy of love, I always mess things up,* or *I'm not smart enough.*

5. Reflect on each belief and try to identify where it may have originated. Was it influenced by a past experience, a significant person in your life, or societal expectations? Write down any insights that come to mind.

6. Consider how these beliefs impact your life today. How do they affect your relationships, self-esteem, or decision-making? Be honest with yourself and jot down any observations.

7. Take a moment to acknowledge that these beliefs were formed in the past and may no longer serve you. Recognize that you have the power to challenge and change them.

8. Finally, write a short positive affirmation or counter-statement for each unhelpful belief. For instance, if the belief is *I'm not worthy of love,* the counter-statement could be *I am deserving of love and affection.*

Remember that second rule of the subconscious—the subconscious mind is extraordinarily literal, which is why reciting positive affirmations work to help change negative core beliefs.

Take your time with this exercise; it is meant to help you gain awareness and begin the process of healing. So, be gentle with yourself, and do everything at a pace that feels right to you.

Reframing Unhelpful Core Beliefs

Imagine your negative or unhelpful core beliefs as old, weathered road signs that line the paths of your mind. These signs, etched with messages of unworthiness, inadequacy, and self-doubt, have been standing for years, guiding your thoughts and perceptions. Like faded markers on a well-traveled road, they silently shape the landscape of your inner world, directing your emotions and influencing your decisions. Despite their worn appearance, these signs remain deeply ingrained, casting shadows of doubt and insecurity as you navigate life's journey.

Our core beliefs play a really big role in our overall health and how we see the world around us in general; that's why we have to teach ourselves to tap into the power of our thoughts and learn to reframe those thoughts that are holding us back.

Reframing is a cognitive technique that involves changing the way we perceive and interpret situations, events, or thoughts. It allows us to shift our perspective and to find new meaning or alternative viewpoints. By reframing our thoughts, we can challenge negative or limiting beliefs and replace them with more positive and empowering ones.

When we reframe, we consciously choose to change the narrative; we choose to focus on the positive aspects of a situation rather than dwelling on the negative. This can help us reduce stress, improve our emotional well-being, and enhance our overall health. Reframing also enables us to see opportunities and solutions where we might have previously seen obstacles or problems.

Here are some examples of common negative core beliefs that we might hold and some tips on what to do to reframe them:

> **Negative Belief:** *I am not good enough.*
> **Reframing Example:** *I am constantly growing and learning, and I have many unique qualities that make me worthy.*

> **Negative Belief:** *I will never succeed.*
> **Reframing Example:** *Every step I take toward my goals is a success, and I am capable of achieving great things.*

> **Negative Belief:** *I am a failure.*
> **Reframing Example:** *Mistakes and setbacks are opportunities for growth, and I am resilient and capable of turning them into success.*

> **Negative Belief:** *I am unlovable.*
> **Reframing Example:** *I am deserving of love and affection, and I have people in my life who care about me deeply.*

> **Negative Belief:** *I am not smart enough.*
> **Reframing Example:** *Intelligence comes in many forms, and I have unique strengths and abilities that contribute to my success.*

> **Negative Belief:** *I am always unlucky.*
> **Reframing Example:** *I have the power to create my own luck, and I attract positive opportunities into my life.*

Negative Belief: *I will never be happy.*
Reframing Example: *Happiness is a journey, and I am capable of finding joy in the present moment and creating a fulfilling life.*

Negative Belief: *I am a burden to others.*
Reframing Example: *I am worthy of support and care, and my loved ones are happy to be there for me.*

Negative Belief: *I am not attractive.*
Reframing Example: *Beauty is subjective, and I have unique qualities that make me attractive in my own way.*

Negative Belief: *I will always be alone.*
Reframing Example: *I am capable of building meaningful connections, and I am open to the possibilities of love and companionship.*

Negative Belief: *I am not talented.*
Reframing Example: *I have untapped potential and skills that I can develop, and I am capable of achieving greatness in my own way.*

Negative Belief: *I am a disappointment.*
Reframing Example: *I am constantly growing and evolving, and I have the power to make positive changes in my life.*

Interactive Element

There are plenty of other exercises that you can try to bring more awareness to your thoughts—things that you can do to make them work for you, instead of against you. Let's have a look at some of them and what exactly you can do to put them into practice.

Keep a Thought Log

Keeping a thought log is a powerful way to increase awareness of your inner dialogue and challenge unhelpful thinking patterns. Follow these steps to integrate this practice into your daily life:

1. Start by finding a quiet and comfortable space where you can reflect without distractions.

2. Take a few deep breaths to center yourself and bring your focus inward, allowing the mind to settle.

3. Begin by writing down a triggering event or situation that brought up strong emotions or negative thoughts.

4. Write down the thoughts, beliefs, or fears that arose in response to that event. Be as specific as possible.

5. Reflect on the validity of these thoughts, and ask yourself: Are these thoughts based on facts, or are they shaped by past experiences, fears, or distortions?

6. Reframe unhelpful thoughts. Challenge negativity by seeking alternative perspectives. Look for evidence that supports a more

constructive or balanced viewpoint.

7. Write down the new, more balanced thoughts and beliefs that you want to cultivate.

8. Take a moment to notice any changes in your emotions or how you feel after reframing your thoughts.

9. Repeat this exercise regularly, noting any patterns or recurring negative thoughts that may require further exploration and healing.

Remember, this is a practice, not perfection. At first, it may feel awkward or forced, but with patience and consistency, it will become second nature. Be kind to yourself in the process—growth takes time, and every small step counts.

Brain Dump

A brain dump is a technique where you write down all the thoughts, ideas, tasks, or concerns that are occupying your mind onto paper or a digital document. It serves as a way to declutter your mind and externalize your thoughts. You are essentially transferring all the information from your mind onto paper, which helps in several ways:

- Externalizing thoughts makes them more tangible and easier to work with. It frees up mental space and reduces the cognitive load.

- Gaining clarity through seeing your thoughts on paper helps make it easier to identify patterns, recurring themes, or areas that need attention. It provides a clearer picture of what's on your mind.

- Letting go of unhelpful thoughts can help you detach from unhelpful or negative thinking patterns, allowing you to let go of them more easily.

Here's how you can do a brain dump on your own:

1. Grab a pen and a blank sheet of paper or open a document on your computer.

2. Set a timer for a specific duration, such as 10 or 15 minutes. This will help you stay focused and prevent the process from becoming overwhelming.

3. Start the timer and begin writing down any thoughts, emotions, memories, or beliefs that come to mind related to your inner child. Allow yourself to freely express anything that arises, without judgment or filtering.

4. Explore any unhelpful beliefs or patterns that you notice. Write them down and reflect on how they may have originated from your childhood experiences or conditioning.

5. Consider how these beliefs or patterns impact your life today. How do they affect your relationships, self-esteem, or overall well-being? Write down any insights or observations.

6. Acknowledge and validate the emotions that arise during this process. Allow yourself to feel and express them in a safe and supportive way.

7. Once the timer goes off, review what you've written. Look for common themes, recurring patterns, or unresolved emotions that may require further attention.

My Memory Timeline and Photo Reflection

Our memories are the threads that weave the fabric of our identity. Some are warm and golden, illuminating moments of joy and connection, while others carry the weight of pain, echoing the wounds we have yet to heal. This exercise invites you to step into the past with curiosity and compassion, allowing old memories to surface—not to dwell in them, but to understand their impact and reclaim your power.

1. **Gather Old Photos.** Start by gathering a selection of old photos from your childhood or significant moments in your life. Photos help to wake up your memory. It will make constructing your timeline a bit easier.

2. **Create a Memory Timeline.** Take a piece of paper or create a digital document to create a timeline. Mark significant events or memories from your past using dates or age ranges.

3. **Reflect on Each Memory.** For each significant memory, take a moment to reflect on the emotions, thoughts, and experiences associated with it. Write down any positive or negative aspects that come to mind.

4. **Identify Problem Areas.** Review your timeline and identify any recurring negative patterns or problem areas that emerge from your reflections. These could be related to relationships, self-esteem, or other aspects of your life.

5. **Explore the Impact.** Consider the impact of these problem areas on your present life. How might these past experiences be influencing your beliefs, behaviors, and emotional well-being today?

6. **Set Intentions for Healing.** Write down specific actions or practices you can engage in to address and heal these problem areas, nurturing your inner child along the way.

When you've completed your timeline, take a moment to breathe deeply. Honor the emotions that surfaced, knowing that they are stepping stones on your path to healing. What patterns have emerged? What insights have you gained? And most importantly, what loving intentions will you now set for the next chapter of your life?

As we work through childhood wounds, we will find many emotions bubbling up—some familiar, some unexpected, and some that feel almost too big to hold. These emotions are not here to overwhelm us but to guide us, revealing the stories we have carried for so long. Learning to navigate them with awareness and compassion is essential to our healing.

In the next chapter, we will explore the role emotions play in our inner world, how they act as messengers, and how we can begin to develop a healthier relationship with them. By building emotional awareness, identifying emotional patterns and triggers, and cultivating resilience, we can shift from being at the mercy of our emotions to understanding and working with them. Emotions are not our enemies—they are signals, invitations, and pathways to deeper self-awareness. Let's learn how to make them a safe space, rather than something we fear.

Chapter Five

Emotions as Energy

Understanding and Transforming Your Inner World

Whatever we plant in our subconscious mind and nourish with repetition and emotion will one day become a reality. –Earl Nightingale

Our emotions are the silent architects of our realities, the unseen brushstrokes that color our experiences, the very fabric from which our perceptions are woven. They guide us through the maze of life, as if holding an invisible thread, tugging gently, or not so gently, at our hearts. They have the power to lift us to the highest peaks of joy, plunge us into the deepest valleys of despair, and everything in between.

Through the ages, emotions have been variously described—the language of the soul, the energy in motion, the heartbeat of our subconscious mind. They are all these and more. We cannot escape them, but we can learn to understand them, to listen to their nuanced messages, to dance with them, and yes, even to heal with them.

Emotions play a crucial role in our mental, physical, and spiritual health. They are not just fleeting internal states but they carry a tangible energy that impacts our bodies, our minds, and our environment. When we suppress or ignore our emotions, we create blockages in our energy flow, which can manifest as health issues, relationship difficulties, or a general sense of dissatisfaction and unrest. Alternatively, when we welcome our emotions, allow them space, and give them a voice, we pave the way for healing and growth.

This powerful statement by Earl Nightingale underlines the immense power our emotions wield. They are the seeds we plant in the fertile soil of our subconscious. If we water these seeds with positive emotions, we grow beautiful gardens of joy, peace, and fulfillment. If we nourish them with negative emotions, we cultivate thorny bushes of fear, stress, and unhappiness. The journey to emotional wellness is a deeply personal one. It requires courage, patience, and a willingness to venture into the often-murky waters of our inner world. But the rewards are invaluable. It is through this journey that we can unlock our full potential, build healthier relationships, and cultivate a deeper sense of peace and contentment.

Our emotions are with us as we open our eyes in the morning, shaping the manner in which we will show up. They walk with us throughout the day, influencing our decisions, our interactions, our responses. They are our constant companions, our guides, our teachers. So, as hard and as uncomfortable as it is, walking the journey of understanding, accepting, and transforming them is a journey that promises not just healing but also growth—not just peace but also power—not just surviving but truly thriving.

Come now, embrace your emotions. Embrace the energy they bring. Embrace the change they promise. It is in this embrace that we can truly heal, grow, and bloom.

Building Emotional Awareness

Our emotional experiences are complex and multifaceted. There are not those that are right or wrong; we must allow ourselves to experience a whole range of them. For example, you might feel a mix of joy and apprehension before a significant event like a job interview. These emotions coexist because they come from different aspects of the situation.

Emotions are not mere fleeting sensations, but profound indicators of our alignment with our deepest values and needs. When negative emotions arise, they gently whisper that our actions have temporarily veered from our authentic path. This signals an unmet need, a call for attention. In those moments, it is crucial to step back, to pause, and to lovingly tend to this depleted aspect of ourselves. Conversely, positive emotions beam as radiant affirmations. They illuminate that our actions and activities are harmoniously aligned with our core values. Moreover, they signify that our experience is beautifully attuned to our fundamental needs. It is in these moments of lightness and joy that we find resonance with our truest selves.

Embracing the fact that our emotions—both the positive and negative—can contribute to our emotional resilience and growth is what allows us to navigate life's challenges with a more balanced perspective. By understanding the purpose of both positive and negative emotions, we unearth a powerful tool for personal growth and self-awareness. Each emotion carries wisdom, inviting us to delve deeper into our inner world. With patience and compassion, we learn to dance with the ebb and flow of our feelings, transforming them into stepping stones toward a more authentic, aligned life.

Our Emotions as Messengers

When we become aware of our emotions and listen to their messages, we can cultivate a deeper understanding of ourselves and our needs. Emotions act as messengers, guiding us toward the areas of our lives that may require attention, healing, or growth. By acknowledging and embracing these messages, we can better care for ourselves and navigate life's challenges more effectively.

Sadness, for example, is often accompanied by feelings of loss and grief. It is an invitation for us to honor and process the emotions associated with any kind of loss, whether it be a loved one, a relationship, or a dream. Allowing ourselves to grieve, we can find healing and move forward with a renewed sense of strength and resilience.

Loneliness is another emotion that calls our attention to the need for connection. It encourages us to seek meaningful relationships and build a support system. Connecting with others can provide us with comfort, understanding, and a sense of belonging, ultimately reducing feelings of isolation.

Anxiety, with its accompanying fear and worry, invites us to delve deeper into our fears and confront them head-on. By working through our anxieties, we can gain a greater understanding of ourselves and develop strategies to navigate challenging situations. This self-awareness enables us to grow and expand our comfort zones, fostering personal development.

Stress, on the other hand, acts as a signal for us to slow down and practice self-care. In today's fast-paced world, it is easy to become overwhelmed and neglect our well-being. By honoring our stress and taking time to relax, rejuvenate, and engage in activities that bring us joy, we can restore balance and improve our overall mental and physical health.

Lastly, **anger** serves as a reminder to identify and establish personal boundaries. It shows us where our limits have been crossed and calls for assertiveness in communicating our needs. That is how we can learn to assert ourselves and foster healthier relationships based on mutual respect.

In the complex landscape of human experience, emotions serve as our internal compass, offering insight into our reactions, desires, and needs. Understanding these emotional signals is a crucial step toward self-awareness and effective communication. Below is a table outlining common emotions and their underlying meaning, providing a valuable reference for navigating the intricate terrain of our feelings.

Listening to our emotions can be hard. There will be moments of discomfort, moments where you want to quit and altogether give up on all and any effort, but it's worth it, I promise you. And most importantly, you want to remember that there is not a one-size-fits-all approach. By becoming attuned to our emotional landscape, we can navigate life with greater clarity, authenticity, and purpose. Let's explore some practical steps to better listen to and engage with our emotions:

- **Cultivate Awareness.** The first step in learning to listen to your emotions is to cultivate a sense of awareness. Take a moment each day to check in with yourself. Set aside time for reflection and introspection. Tune into how you are feeling in the present moment, without judgment or analysis. Simply observe and acknowledge your emotions as they arise.

- **Learn the Language of Your Emotions.** Just as a foreign language requires study and practice, understanding your emotional language takes time and effort. Start by exploring the fundamental emotions such as joy, sadness, anger, fear, and disgust. Reflect on what triggers these emotions in your life and how they manifest physically and mentally. The more you familiarize yourself with the nuances and unique expressions of your emotions, the better you can decipher their messages.

- **Connect With Your Body.** Emotions may originate in the mind with our thoughts, but it is our physical bodies that actually "feel" and experience an emotion. Notice how your emotions feel in different parts of your body. For example, anger might be felt as a tightness in your chest, while fear or anxiety might cause a knot in your stomach. By tuning into these bodily cues, you can gain insight into the underlying emotions and their associated needs.

- **Practice Mindfulness.** Mindfulness is a powerful tool for emotional awareness and active listening. Engaging in mindfulness activities such as meditation, deep breathing, or yoga can help you develop a non-judgmental, accepting stance toward your emotions. By observing your thoughts and feelings without attachment or avoidance, you create a space for self-discovery and understanding.

- **Reflect and Journal.** Writing down your thoughts and emotions in a journal can be an invaluable practice for listening to your emotional landscape. Set aside regular time to reflect on your experiences and record your thoughts, feelings, and insights. Journaling allows you to gain clarity, process your emotions, and identify patterns or triggers.

- **Build Emotional Acceptance.** Building emotional acceptance is all about softening our hearts toward our own experiences and being gentle when the anxiety strikes and being tender toward our triggers. It's not a journey about suppressing or ignoring them, but lovingly accepting them as a part of our human experience.

Be gentle with yourself, and remember that your emotions are invaluable guides; you do not have to feel ashamed or embarrassed about what it is that you are or aren't feeling.

Developing Self-Awareness Through Introspection and Mindfulness

Let's take a moment to really dissect the difference between self-awareness, introspection, and mindfulness. Understanding the difference between these three seemingly interchangeable terms is necessary for us to significantly enhance our understanding of our inner child and overall emotional health.

Self-awareness involves recognizing and understanding our own emotions, thoughts, and behaviors. It is about seeing ourselves clearly and objectively, reflecting on how our experiences and actions align with our own values and desires.

Mindfulness, on the other hand, is the practice of being present in the moment, observing our thoughts and feelings without judgment. While self-awareness and mindfulness are closely related, they serve distinct purposes and involve different processes.

Introspection is the act of looking inward to examine our own thoughts, feelings, and motives. It involves setting aside time to reflect on our experiences and how they shape our current behavior and emotional state. To develop self-awareness through introspection, consider keeping a journal where you can document your daily thoughts and feelings. This practice allows you to track patterns and identify triggers for certain emotions. Asking yourself questions like *Why did I react that way?* or *What am I truly feeling right now?* can also facilitate a deeper understanding of your inner worlds.

Mindfulness complements introspection by encouraging a non-judgmental awareness of the present moment. It involves practices such as meditation, deep breathing exercises, and mindful observation of our surroundings and internal experiences. By regularly practicing mindfulness, we can develop a heightened awareness of our immediate thoughts and feelings, which can prevent us from being overwhelmed by them. For example, mindfulness can help you notice the early signs of stress or anxiety, allowing you to address them before they escalate. Mindfulness helps cultivate a sense of calm and clarity, enabling you to respond to situations more thoughtfully rather than reacting impulsively.

The difference between self-awareness and mindfulness lies in their focus and application. Self-awareness is about understanding the "why" behind our emotions and behaviors, delving into past experiences and patterns. While mindfulness is about the "what" and "how" of the present moment, noticing our current state without getting entangled in it. While self-awareness can lead to deeper insights and long-term growth, mindfulness provides immediate tools for managing our emotional and mental states.

Combining both practices can be incredibly powerful. For instance, you might start with a mindfulness session to calm your mind and become more present, followed by introspective journaling to explore any emotions or thoughts that surfaced during your practice. Over time, this integrated approach can enhance your overall self-awareness, emotional regulation, and ability to heal and nurture your inner child.

Awareness of our emotions begins with a simple yet profound practice—tuning into how we feel in the present moment. From that place of mindfulness, we can begin to set new intentions for ourselves and reshape our emotional landscape.

- **Acknowledge Your Emotions.** As feelings arise, take a moment to recognize them. If it helps, give them a name or label—this can make them feel less overwhelming and easier to process.

- **Pause and Breathe.** Instead of reacting impulsively, take a few slow, deep breaths. Allow yourself to fully experience the emotion without judgment or resistance.

- **Release Tension.** If you notice any physical tightness or constriction, consciously relax your body. Let go of the tension that the emotion has created. If a productive action comes to mind—one that aligns with your growth—lean into it rather than falling into old, unhealthy habits.

- **Commit to the Process.** Emotional awareness is a skill that takes time to develop. Be patient with yourself as you unlearn old patterns and create new, healthier ways of responding to your emotions.

Identifying and Understanding Individual Emotional Patterns and Triggers

Understanding and identifying individual emotional patterns and triggers is a crucial step in inner child healing. Emotional patterns are the habitual ways in which we respond to different situations, often rooted in our past experiences, particularly those from childhood. These patterns shape how we perceive and react to the world around us, influencing our thoughts, behaviors, and relationships.

Emotional triggers are specific stimuli that evoke strong emotional responses, often disproportionate to the situation at hand. These triggers, like our emotional patterns, are typically tied to unresolved emotional wounds from our past.

Trying to reason our way out of our emotional triggers might seem like the logical thing to want to do at the moment, but it's not effective. It's the equivalent of trying to use a water gun to put out a fire.

The rational brain is built on top of our emotional brain, just like the crust of the earth is on top of the mantle. If the mantle quakes, then the crust won't be able to hold it all together. So when we are triggered, we need to find a way to soothe the emotional responses and swing it back the other way. Some of the most common emotional triggers that people feel include:

- **Rejection.** Feeling excluded or unappreciated can trigger intense feelings of inadequacy and abandonment.

- **Criticism.** Negative feedback or perceived judgment can evoke feelings of worthlessness or failure.

- **Control.** Situations where one's autonomy is threatened can trigger feelings of helplessness and frustration.

- **Neglect.** Feeling ignored or overlooked can bring up feelings of invisibility and unimportance.

- **Low Self-Worth or Lack of Confidence:** A belief that your opinions are not valuable enough to be shared or that you will not be able to convey your message effectively can result in a feeling as though you cannot speak up or speak your mind.

- **Betrayal:** Experiences of deceit or disloyalty can trigger deep feelings of mistrust and anger.

By practicing self-awareness through combining introspection and mindfulness, we can develop a comprehensive understanding of our emotional patterns and triggers. Here are some practical steps to apply introspection and mindfulness—concepts we explored in the previous section—specifically for understanding your emotional triggers:

1. **Awareness.** Work on identifying those things that are usually your biggest triggers. For instance, is it when people make unsolicited comments about your weight or appearance? Or when certain outcomes don't pan out as you'd hoped? Take note of these so that the aspects that need to heal are clarified.

2. **Track Emotional Reactions.** Keep a journal where you record your reactions throughout the day. Note the context, your thoughts, and physical sensations associated with each emotion. Over time, this record will help you identify patterns and reoccurring triggers.

3. **Reflect on Patterns.** Regularly review your journal entries and reflect on the patterns that emerge. Ask yourself questions, such as *What situations consistently trigger strong emotions?* This reflection will deepen your self-awareness and highlight areas for growth.

4. **Track the Trigger's Origin.** While journaling, try to uncover where the trigger originated. Did you have a parent who was

overly critical of your weight? Was your potential constantly undermined or were you a little neglected, so that ended up making you feel like you were unlovable? Pinpointing the origin of the trigger can give you a starting point of where to focus your energy for healing.

5. **Practice Mindfulness Meditation.** Engage in mindfulness meditation to cultivate a habit of present-moment awareness. Set aside time each day to sit quietly, focus on your breath, and observe your thoughts and emotions without judgment. This practice will enhance your ability to stay present and non-reactive when faced with emotional triggers.

6. **Seek Professional Support.** If you find it challenging to identify and understand your emotional patterns, consider seeking support from a therapist or counselor. A professional can provide guidance, offer new perspectives, and help you develop effective coping strategies for managing emotional triggers.

Start with one trigger and then consciously work toward reframing it. Remember that exercise that we did in Chapter Four? Reframing is a powerful tool used to shift one's perspective on a situation or emotional trigger, thereby altering its emotional impact. Here is a brief recap of the steps involved:

- **Identify the Trigger.** Recognize the specific situation or thought that elicits a strong emotional response. For example, if a person feels intense anxiety when speaking in public, the act of public speaking is the trigger.

- **Acknowledge the Emotion.** Accept and label the emotion associated with the trigger. Understanding the exact feeling (e.g., fear, anxiety, frustration) is crucial for effective reframing.

- **Examine the Thought.** Analyze the automatic thoughts that arise in response to the trigger. These are often negative and irrational, such as *I will make a fool of myself* or *Everyone will judge me.*

- **Challenge the Thought.** Question the validity of these negative thoughts. Ask yourself if they are based on facts or assumptions. Consider alternative viewpoints and gather evidence that contradicts the negative belief.

- **Create a New Frame.** Develop a new, more positive or neutral perspective on the situation. For instance, instead of thinking, *I will fail and everyone will judge me,* reframe it to, *This is an opportunity to share my ideas, and I can learn and improve from the experience.*

- **Practice the New Frame.** Consistently apply the new perspective whenever the trigger arises. This may involve using positive affirmations or visualizations to reinforce the new frame.

An example of reframing an emotional trigger might look like this:

Imagine someone feels unworthy because they didn't receive a promotion at work. The initial thought might be, *I am not good enough for this job*. By challenging this thought, they could consider other factors that might have influenced the decision, such as the availability or more experienced candidates or organizational restructuring. The reframe could be, *this is a chance to develop my skills further and explore other opportunities for growth.*

Act as if you are healed already. At the beginning of your healing process, you might need to take on a bit of a fake-it-till-you-make-it approach, because you might not have the belief that everything is fully integrated yet. Sometimes, enlightened behavior is what is needed to help let a new feeling sink in and for it to become all that more real. Although it may sound superficial at first, this approach involves adopting positive behaviors and attitudes, even if they do not initially feel genuine or natural. By doing so, we can create a new, healthier framework for our thoughts and emotions, which can gradually lead to genuine transformation.

Managing Emotions

Imagine your emotions as a vast, untamed sea, with waves that range from gentle ripples to towering, tumultuous swells. Navigating these waters requires skill, patience, and a steadfast compass. The process of managing emotions parallels that of becoming a seasoned sailor, one who learns to read the winds of change and steer through storms with grace and resilience. This journey is not without its challenges, but it is essential for reaching the serene shores of inner peace and self-understanding.

Managing emotions is a cornerstone of inner child healing, as it enables us to transform the raw, often overwhelming energy of our feelings into a source of strength and insight. Emotions, like the weather, are ever-changing and unpredictable, yet they hold profound wisdom if we learn to listen. By acknowledging and skillfully navigating our emotional landscape, we can heal old wounds, cultivate emotional resilience, and foster a deeper connection with our true selves.

The benefits of mastering this art are manifold. Just as a well-tended garden flourishes and brings forth beauty, a well-managed emotional life allows us to thrive, nurturing healthier relationships and a more fulfilling existence. Learning to manage our emotions empowers us to respond to life's challenges with clarity and calm, rather than being swept away by the tides of reactive impulses.

In this section, we will explore various techniques and strategies for managing emotions effectively. From tips on how to develop healthy coping mechanisms to transforming negative emotions and building emotional resilience, these strategies will equip you with the skills needed to navigate your emotional seas. Embrace this journey with an open heart and mind, for within these practices lies the key to unlocking a deeper sense of harmony and balance in your life.

Developing Healthy Coping Mechanisms for Handling Intense Emotions

Our coping mechanisms are personal, and what works for one person may not work for another. It's important to explore and find strategies that resonate with you and support your emotional well-being. Here are a few great places where you can start:

- **Self-Care Practices.** Engaging in self-care activities can help regulate and manage intense emotions. This can include activities like exercise, getting enough sleep, practicing relaxation techniques such as deep breathing or meditation, or engaging in hobbies that bring joy and relaxation.

- **Seeking Friendly Support.** Reach out to trusted friends or family members to talk about your emotions. Sharing your feelings with a loved one who can provide support and understanding can be incredibly helpful in processing intense emotions.

- **Journaling.** Writing down your thoughts and emotions in a journal can be a cathartic and reflective practice. It allows you to explore and express your emotions in a safe and private space, helping you gain clarity and perspective.

- **Mindfulness and Grounding Techniques.** Practicing mindfulness involves bringing your attention to the present moment without judgment. This can help you observe and accept your emotions without getting overwhelmed by them. Grounding techniques, such as focusing on your senses or engaging in deep breathing exercises, can also help bring you back to the present moment and provide a sense of calm.

- **Engaging in Creative Outlets.** Expressing your emotions through creative outlets like art, music, or writing can be a healthy way to channel intense feelings. These activities allow for self-expression and can provide a sense of release and emotional catharsis.

- **Setting Boundaries.** Recognize your limits and establish healthy boundaries in your relationships and daily life. This can help prevent emotional overload and provide a sense of control over your emotions.

- **Seeking Professional Help.** If intense emotions persist or significantly impact your daily functioning, consider reaching out to a mental health professional. They can provide guidance, support, and additional coping strategies tailored to your specific needs.

Transforming Negative Emotions

Our negative emotions, like anger, sadness, fear, and anxiety, often get a bad rap in society. We tend to label them as undesirable or inconvenient, as if they serve no purpose other than to burden us. However, when we shift our perspective and view these emotions as messengers, we can gain a deeper understanding of their purpose and the messages they hold.

Imagine for a moment that you're walking through a dense forest, and suddenly you hear the sound of a twig breaking behind you. Immediately, fear takes over your body, triggering a physiological response: Your heart begins to race, your muscles tense up, and your senses become hyperaware. In this scenario, fear isn't just an unwelcome feeling; it's a message from your body, warning you of potential danger and preparing you to take necessary action to ensure your safety.

The same goes for our negative emotions in daily life. They are messengers that communicate important information about our needs, desires, and boundaries. When we experience sadness, for example, it often signifies a loss or a need for healing. It compels us to reflect on our experiences, process our emotions, and ultimately, find ways to navigate through our pain.

Anger, on the other hand, can indicate a violation of our boundaries or values. It prompts us to assert ourselves, stand up for what we believe in, and create healthier boundaries to protect our well-being. By paying attention to our anger and understanding its message, we can make positive changes in our lives and relationships.

Negative emotions also serve as valuable feedback about our external circumstances and internal states. They can alert us to situations that are not aligned with our values, or indicate areas of personal growth and development. By acknowledging and exploring these emotions, we can gain insights into ourselves and make more informed choices for our well-being.

It's important to remember that our emotions are not meant to control us, but rather guide us. They are simply messengers, delivering valuable information that can help us navigate life more effectively. By embracing and exploring our negative emotions, we can transform them into catalysts for personal growth, self-discovery, and ultimately, a greater sense of well-being.

Tips and Techniques for Transforming Negative Emotions

- **Curiosity and Inquiry.** Instead of immediately pushing away negative emotions, adopt a curious mindset. Ask yourself questions like, *what is this emotion trying to tell me?* or *what need or value is being challenged?* By approaching your emotions with genuine curiosity, you can uncover deeper insights and gain a better understanding of yourself.

- **Self-Compassion.** Negative emotions often come bundled with self-criticism and harsh judgments. Practicing self-compassion involves treating yourself with kindness and understanding, just as you would a close friend who is experiencing difficulty. Remind yourself that it's okay to feel these emotions and that you are doing the best you can under the circumstances. (See "The Principle of Maitrī," in the next section, for a more in-depth discussion about self-compassion).

- **Reframing and Perspective-Shifting.** One powerful technique is to consciously reframe your negative emotions by examining them from a different perspective. For example, if you're feeling anxious about a public speaking engagement, try reframing it as an opportunity for personal growth and development. By shifting your focus from fear to learning, you can harness the energy of the emotion toward positive outcomes.

- **Emotional Write-Down.** Writing down your negative emotions can be a therapeutic and purifying exercise. Take a few moments to jot down your thoughts and feelings on paper, allowing yourself to fully express and process them. This practice enables you to create distance from the emotions and gain perspective on them, making it easier to reframe and reevaluate their significance.

- **Gratitude and Positivity.** Counterbalancing negative emotions with gratitude and positivity can help shift your perspective. Take some time each day to focus on the things you're grateful for, no matter how small they may seem. This practice cultivates a positive mindset and helps rewire your brain to notice and appreciate the good in your life, reducing the intensity of negative emotions.

Remember, reframing and shifting perspectives on negative emotions is an ongoing practice. Be patient with yourself and allow room for growth. With time and consistent effort, you'll find that you have the power to transform negative emotions into opportunities for personal development and well-being.

Cultivating Emotional Resilience

In the depths of our human experience, emotional resilience is the guiding light, illuminating our path through the twists and turns of life's labyrinth. It is a beacon of strength that allows us to navigate the storms within and around us, fostering a profound connection with our innermost selves. Just as the sun casts its warm glow upon the earth, emotional resilience radiates from within, empowering us to weather the tempests with grace and courage.

At the heart of emotional resilience lies the remarkable ability to pause, to quiet the external clamor, and to turn our gaze inward to the landscape of our emotions. In these moments of stillness, we embark on an introspective journey, traversing the terrain of our inner world with a compassionate curiosity that mirrors the work of a great explorer. With unwavering courage, we delve into the depths of our emotions, embracing the discomfort, the vulnerability that arises. Like archeologists unearthing ancient treasures, we excavate our past experiences, unearthing buried emotions that yearn to be acknowledged and embraced. We recognize that emotional resilience is not about evading or numbing the pain, but rather about embracing it as an integral part of our human experience.

As we traverse this introspective path, we encounter a myriad of emotions, each with its unique story to tell. We learn to sit with discomfort, to lean into vulnerability, and to honor the full spectrum of our feelings. We allow ourselves to be bathed in the tender glow of self-compassion, extending to ourselves the same kindness and understanding we would offer to a beloved friend. In this sacred space of self-reflection, we nurture the seeds of emotional resilience, cultivating the fertile ground for growth and transformation.

Within the sanctuary of our internal world, we confront our fears, our insecurities, and our shadows. We engage in a dance of introspection, embracing the light and the shadow, acknowledging that both are necessary for our growth and evolution. With each step forward, we shed the weight of judgment and shame, embracing our imperfections as the tapestry of our humanity.

Pause and honor the power of looking within. In the depths of your emotions lies a wellspring of wisdom, a compass that guides you toward authenticity and wholeness. As you develop the courage to face your inner landscape, to navigate the labyrinth of emotions, you discover that emotional resilience is not a fixed destination but a continuous journey of self-discovery. May you find solace in vulnerability, and may your journey unveil the strength and wisdom that lie dormant within your soul.

Practicing Emotional Resilience: The Principle of Maitrī

Imagine you're sitting across from a friend who's had a tough day. They're feeling down, questioning their worth, maybe even blaming themselves for things that went wrong. How would you respond to them? You'd likely extend a hand of comfort, assure them of their worth, remind them that it's okay to have off days and that tomorrow is a new start. Now, think about how you treat yourself when you're having a hard day. Do you extend the same kindness and understanding to yourself? Or are you your own harshest critic?

For many of us, the latter is often true. We berate ourselves for our shortcomings, we hold ourselves up to impossible standards, and we refuse to offer ourselves the compassion we so readily give to others. This is where the principle of maitrī comes in. Maitrī, a Sanskrit term often translated as "loving-kindness" or "unconditional friendliness," is a fundamental principle in Buddhist teachings. It involves cultivating a deep sense of compassion and kindness towards oneself and others. Practicing maitrī means extending warmth, acceptance, and non-judgmental care, first towards oneself and then outward to others. It is recognizing that you, too, are deserving of compassion and understanding. It's about acknowledging your humanness—the fact that you're not perfect and that's okay. It's about meeting your flaws and your mistakes with kindness, not criticism.

In the context of inner child healing, maitrī plays a crucial role in cultivating emotional resilience. By practicing maitrī, we learn to treat ourselves with the same kindness and understanding we would offer a close friend. This self-compassion helps to soothe the wounded inner child and provides a foundation for healing deep-seated emotional pain. When we embrace ourselves with unconditional friendliness, we can face our emotions without fear or resistance, allowing us to process and integrate them more effectively.

Maitrī helps in building emotional resistance by promoting a mindset of self-acceptance and non-judgment. Instead of criticizing ourselves for our emotional responses or perceived shortcomings, we acknowledge our feelings and experiences with compassion. This approach reduces the internal conflict that often exacerbates emotional distress and allows us to recover more quickly from setbacks. By fostering a gentle and supportive relationship with ourselves, we develop the strength and flexibility needed to navigate life's challenges with greater ease.

Moreover, maitrī encourages mindfulness and presence, as it requires us to be fully aware of our thoughts and feelings in the moment without pushing them away or becoming overwhelmed by them. This mindful approach enables us to observe our emotional patterns and triggers with clarity, creating space for conscious responses rather than automatic reactions.

Here's how you can start practicing maitrī:

- **Mindfulness.** Notice when you're being hard on yourself, and gently redirect your thoughts toward kindness and understanding. It's not about ignoring your mistakes, but about acknowledging them without self-blame or judgment.

- **Self-Kindness.** Talk to yourself as you would to a friend. When you stumble, extend a hand of understanding to yourself. Remind yourself that it's okay to be human, to make mistakes, to be less than perfect.

- **Common Humanity.** Remember that everyone has their struggles, their own off days, their own doubts and fears. You're not alone in your feelings. It's a shared human experience, and there's comfort to be found in that.

- **Non-Judgmental Acceptance.** Acceptance doesn't mean complacency. Instead, it's about recognizing where you are at this moment without judgment. It's about embracing the reality of your experience, whether it's pleasant or painful, and treating yourself kindly regardless.

Remember, maitrī is a practice. It's something you cultivate over time. And just like any practice, some days will be easier than others. There might be days where self-compassion feels almost impossible, and that's okay. Be patient with yourself. After all, practicing maitrī is about extending love and kindness to yourself, even—and especially—when it's hard.

Just as Brené Brown said, "Talk to yourself like you would to someone you love." That's the heart of maitrī. It's about being your own friend, your own cheerleader, your own safe haven. It's about recognizing that you, too, are worthy of love and kindness—especially from yourself.

Embracing Positive Emotions

Remember to allow yourself to feel positive emotions.

It might seem like a silly piece of advice to bring up, but the truth is that we're entangled in a complex dance with our emotions every day. They swing us high, dip us low, and whirl us around in circles. Sometimes, it feels like we're being led by our negative emotions, the ones that step on our toes and make us trip over our own feet. Anger, frustration, pessimism—these are the dance partners we've become all too familiar with. They're easy to follow, their steps predictable and well-rehearsed, but they lead us into a dance that is not our own. But what if we changed our dance partners? What if we chose to embrace optimism, joy, love, and peace instead? These partners might not be as familiar, their steps might be more complex, but the dance they lead us in is one of growth, fulfillment, and positivity.

Ask yourself this: When was the last time you truly celebrated a victory, no matter how small? Have you ever savored a moment of peace and tranquility, letting it seep into your being until you're brimming with serenity? Have you ever embraced optimism, allowing it to light up your path and guide your steps? If not, why not?

You see, when we constantly give center stage to our negative emotions, we're missing out on the radiant performance of our positive emotions. We're backstage, trapped in the shadows, while the spotlight shines brightly on the empty stage.

But we can change that. We can pull back the curtains and let our positive emotions take the lead. We can learn their steps, follow their rhythm, and dance to their tune. And in doing so, we'll find that we're not just spectators in our emotional journey but active participants. And the dance becomes not just a performance but a celebration of life's beautiful complexities. Embracing our positive emotions is not about ignoring our negative emotions or pretending they don't exist. It's about choosing which emotions get to lead our dance. It's about acknowledging that every emotion has its place and time and choosing to give our positive emotions the spotlight they deserve, and perhaps even more profound is the shift in perspective that positive emotions bring. They alter the way our mind operates, allowing us to perceive opportunities where once we saw limitations. This transformation in perception has the power to shape our future in ways we may have never imagined.

Interactive Element

Emotional Release

Imagine your inner world as a magnificent river, flowing through lush landscapes, winding through valleys, and cascading over waterfalls. This river represents the currents of emotions, memories, and experiences within you.

Emotional release is like allowing the river to flow freely and uninhibited. It's about removing any obstacles or dams that block the natural movement of the water. By doing so, you create a channel for emotions to be expressed and released, which allows for healing and restoration.

Here are several practical activities to help you achieve emotional release:

- **Writing**: Imagine your emotions as words and sentences carried by the river's current. Writing is like dipping your pen into the flowing river, allowing the words to spill onto the page. Take time each day to journal about your thoughts and feelings. Don't censor yourself; let the words flow naturally. Write about your emotions, memories, and experiences. This process helps articulate and release what's inside, transforming your emotions into something tangible and manageable.

- **Visual Art**: Picture your emotions as vivid colors and shapes swirling within the river. Engage in visual art, such as painting, drawing, or sculpting. As you create, focus on how your emotions translate into colors and forms. The act of transferring your feelings onto a canvas or into a sculpture externalizes and expresses your emotions. It's a therapeutic way to reflect the movement and energy of your inner river.

- **Movement and Dance**: Envision your body as a vessel for the river's current. Through movement and dance, you become the embodiment of your emotions. Find a quiet space and let your body move to the rhythm of your feelings. Dance freely, allowing each step, sway, or leap to channel the river's flow. This physical expression helps release the energy stored within your body, offering a profound sense of liberation and connection to your emotions.

- **Music and Sound**: Imagine the river's flow creating a symphony of melodies and rhythms. Music and sound can be powerful vehicles for emotional release. Listen to music that resonates with your current emotions or play an instrument to express how you feel. Experiment with vocalization, such as humming, singing, or even shouting, to harmonize with the river's currents. Allow the music and sound to penetrate deep within, helping you connect with and express your emotional depths.

- **Nature Connection**: Visualize yourself immersed in the river's surroundings, surrounded by the beauty of nature. Spending time in natural environments, like forests, mountains, or by the ocean, provides a powerful means of emotional release. Nature has a way of mirroring our emotions, offering solace, grounding, and perspective. Take walks, sit quietly in a natural setting, and observe the beauty around you. Let the tranquility of nature help you release your emotions and restore your inner balance.

By incorporating these activities into your routine, you can facilitate the free flow of emotions, aiding in the release of negative feelings and fostering emotional healing. Remember, emotional release is an ongoing process, and these practices can help maintain the health and vitality of your inner river.

Breathing and Relaxation Techniques to Manage Emotions

You deserve a life where your emotions are tools, not your masters. There are so many wonderful and helpful techniques you can try to cultivate greater emotional awareness, resilience, and self-awareness.

Below are some effective practices to explore. Start with just a few minutes each day and gradually increase the duration as you become more comfortable. Feel free to experiment and find what works best for you. Incorporating these techniques into your routine can have a significant impact on managing your emotions and promoting overall well-being.

- **Deep Belly Breathing:** One of the simplest and most effective techniques is deep belly breathing. Find a comfortable position, either sitting or lying down. Place one hand on your belly and the other on your chest. Take a slow, deep breath in through your nose, allowing your belly to rise as you fill your lungs with air. Exhale slowly through your mouth, feeling your belly fall. Focus on the sensation of your breath and repeat this process for a few minutes. Deep belly breathing helps activate the body's relaxation response, reducing feelings of stress and anxiety.

- **Box Breathing:** Box breathing is a technique that involves inhaling, holding the breath, exhaling, and holding the breath again, all for the same duration. Start by inhaling deeply through your nose to a count of four, then hold your breath for a count of four. Exhale slowly through your mouth for a count of four, and hold your breath again for a count of four. Repeat this cycle several times, visualizing the sides of a box as you go. Box breathing helps regulate your breathing pattern, promoting relaxation and mental clarity.

- **Progressive Muscle Relaxation:** Progressive muscle relaxation is a technique that involves systematically tensing and then releasing different muscle groups in your body. Find a quiet space and begin by focusing on your breathing. Start with your toes— tense the muscles for a few seconds, and then release, feeling the tension melt away. Gradually work your way up through your legs, abdomen, arms, and shoulders, tensing and releasing each muscle group. This technique helps promote physical relaxation and reduces muscle tension associated with stress and emotional turmoil.

- **Guided Imagery:** Guided imagery involves using your imagination to create calming and peaceful images in your mind. Find a quiet space and close your eyes. Imagine yourself in a serene place, such as a beach, forest, or mountain. Engage all of your senses to make the scene as vivid as possible. This technique helps reduce stress and promotes relaxation by shifting your focus away from negative emotions and towards positive, soothing images.

Here are some practical tips on how to engage all five senses in order to maximize the benefits of guided imagery:

1. **Sight.** Visualize a peaceful scene as vividly as possible. Imagine the colors, shapes, and details of your surroundings. Whether it's a beach, a forest, or a mountain, picture every element clearly. For example, if you're imagining a beach, see the blue waves gently crashing against the shore, the golden sand, and the clear sky.

2. **Sound.** Incorporate sounds that you would hear in your chosen setting. Imagine the sound of waves crashing, birds chirping, or leaves rustling in the wind. You can also listen to a recording of nature sounds to enhance your experience.

3. **Smell.** Think about the scents you would experience in your peaceful place. At the beach, you might smell the salty sea air. In a forest, you could imagine the fresh, earthy scent of pine trees. Engage your olfactory senses to deepen the immersion.

4. **Touch.** Focus on the sensations you would feel in your serene environment. Imagine the warmth of the sun on your skin, the coolness of the breeze, or the texture of the sand or grass beneath your feet. This tactile engagement helps ground you in the experience.

5. **Taste.** Although taste is less commonly engaged, you can imagine the taste of something pleasant that fits the scene. For example, if you're imagining a beach, you might taste the salt in the air or a sip of refreshing coconut water.

Example of a Guided Imagery Meditation

Here is a step-by-step example of a guided imagery meditation that you can try:

1. **Find a Quiet Space.** Sit or lie down in a comfortable position in a quiet, distraction-free environment. Close your eyes and take a few deep breaths to relax.

2. **Begin the Visualization.** Start by imagining yourself in a beautiful, serene place. For this example, let's use a tranquil beach.

3. **Engage Your Senses.**

    - **Sight.** Visualize the scene in detail. See the crystal-clear water stretching out to the horizon. Notice the gentle waves lapping at the shore and the bright, golden sand.

    - **Sound.** Listen to the rhythmic sound of the waves crashing and the distant call of seagulls. Imagine the gentle rustle of palm leaves swaying in the breeze.

    - **Smell.** Breathe in deeply and imagine the salty scent of the sea air mixed with the faint aroma of tropical flowers.

    - **Touch.** Feel the warmth of the sun on your skin and the coolness of the gentle sea breeze. Notice the soft sand beneath your feet and how it shifts slightly as you walk.

    - **Taste.** Imagine taking a sip of cool, refreshing coconut water, feeling its sweetness on your tongue.

4. **Immerse Yourself.** Spend several minutes fully immersed in this peaceful scene. If your mind wanders, gently bring your focus back to your imagined environment and the sensations you're experiencing.

5. **Gradual Return.** When you're ready to end the meditation,

slowly bring your awareness back to the present moment. Wiggle your fingers and toes, and take a few deep breaths. Open your eyes and take a moment to notice how you feel.

By regularly practicing guided imagery, you can create a mental sanctuary that helps you manage stress and emotions, providing a powerful tool for emotional regulation and healing.

Attentional Control as a Practice

Attentional control is a powerful tool for emotional regulation, enabling us to consciously direct our focus toward specific aspects of our emotions, thoughts, or situations. By mastering this practice, we can shift our attention away from negative or distressing emotions and redirect it toward more positive or adaptive aspects of our experiences. Here's how you can actively practice attentional control in your daily life:

1. **Shifting Attention.** To begin, identify when you are caught up in negative thoughts or emotions. Notice if you are ruminating or dwelling on a problem.

    - **Practical Exercise:** When you find yourself spiraling into negative thoughts, pause and take a deep breath. Consciously choose to shift your attention to something neutral or positive around you. For example, focus on the details of a nearby object, listen to soothing music, or engage in a hobby that you enjoy. By doing so, you can prevent yourself from being overwhelmed by distressing emotions.

2. **Refocusing Attention.** Once you've shifted your attention, the next step is to refocus it on something that can help you feel more grounded and calm.

- **Practical Exercise:** If you're feeling anxious, try redirecting your focus to your breath. Practice deep breathing exercises, such as box breathing—inhaling deeply through your nose for a count of four, holding the breath for a count of four, and exhaling slowly through your mouth for a count of four, then holding again for a count of four. Alternatively, engage in a relaxing activity, like taking a walk in nature or practicing yoga. This refocusing helps reduce anxiety and promotes a sense of calm.

3. **Cognitive Reappraisal.** Use attentional control to reinterpret a negative situation by consciously adopting a more objective or positive perspective.

    - **Practical Exercise:** Think of a recent situation that upset you. Write down the negative thoughts associated with it. Next, challenge these thoughts by writing down alternative perspectives or reframing the situation in a more positive light. For instance, if you think, *I failed at my presentation*, reframe it as, *I learned valuable lessons that will help me improve for next time.*

4. **Selective Attention.** Practice selectively attending to positive or rewarding stimuli in your environment.

    - **Practical Exercise:** Make it a daily habit to intentionally seek out and focus on positive aspects of your surroundings or experiences. Create a "gratitude journal" where you write down three positive things that happened each day, no matter how small. Engage in activities that bring you joy and fully immerse yourself in them, whether it's reading a good book, spending time with loved ones, or enjoying a favorite hobby.

Incorporating Attentional Control into Your Routine

1. **Set Intentions.** At the start of each day, set an intention to practice attentional control. Remind yourself to shift, refocus, reappraise, and selectively attend to positive stimuli.

2. **Mindfulness Reminders.** Use reminders, such as alarms on your phone or sticky notes, to prompt you to practice attentional control throughout the day.

3. **Reflection.** At the end of each day, reflect on how well you managed to control your attention. Note any progress or challenges, and adjust your approach as needed.

By integrating these practices into your daily routine, you can enhance your ability to manage emotions, reduce stress, and cultivate a more positive and balanced emotional state.

We are not just the mind, not just the body, we are also heart and spirit. By understanding and nurturing the interconnectedness of these elements, we open the door to profound healing and transformation. In the next chapter, we will explore how to harmonize these aspects of ourselves, guiding you towards a journey of holistic well-being and authentic living.

Chapter Six

Sacred Alignment

Integrating the Mind, Body, Spirit, and Heart

In nature we never see anything isolated, but everything in connection with something else which is before it, beside it, under it, and over it. –Johann Wolfgang von Goethe

In the realm of inner child healing, we get to a point where we recognize that we are not merely fragmented parts but an interconnected tapestry of mind, body, spirit, and heart. We are much more than the sum of our individual components; we are a symphony of energies, intricately woven together to create the essence of who we are.

Imagine, if you will, a dance among the mind, body, spirit, and heart. It is a dance of harmony, where each partner moves in sync, supporting and nourishing the other. When we are attuned to this interconnectedness, a gateway to profound healing opens before us, offering the potential for transformative growth and inner liberation.

Our mind is the architect of thoughts and beliefs, shaping our perceptions and narratives. It holds the power to create boundless possibilities or confine us within self-imposed limitations. Our body, the vessel that carries us through life, whispers to us its stories of sensations, emotions, and physical manifestations. It is a wise messenger, revealing the imprints of our experiences and the keys to unlocking our deepest healing.

But we must not forget the heart, the wellspring of our emotions, compassion, and connection. It is the seat of vulnerability and courage, guiding us toward authentic self-expression and the capacity to love and be loved. And intertwined with it all is our spirit, our essence, the eternal flame that ignites our purpose and guides us on our unique journey.

In this chapter, we dive deep into the profound connection between the physical body, the mind, emotional memory, and the spirit. By understanding how emotional trauma manifests in the body, we can begin to identify where these hidden wounds lie and unlock the healing potential within. We'll explore the spirit's relationship to the mental, emotional, and physical bodies, and how the chakra system serves as a vital link in this interplay. Through practices like somatic experiencing and chakra healing, we will discover how to release stored trauma and integrate therapeutic approaches for holistic inner child healing, restoring balance and harmony to the mind, body, spirit, and heart.

When we embrace the power of this interconnectedness, when we honor and nurture each aspect of our being, we unlock the true transformative potential of healing. It is in this recognition that we discover the threads that weave together our stories of resilience, growth, and transformation.

The Physical Body and Emotional Memory

When we think about the body, we often focus on its physical functions—its strength, endurance, and ability to carry us through life. Yet, the body is not simply a vessel for movement and survival; it is also a profound repository for our emotions and experiences. From the gentle flutter of butterflies in your stomach before an exciting event to the weighty pressure in your chest after a heartbreak, our bodies carry the echoes of our emotional lives in a language all their own.

The interplay between the body and emotions is something we all instinctively know, even if we don't always have the words for it. After all, how many times have you experienced a knot in your stomach when faced with anxiety or tension in your shoulders during stressful periods? These aren't just random occurrences; they are our bodies reacting to and remembering emotions. The physical manifestations of our inner emotional world are undeniable—woven into the very fabric of our being.

As we embark on this chapter, we'll explore how the body holds emotional memories and how past traumas can create physical sensations, tension, and even chronic conditions. This connection between our emotional experiences and physical body, known as somatic experiencing, forms the foundation for understanding more complex concepts like the spirit's relationship to our mental and emotional bodies, and how energy systems like the chakras help bridge these connections.

Somatic Experiencing: The Body Remembers

Somatic experiencing (SE) is a body-centered therapeutic approach to healing trauma that recognizes the deep connection between the physical body and emotional memory. Founded by Dr. Peter Levine, this method focuses on the idea that trauma is not just an event experienced by the mind, but a bodily experience that imprints itself into our nervous system, often manifesting as tension, pain, or other physical symptoms. The body, in its wisdom, "remembers" what the mind may suppress or avoid, and somatic experiencing aims to help individuals release these trapped memories.

At its core, somatic experiencing taps into the body's natural ability to process and release trauma. It's based on the understanding that animals in the wild, when faced with a threat, go through a process of literally shaking off the residual energy after the danger has passed. This helps them return to a state of equilibrium. In humans, however, traumatic experiences can leave us "frozen," disrupting the body's autonomic nervous system, which controls automatic bodily functions. This can result in dysregulation of the sympathetic and parasympathetic branches of the nervous system. The sympathetic branch, responsible for the "fight-or-flight" response, may become overactive, leading to heightened arousal, anxiety, and a hyper-vigilant state. On the other hand, the parasympathetic branch, responsible for relaxation and restoration, may become underactive, making it challenging for the body to calm down and recover from stress.

In somatic experiencing, the focus isn't just on talking through the trauma but on the bodily sensations associated with it. The goal is to guide individuals through gentle, mindful awareness of these sensations, allowing the body to complete the natural cycles of processing the trauma that may have been interrupted. It's like letting the body exhale the pent-up breath it's been holding for too long.

This method is a powerful reminder that trauma is not just locked in our minds or our emotions—it's stored within our tissues, muscles, and nervous system. Somatic experiencing provides a pathway to release these trapped memories, allowing the body to heal in ways that talking alone might not reach.

Physical Manifestations of Emotional Trauma

The connection between somatic experiencing and emotional memory becomes clear when we understand that the body doesn't just respond to trauma in the moment—it carries those emotional imprints long after the event has passed. Physical manifestations of emotional trauma are real and tangible; they are the body's way of signaling unresolved feelings that have not been fully processed. Understanding how trauma shows up in the body physically can shed light on the complex interconnections between our emotional and physical states.

Here are some common examples of how emotional trauma or stress can manifest physically:

- **Tightness in the Chest.** Grief, sadness, and unresolved emotional pain often find their home in the chest area, particularly around the heart. This is why people experiencing emotional distress frequently describe sensations of the heart "aching" or feeling constricted. In severe cases, it can lead to panic attacks or trouble breathing.

- **Tension in the Shoulders and Neck.** The weight of the world often rests on our shoulders—both metaphorically and physically. Stress, responsibility, and fear of losing control commonly manifest as tightness or stiffness in the neck and shoulders, as if the burdens we carry are physically holding us back.

- **Digestive Issues.** The gut is the second brain, rich with nerve endings and intricately tied to our emotional state. Anxiety, fear, and unresolved trauma can lead to digestive disturbances such as nausea, irritable bowel syndrome, or stomach cramps. It's no coincidence that we refer to emotions as "gut feelings."

- **Back Pain.** Repressed emotions, particularly anger, can often manifest as chronic lower back pain. The back is where we physically "support" ourselves, and emotional instability can undermine this, leading to ongoing discomfort.

- **Headaches and Migraines.** Emotional tension, particularly that which stems from overthinking or anxiety, is often accompanied by headaches. These sensations can act as a physical manifestation of emotional pressure or mental overload.

- **Fatigue and Chronic Pain.** When emotional wounds linger, they can drain our physical energy. Those dealing with unprocessed trauma may experience persistent fatigue, as the body exhausts itself in an effort to hold onto these emotional memories. This is a common trait in people with chronic pain conditions, which are often linked to emotional trauma or long-term stress.

So it becomes clear that the relationship between our physical body and our emotional experiences is a two-way dialogue. When we experience an emotion, our body often responds before we even consciously recognize the feeling. For instance, fear may trigger the release of adrenaline, causing our heart to race and our muscles to tense. Similarly, sadness may result in a heaviness in our chest or tears welling up in our eyes. The body speaks the language of emotion in sensations, movements, and tensions.

Just as emotions can affect the body, the reverse is also true. The state of the body can influence how we feel emotionally. Chronic tension in the body, for example, may lead to irritability or an ongoing sense of unease. This reciprocal relationship makes it crucial for us to pay attention to the physical signals our bodies send, as they can reveal hidden emotional truths we may not be consciously aware of.

This link between the body and emotion becomes particularly important when we discuss healing trauma. Unresolved emotional experiences are not simply forgotten by the mind; they become stored in the body, creating tension and pain until they are acknowledged and released. The body remembers, even when the conscious mind does not.

The Concept of Somatic Experiencing and Its Role in Healing Trauma

Imagine, if you will, a glorious orchestra, each instrument tuned to perfection, ready to create a symphony of sound. The orchestra is your body, the instruments are your cells, the conductor is your brain, and the symphony, your life experiences. But, what happens when a discordant note is played, a note of trauma, that reverberates through the orchestra, causing a disharmony that simply won't fade? The answer lies in the remarkable approach of somatic experiencing.

Somatic experiencing, being the artful maestro, steps in to retune the orchestra, to restore harmony. It is a therapeutic approach that understands that trauma is not just an experience of the mind but an echo in the body, a dissonant note that the body remembers and reacts to, often in ways that confound the conscious mind.

Think of your body as a library. Each book, each page, each word, is a record of your experiences, your emotions, your traumas. Some books are dusty and untouched, long-forgotten memories. Others are worn and dog-eared, constantly revisited. The trauma, those dissonant notes, are like books hastily shoved onto a shelf, not properly filed, their pages threatening to spill out and disrupt the quiet order of the library.

Somatic experience is the librarian that ensures every book is in its rightful place, every page is smoothed out, and every word is acknowledged. It does not throw the book of trauma away, but it helps you to read it, understand it, and put it back on the shelf in a way that it no longer disrupts your peace.

It is a bodily journey through the landscapes of your past traumas. The therapist, like an experienced navigator, helps you traverse these landscapes, not to relive the traumas, but to understand them, to feel them, to release the pent-up energy they've locked within your physical being. Like a river that has been dammed, these energies, once freed, can flow naturally, taking the path of least resistance, purging the toxicity of unresolved trauma.

The role of somatic experiencing in healing trauma is like that of a gentle gardener. It does not forcefully pull out the weeds of trauma, risking damage to the delicate roots of your psyche. Instead, it gently loosens the soil, allowing space for the trauma to breathe, to be seen, to be understood. It carefully extracts the trauma from your being, ensuring that it takes with it the roots of pain, fear, and physical tension.

And so, in the grand orchestra of your body, the dissonant notes are resolved, the trauma acknowledged and released. Your body, mind, and soul, like a well-tuned orchestra, can once again play the symphony of life, a symphony of healing, resilience, and wholeness. The art of somatic experiencing, the gentle gardener, the skilled librarian, the adept maestro, guides you on this journey to harmony, a testament to the resilience of the human spirit.

Examples of Somatic Experiencing Exercises

Somatic experiencing exercises offer a gentle yet powerful way to reconnect with your body, release stored tension, and cultivate a sense of safety within yourself. By tuning into physical sensations, you create space for healing that goes beyond words. Below are a few foundational exercises to help you begin this process, guiding you toward greater awareness and emotional regulation.

Grounding Exercise

1. Find a comfortable sitting or standing position.

2. Close your eyes and take a few deep breaths, focusing on the sensation of your breath entering and leaving your body.

3. Bring your attention to your feet and notice the connection between your feet and the ground.

4. Feel the support of the ground beneath you, imagining roots growing from your feet, anchoring you to the earth.

5. Pay attention to the sensations in your body, noticing any areas of tension or discomfort. Allow them to be present without judgment.

6. Take a few more deep breaths, and when you're ready, gently open your eyes.

Body Scan

1. Lie down comfortably on your back or sit in a chair with your feet flat on the floor.

2. Close your eyes and take a few deep breaths, allowing your body to relax.

3. Start at the top of your head and slowly scan your body from head to toe, noticing any sensations or areas of tension.

4. As you come across areas of tension or discomfort, bring your attention to those areas and imagine sending your breath into them, allowing them to soften and release.

5. Continue scanning your entire body, paying attention to each part and allowing any sensations to be present without judgment.

6. Take your time with this exercise, spending as much time as you need to connect with your body and release tension.

Pendulation

1. Sit or lie down comfortably, closing your eyes and taking a few deep breaths.

2. Bring your attention to an area of your body that feels relatively comfortable and pleasant.

3. Notice the sensations in that area, allowing yourself to fully experience them.

4. Now, gently shift your attention to an area of your body where you feel tension, discomfort, or distress.

5. Observe the sensations in that area, but try not to get overwhelmed. If it becomes too intense, return your attention to the comfortable area for a moment.

6. Continue to pendulate back and forth between the comfortable area and the distressed area, allowing yourself to experience both sensations.

7. Over time, you may notice a softening or easing of the distressing sensations as you practice this exercise.

Remember, these exercises are just a starting point, and it's essential to listen to your body and adjust them as needed. Also, do not underestimate the power of these exercises. They are designed to begin the process of building a bridge between your mental, emotional, and physical bodies.

The Spirit and Its Relationship to the Mental, Emotional, and Physical Bodies

The spirit, or soul, is often described as the pure essence of who we are, the part of us that transcends time, the body, and the mind. It is the deep, inner light that guides us through the journey of life. While intangible and difficult to define, the spirit is that whisper of intuition, the pull toward meaning, purpose, and connection to something greater than ourselves.

In many traditions and philosophies, the spirit is seen as the highest form of consciousness, connected to both the emotional and mental bodies but not bound by them. It is like the sun, radiating energy that touches all aspects of our being—the mental, emotional, and physical bodies are like planets orbiting this central force. Though the spirit is beyond physical form, it acts as the glue that ties together the different layers of who we are, helping to unify our experiences.

Spirit and Mental Body

The mental body is where thoughts, ideas, and cognitive processes reside. It is the space of intellect, reasoning, beliefs, and perception. While the mental body is highly active and analytical, the spirit operates in the realm of higher wisdom. The mental body is like the wind—it can blow fiercely or gently, shaping the landscape of our consciousness, but the spirit is like the sky that contains it, vast and unchanging. When our spirit and mental body are aligned, we are able to think more clearly and make decisions that resonate with our deeper truths.

The spirit guides the mental body, offering a higher perspective, allowing us to think beyond mere logic and understand the wisdom hidden in life's mysteries. The mental body is connected to the spirit through practices such as meditation, reflection, and spiritual inquiry.

Spirit and Emotional Body

The emotional body is where we experience feelings—joy, sorrow, love, fear. Emotions are fluid, like water, and just as waves can be calm or turbulent, our emotional body can rise and fall with the tides of life. The spirit is like the moon, pulling on the emotional currents but not being consumed by them.

When our emotional body is in harmony with our spirit, we feel more connected to ourselves and others. Love, compassion, and forgiveness flow naturally when the emotional body is attuned to the spirit. However, if our emotional body becomes disconnected from the spirit, we may experience emotional turmoil, confusion, or disconnection.

Practices like, prayer, mindful breathing, and heart-centered meditation help to strengthen this connection, grounding our emotions in a deeper spiritual foundation.

Spirit and Physical Body

The physical body is the vessel through which we experience life. It is our temple, where we store both our vitality and our weariness. Though it seems separate, the physical body is deeply intertwined with the spirit. Think of the body as the earth itself, solid and tangible, and the spirit as the life-giving sun that nourishes it. Without the warmth and light of the spirit, the body would wither.

The spirit flows through the physical body, energizing it, providing us with the life force that keeps us moving. In many spiritual traditions, it is believed that when we care for our bodies—through proper nutrition, exercise, and rest—we are also nurturing our spirit.

Practices such as yoga, tai chi, and energy healing are great ways to connect the physical body with the spirit, ensuring a harmonious balance between the two.

The Mental, Emotional, and Physical Bodies' Interconnection

Just like threads in a tapestry, the mental, emotional, and physical bodies are interwoven. The mental body influences the emotional body—thoughts can trigger feelings, as when a worrying thought creates anxiety, or a joyful memory brings happiness. The emotional body, in turn, impacts the physical body. Stress, anger, or fear can manifest physically as tension, headaches, or illness, while feelings of love and contentment promote health and vitality.

The physical body also informs the emotional and mental bodies. Physical pain can cause frustration or sadness, while physical wellness can create a sense of peace. These bodies exist in a delicate dance, each one influencing the other in ways both subtle and profound. For example, exercise not only strengthens the physical body but also releases endorphins, enhancing the emotional body and sharpening mental clarity.

How the Chakra System Connects These Bodies

The concept of chakras, derived from ancient Indian spiritual traditions, paints a vivid picture of our internal universe. The chakra system is often seen as the energy bridge that connects the spiritual, mental, emotional, and physical bodies. Chakras are like spinning wheels or vortexes of energy, each responsible for different areas of our well-being, from our most basics needs for survival to our highest aspirations for spiritual connection. Like a cascading waterfall, energy flows from the crown of your head to the base of your spine, linking all of the aspects of your being. There are seven main chakras that each connect to an aspect of your being—mind, body, spirit, heart.

1. **Root Chakra (Physical Body).** Sits at the base of your spine like a shimmering red ruby. Like the deep roots of a mighty oak, the root chakra grounds us, fostering our sense of security, safety, and physical health.

2. **Sacral Chakra (Emotional Body).** Just above the Root Chakra, but just below the navel, sits the warm orange glow of the Sacral Chakra. It governs how we experience and process our emotions. When in equilibrium, it allows us to relish life's pleasures without guilt and fosters a strong sense of self-worth.

3. **Solar Plexus Chakra (Mental Body).** Next, glowing like a

golden sun in our solar plexus or diaphragm region is the Solar Plexus Chakra. This is the core of our personal power, self-esteem, and willpower. It plays a key role in how we think about ourselves. When harmonized, it fuels our ambition and gives us the strength to take control of our life.

4. **Heart Chakra (Spirit and Emotional Body).** At the center of our chest, glistening with an emerald light, is the Heart Chakra. It is the bridge between the lower chakras and the higher spiritual chakras—the meeting point of the physical and spiritual, governing love, compassion, altruism, and spiritual connection.

5. **Throat Chakra (Mental Body).** Situated in the throat is the Throat Chakra, a turquoise vortex of energy. It is the voice of our spirit. It encourages truth, communication, and self-expression. When balanced, it helps us to articulate our deepest truths with clarity and conviction, aligning our thoughts with our words and actions.

6. **Third Eye Chakra (Mental and Spiritual Body).** Between the eyebrows, glowing a bright, beautiful indigo, like the evening sky or a luminous bowl of blueberries, is the Third Eye Chakra. It is the seat of intuition, insight, and higher consciousness. When awakened, it allows us to see beyond the physical world, perceiving deeper truths beyond logic.

7. **Crown Chakra (Spirit).** The highest chakra, at the crown of our head, is associate with either a brilliant violet or crystalline white hue. It is our spiritual gateway, connecting us to divine consciousness and universal wisdom. When aligned, it brings enlightenment, peace, and a profound sense of unity with all that is.

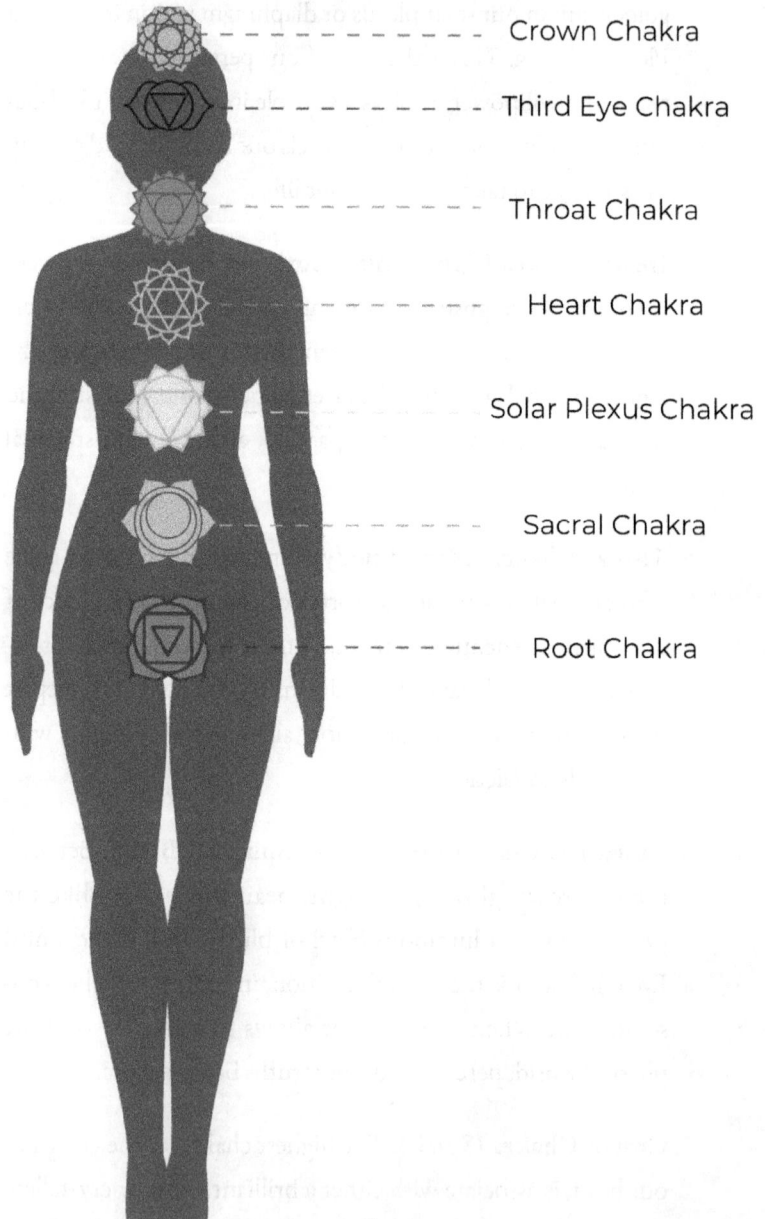

Image 6.1 The seven main chakras and their placement on the human body.

Together, the chakras serve as the energetic roadmap that helps balance and harmonize the physical, emotional, mental, and spiritual bodies. When these chakras are open and aligned, we experience a sense of flow and ease across all levels of our being, allowing us to tap into our inner wisdom, heal from emotional wounds, and find balance and purpose in life.

Using Chakras to Heal

To understand how the chakras tie into inner child healing, we must first recognize that inner child wounds are often buried deep within us—locked away in the very essence of our being. These wounds are not just mental or emotional; they can reside within our body and soul, distorting how energy flows through our chakra system. Each chakra represents a different aspect of our inner world, and when these energy centers are imbalanced, the residue of unhealed trauma can manifest in many ways.

Let's explore how specific inner child wounds can affect each chakra, what the symptoms of trauma might look like, and how we can begin to heal these wounds through chakra work.

Root Chakra (Muladhara) — Security and Belonging

The root chakra is the foundation of our existence, connected to our sense of safety, survival, and belonging. Inner child wounds related to abandonment, neglect, or feeling unsafe in childhood often show up here. If you grew up in an unstable environment or lacked a sense of security, your root chakra may be blocked or imbalanced.

Symptoms of Root Chakra Imbalance:

- Chronic fear or anxiety, often without an apparent cause.

- Feeling "ungrounded," restless, or disconnected from your body.

- Financial instability or deep fear of loss.

- Physical issues such as leg pain, lower back problems, or chronic fatigue.

Healing the Inner Child through the Root Chakra: To heal the root chakra, start by reestablishing a sense of safety within your body.

Grounding exercises: Spend time in nature, walk barefoot on the earth, or sit under a tree, visualizing roots extending from your body deep into the ground. This reconnects you with the stability of the Earth.

Affirmations: Repeat affirmations like "I am safe," "I am grounded," or "I belong."

Emotional work: Address memories where you felt abandoned or unsafe. Journaling can help, as can visualizing your adult self embracing your inner child, assuring them they are protected now.

Sacral Chakra (Svadhisthana) — Emotions and Creativity

The sacral chakra is the center of emotional flow, creativity, and pleasure. Inner child wounds often arise from a lack of emotional validation or suppression of creativity during childhood. If you were taught to suppress your emotions, were shamed for expressing your true self, or experienced emotional neglect, your sacral chakra may carry this pain.

Symptoms of Sacral Chakra Imbalance:

- Difficulty expressing emotions or connecting with your desires.

- Suppressed creativity or feelings of shame around self-expression.

- Addictions or unhealthy coping mechanisms to avoid feeling emotions.

- Sexual dysfunction or disconnection from pleasure.

Healing the Inner Child through the Sacral Chakra: To heal this chakra, you need to restore emotional flow and reclaim your creative essence.

Creative expression: Engage in activities like painting, dancing, or writing, without judgment. Let your inner child explore and play through these mediums.

Emotional release: Practice emotional release techniques like crying, screaming into a pillow, or journaling to release pent-up emotions.

Affirmations: Say, "It is safe to feel," and "My emotions are valid," while holding space for your inner child's unexpressed feelings.

Water connection: Spend time near water, such as a lake or ocean, or take mindful baths, imagining the water soothing and healing emotional wounds.

Solar Plexus Chakra (Manipura) — Personal Power and Self-Worth

The solar plexus chakra governs our sense of personal power, self-esteem, and confidence. Inner child wounds in this chakra are often tied to criticism, control, or feelings of worthlessness. If you grew up in a rigid, authoritarian environment where your choices were stifled or belittled, this energy center may be blocked.

Symptoms of Solar Plexus Chakra Imbalance:

- Low self-esteem or difficulty asserting boundaries.

- People-pleasing tendencies, or feeling powerless in relationships.

- Digestive issues, such as ulcers or indigestion.

- Chronic fatigue or lack of motivation.

Healing the Inner Child through the Solar Plexus Chakra: To heal the solar plexus chakra, focus on reclaiming your sense of personal power and self-worth.

Empowerment exercises: Take small actions that honor your independence, like setting boundaries or pursuing a passion project.

Affirmations: Speak empowering words such as "I am enough," or "I am powerful," directly to your inner child, offering them the confidence they lacked.

Sun meditation: Visualize a golden sun in your solar plexus, expanding outward, filling you with warmth and confidence.

Heart Chakra (Anahata) — Love and Compassion

The heart chakra is the seat of love, compassion, and connection. Inner child wounds in this chakra often stem from a lack of affection, emotional abandonment, or rejection during formative years. When your heart chakra is blocked, it can manifest as fear of intimacy, distrust, or difficulty loving yourself and others.

Symptoms of Heart Chakra Imbalance:

- Difficulty giving or receiving love.

- Emotional numbness or disconnection from others.

- Loneliness, even in the presence of others.

- Chest tightness, heart issues, or poor circulation.

Healing the Inner Child through the Heart Chakra: To heal the heart chakra, we must cultivate self-love and open the heart to connection.

Loving-kindness meditation (Maitrī): Practice sending love to yourself, your inner child, and others. Picture your heart glowing with green light, expanding outward to embrace both past and present versions of yourself.

Heart-opening exercises: Engage in breathwork or yoga poses like camel or cobra that physically open the chest area, releasing stored grief or sadness.

Affirmations: Gently speak words like, "I am worthy of love," or "I open my heart to healing," to your inner child, helping them understand they deserve love.

Throat Chakra (Vishuddha) — Expression and Communication

The throat chakra is the center of communication and expression. Inner child wounds here are often linked to being silenced, ignored, or ridiculed for speaking your truth as a child. If you were told to "be quiet" or "stay in your place," you may have a blocked throat chakra.

Symptoms of Throat Chakra Imbalance:

- Fear of speaking up or expressing opinions.
- Difficulty in communication or feeling misunderstood.
- Persistent sore throat or thyroid problems.
- Social anxiety or trouble being authentic.

Healing the Inner Child through the Throat Chakra: To heal the throat chakra, practice speaking your truth and reclaiming your voice.

Journaling or vocalization: Write or say aloud everything your inner child was unable to express. You might even try chanting or singing as a way to free your voice.

Affirmations: Use empowering statements like "My voice matters," and "It's safe for me to express myself."

Blue visualization: Imagine a blue light in your throat, dissolving any blocks, as you visualize your inner child speaking freely and fearlessly.

Third Eye Chakra (Ajna) — Intuition and Insight

The third eye chakra governs intuition and inner wisdom. Inner child wounds in this chakra are tied to disbelief in one's inner knowing or feeling confused about reality due to mixed messages in childhood. If your intuitive gifts were dismissed or you were gaslighted as a child, this chakra might be imbalanced.

Symptoms of Third Eye Chakra Imbalance:

- Difficulty trusting your intuition or making decisions.
- Overreliance on external validation or logical thinking.
- Headaches, vision issues, or sinus problems.

Healing the Inner Child through the Third Eye Chakra: To heal this chakra, cultivate your intuition and trust your inner wisdom.

Meditation: Practice visualization exercises, such as imagining a glowing indigo light between your eyebrows, expanding outward to bring clarity.

Affirmations: Remind your inner child, "I trust myself," or "I see clearly."

Journaling dreams: Keep a journal to track dreams, insights, or intuitive feelings, which helps reconnect with the inner child's wisdom.

Crown Chakra (Sahasrara) — Connection to Spirit

The crown chakra represents our connection to the divine, higher self, or universal consciousness. Inner child wounds in this chakra often reflect a disconnection from spirituality or a loss of faith due to trauma, hardship, or existential fear as a child.

Symptoms of Crown Chakra Imbalance:

- A sense of meaninglessness or spiritual disconnection.
- Feeling disconnected from life's purpose.
- Depression or mental fatigue.

- Migraines or a foggy mind.

Healing the Inner Child through the Crown Chakra: To heal the crown chakra, focus on restoring spiritual connection and trust in life's flow.

Meditation or prayer: Engage in practices that connect you with your higher self or a sense of divine guidance. Picture a violet or white light at the top of your head, connecting you to the universe or whatever spiritual source resonates with you.

Affirmations: "I am connected to something greater," and "I trust the flow of life," can help bring peace to your inner child's spiritual wounds.

Healing your inner child through the chakras is about restoring balance and harmony within your energy system. Each chakra holds the key to unlocking and releasing the memories, traumas, and patterns we've carried from childhood. By working through these energy centers, you're not only healing your past but creating space for wholeness, growth, and authentic living. Embracing the healing energy of the chakras opens us to a deeper connection with ourselves, allowing our inner child to feel seen, loved, and whole once again.

Combining Therapeutic Approaches

Combining traditional therapeutic approaches like psychotherapy or counseling with chakra healing work creates a synergistic path toward deep and lasting healing. Each approach complements the other, bridging the gap between the seen and the unseen, the tangible and the intangible. While therapy helps us process our thoughts, emotions, and patterns of behavior, chakra work taps into the energetic undercurrents that influence those same aspects of our being. Together, these two modalities offer a more holistic healing experience that addresses the mind, body, emotions, and spirit in unison.

The Advantages of Integrating Therapies

Bringing the Unconscious to Light

Psychotherapy allows us to explore the layers of our subconscious, uncovering hidden beliefs and behaviors that may be holding us back. However, many emotional wounds reside not just in the mind but in the body's energy system—memories stored not in words, but in the vibrations and blockages that disrupt the flow of our chakras. Chakra healing helps us access this energetic realm where traumas and limiting beliefs are often lodged.

By combining these two approaches, we engage both the conscious and unconscious aspects of healing, bringing the light of awareness to the mental patterns explored in therapy, while simultaneously clearing the energetic debris left behind by these patterns through chakra work.

Therapeutic Structure Meets Energetic Flow

Therapy gives us structure—a safe, consistent space to talk, feel, and reflect. It encourages self-awareness and provides a cognitive framework for understanding our experiences. Chakra healing, on the other hand, enhances this by addressing energy imbalances that traditional therapy might not reach. While therapy helps us intellectually process our traumas, chakra work moves the energy of those traumas through and out of the body. It loosens emotional knots and restores energetic flow, creating space for the body to recalibrate.

In this way, the two practices harmonize like the flow of a river against the banks of structure, creating a dynamic current of healing that is both intellectual and somatic, emotional and energetic.

Healing Beyond Words

Some wounds run so deep they elude language. Trauma, especially early in life, can be so overwhelming that it's stored in the body, bypassing the cognitive mind altogether. Traditional talk therapy can be limited in its ability to reach such primal places because some pain lives beyond words. This is where chakra work becomes invaluable.

When combined with therapy, chakra healing accesses nonverbal layers of trauma—those experiences stored as tension in the body, energetic stagnation in the chakras, or emotional memories that don't readily surface in conversation. By releasing these stored energies, chakra work frees the mind and emotions to integrate what has been previously inaccessible, creating a deeper healing that may not have been possible through dialogue alone.

Mind-Body Integration

Therapy often focuses on the mental and emotional bodies, encouraging us to reflect, gain insight, and challenge harmful thought patterns. While this is crucial, it's equally important to integrate the wisdom of the body. Our physical selves are intricately connected to our emotional, mental, and spiritual experiences. Trauma impacts the entire system, and it's not uncommon for deep healing to require work on multiple levels.

Chakra healing works directly with the body's energy centers, ensuring that what we process mentally and emotionally is also released and healed physically. This holistic approach facilitates a true mind-body connection, where healing isn't just thought about or talked about, but also felt and experienced on a cellular and energetic level.

How to Integrate Chakra Healing with Traditional Therapy

To fully benefit from this integrative approach, it's essential to intentionally weave both methods into your healing practice. Here's how:

- **Work with a Therapist and Chakra Healer Simultaneously.** Find a therapist who understands or is open to the concept of energy work, and simultaneously engage with a chakra healer who can guide you in balancing your energy centers. By working with both, you create a supportive team that addresses all facets of your being. Your therapist will help you explore cognitive patterns and emotional wounds, while your chakra healer works on clearing energetic blockages that contribute to those patterns.

- **Use Chakra Meditation After Therapy Sessions.** After an intense therapy session, emotions and memories can surface in ways that feel raw or overwhelming. To help integrate what you've processed, try chakra mediation. Focus on each chakra, particularly those most affected by the topics you've discussed in therapy. For example, if you've been working on issues related to self-worth, focus on your solar plexus chakra, visualizing golden light expanding from your core.

- **Journaling and Energy Work.** After a therapy session, journal about the insights or breakthroughs you had. Then, note any physical sensations or emotions you experienced during the session. Use this information to guide your chakra healing work. If you noticed tension in our throat while talking about a past experience, for instance, spend extra time working with your throat chakra to release any blocks around self-expression or suppressed emotions.

- **Move the Body to Release Stagnation.** Trauma is stored not only in the chakras but also in the muscles, fascia, and tissues. Incorporating movement practices like yoga, tai chi, or qi gong alongside therapy and chakra healing helps the body release stored tension. This allows energy to flow more freely and facilitates a more integrated healing process.

- **Set Intentions for Healing.** In both therapy and chakra healing, the power of intention plays a vital role. Before each session, set an intention for what you hope to achieve or release. For example, if you're working through abandonment wounds with your therapist, you might set an intention with your chakra healer to balance the root and heart chakras, which govern feelings of safety and love.

When we combine psychotherapy with chakra healing, we engage in a fuller spectrum of healing that honors both our earthly and spiritual selves. Like a lotus flower emerging from the mud, this integrative approach allows our deepest wounds to rise to the surface, heal, and transform into sources of growth and beauty. It brings together the structured scaffolding of therapy with the intuitive flow of energy healing, ensuring that the mind, body, heart, and spirit are all cared for, nourished, and restored.

In this dance between science and spirituality, we are invited to witness the power of true integration—where emotional scars soften, energetic blockages dissolve, and the self emerges whole, vibrant, and free.

Interactive Element

This interactive exercise will guide you through a holistic healing process, combining psychotherapy, somatic experiencing, and chakra healing. Whether you're working with a therapist or on your own at home, this step-by-step approach is designed to bring harmony between your mind, body, spirit, and emotions. By following these steps, you'll not only engage in emotional processing but also release any stored trauma from your physical body and energy centers (chakras).

Step 1: Create a Safe and Sacred Space

Before beginning any healing work, it's important to create an environment where you feel safe, relaxed, and grounded. This is your sanctuary for transformation.

- Find a quiet space where you won't be interrupted.
- Light candles, burn incense, or use an essential oil diffuser with grounding scents like sandalwood, frankincense, or lavender.
- Play soft, calming music or nature sounds in the background to promote relaxation.

Optional: Have a journal nearby to record any insights or emotional breakthroughs during the process.

Step 2: Grounding Your Energy (Root Chakra Activation)

We begin by grounding the body and connecting to the earth, which is crucial for healing trauma and accessing stored emotions.

- Sit comfortably either on the floor or in a chair, ensuring your spine is straight.

- Close your eyes and take a few deep breaths, allowing your body to settle into the present moment.

Visualization: Imaging roots extending from the base of your spine (Root Chakra) and the soles of your feet, growing deep into the earth. With each breath, feel your connection to the earth strengthening, as though the ground is pulling away any negative energy, stress, or tension.

- Breathe deeply for 3-5 minutes, visualizing this connection growing stronger with each exhale.

Step 3: Emotional Awareness and Body Scanning (Somatic Experiencing)

Next, we'll tune into the body, allowing any stored trauma, tension, or emotional discomfort to come to the surface.

- Begin a body scan: Starting from the crown of your head, move your awareness slowly down through your body—your face, neck, shoulders, chest, abdomen, legs, and feet.

- As you scan, notice any areas of tension, discomfort, or tightness. Pay attention to any physical sensations such as numbness, heaviness, restlessness, or warmth. These sensations may be the body holding onto emotional memories or unresolved trauma.

Journal Prompt: Write down any observations. Where do you feel tension? What emotions or memories arise when you focus on those areas?

Example: "I feel a knot in my stomach when I think about my childhood fear of being abandoned."

Step 4: Emotional Processing Through Psychotherapy Techniques

Now that you've identified areas of tension or emotional memory, we'll move into processing these emotions using self-reflective therapeutic techniques.

1. **Self-Inquiry Journaling**

    - In your journal, try answer the following questions:

        - *What is this tension or discomfort trying to tell me?*

        - *What emotions are associated with this part of my body?*

        - *Is there a memory, event, or experience from my past that is connected to this sensation?*

2. **Dialogue with the Inner Child**

    - Imagine sitting down your younger self, the child who experienced the original wound or trauma. In your mind, have a conversation:

        - *What do you need right now?*

        - *How can I support you?*

    - Allow your inner child to express their feelings, fears, or unmet needs. This process can be highly emotional, so give yourself permission to feel whatever arises.

Step 5: Chakra Healing for Energetic Release

Now that you've uncovered emotional memories and engaged in self-reflection, it's time to release stored trauma from your energy centers (chakras).

On the next page, *Table 6.1* shows common trauma or wounds associated with each chakra and how to release that energy using simple practices.

Visualization Example for Chakra Healing

Focus on the Heart Chakra for emotional wounds related to rejection or abandonment:

- Close your eyes and imagine a soft, green light glowing in your chest. As you inhale, the light grows brighter, filling your heart space with warmth and compassion.

- On the exhale, imagine releasing any sadness, grief, or rejection you've been carrying. Allow the energy to flow out and dissipate, leaving only love and forgiveness behind.

Note: You can use this visualization technique on any of the chakras, just change the color and location to the corresponding chakra. As for the emotional connection, whatever emotion you are trying to release on the exhale, try to bring in the opposing emotion on the inhale. (See *Image 6.2* for a list of opposing emotions).

Chakra	Location	Wounds/Trauma Stored	Healing Practice
Root	Base of the spine	Fear, insecurity, lack of safety	Grounding meditation (visualize roots); Stomp your feet on the ground to feel connected.
Sacral	Below the navel	Shame, guilt, emotional repression	Gentle hip-opening yoga poses; Visualize orange light swirling in your lower abdomen while repeating the mantra, "I am free to feel and express."
Solar Plexus	Upper abdomen	Low self-esteem, control issues	Practice deep belly breathing; Visualize yellow light in your abdomen and affirm, "I reclaim my personal power and confidence."
Heart	Center of the chest	Grief, heartbreak, rejection	Perform heart-opening stretches; Visualize green light expanding from your chest and say, "I am worthy of love and connection."
Throat	Throat	Inability to express truth, fear of speaking	Chant or hum gently to activate the voice; Visualize blue light around your throat, saying, "I am free to express myself authentically."
Third Eye	Between the eyebrows	Confusion, lack of clarity, distrust	Meditate with your focus on your forehead; Visualize indigo light expanding and affirm, "I trust my intuition and inner guidance."
Crown	Top of the head	Disconnection from spirit or purpose	Meditate in silence; Visualize white or violet light connecting your crown to the universe, affirming, "I am connected to the divine and aligned with my higher self."

Table 6.1 Chakra healing practice.

Image 6.2 List of basic opposing emotions to channel for healing.

Step 6: Somatic Release and Integration

The final step is to release any remaining tension or emotional residue through movement and breathwork.

> 1. **Emotional Release through Movement**
>
>   ○ Stand up and shake your body gently—starting with your hands, then your arms, torso, legs, and feet. Shake out any remaining tension, stress, or emotions that feel stuck. Let your movements be fluid and intuitive.

2. **Breathwork to Reset**

    ○ Practice box breathing to reset your nervous system:

    - Inhale for 4 counts, hold for 4 counts, exhale for 4 counts, hold for 4 counts. Repeat this for 2-3 minutes, allowing your body and mind to come into a state of calm and equilibrium.

Step 7: Closing the Session

End your session by expressing gratitude to yourself for showing up, doing the work, and facing any difficult emotions or memories that arose.

Closing Affirmation. Place your hands on your heart and say:

> "I honor my body, mind, and spirit for holding me through this process. I trust in my ability to heal, and I release all that no longer serves me."

Sit in stillness for a few moments, breathing deeply and allowing yourself to integrate the work you've done.

Optional: Draw a symbol, image, or word in your journal that represents the healing you experienced during this session.

As we've explored in this chapter, the body holds more than just our physical form—it carries our emotional memories, our stories, and the imprints of past experiences. By understanding the deep connection between the mind, body, spirit, and the energies within, we open ourselves to profound healing. We have laid the groundwork for recognizing the importance of addressing the physical and energetic layers of trauma, and how they intertwine with our emotional and mental states.

Now that we've established the connection between these aspects of our being, it's time to take the next step—learning how to heal and release the trauma that may be embedded within. In the following chapter, we will dive deeper into practical methods for releasing trauma, healing old wounds, and reclaiming our wholeness. Through the power of intentional healing, we can begin to shed the burdens that no longer serve us, paving the way for renewed vitality and emotional freedom.

Chapter Seven

Heal and Release

Alchemizing the Past Through Forgiveness

Forgiveness is giving up the hope that the past could have been any different, but we cannot move forward if we're still holding onto the pain of that past and wishing it was something else. –Oprah Winfrey

Like a songbird releases its melody into the dawn, we too must learn to release the chords of our past, allowing them to flutter into the silence of forgiveness.

We've made it this far. Take a moment to honor yourself and bask in the warmth of gratitude—not only for the progress you've made on this journey, but for having the courage to embark on the path of healing in the first place. This chapter is not just about a conclusion, it's about a beginning. It's about taking these fragmented pieces of our past, these shards of our inner child's pain, and tenderly, lovingly allowing them to dissolve in the gentle waves of forgiveness. It's a chapter about healing, about release, and ultimately, about freedom. We've journeyed together through the valleys of self-discovery, climbed the mountains of acceptance, waded through the rivers of sorrow, and now we stand on the brink of a grand ocean—the ocean of forgiveness. This chapter is not an end, but a bridge. A bridge to a life that's not held hostage by the past, but is instead invigorated and inspired by the power of healing and release.

We've spent time nurturing our inner child, listening to their cries, acknowledging their wounds, and now, it's time to let them know that they are free. Free from the chains of past hurt. Free from the expectation of a different past. Free to be the joyful, loving, and wonderful soul they have always been, unburdened by the weight of yesterday's pain.

This chapter is about embracing that freedom, embodying it, and releasing it into the world. It's about healing our inner child and letting them run free in the open fields of our hearts. It's about telling them, "You are forgiven. You are loved. You are free."

So, as we prepare ourselves to unwrap the delightful surprise that it has for us, may we take a deep breath, hold our inner child's hand, and step into the light of forgiveness. It's time to heal and release, to give up the hope that the past could have been any different and embrace the powerful truth: We are not our past. We are the healers of our inner child, the architects of our present, and the authors of our future.

May we allow ourselves the freedom to write a story of healing—a story of release. Let us write a story of forgiveness because in doing so, we're not just writing a story. We are setting our inner child free. We are setting ourselves free.

Reparenting Yourself

Imagine standing at the edge of a dense and enchanting forest. The air is filled with the scent of moss and wildflowers, and sunlight peeks through the canopy, casting dappled shadows on the ground. As you venture deeper into the woods, you come across a small, weathered cottage nestled amidst the towering trees.

This humble cottage holds the key to a profound transformation—the concept of reparenting your inner child. It is here that you set out on a journey of rediscovery, compassion, and healing.

As you step inside, you're greeted by a flickering fire in the hearth, casting a warm and comforting glow. The walls are adorned with paintings, each telling a story of innocence, joy, and vulnerability. You find yourself drawn to a portrait of a young child, radiating with curiosity and untamed enthusiasm. This child represents your inner self—the part of you that experienced the world before the weight of responsibilities, expectations, and disappointments took hold. It embodies your innate needs, desires, and emotions, which may have been suppressed or neglected over time.

In this enchanted cottage, you take on the role of a caring and nurturing parent to your inner child. You realize that this child within you is wounded, seeking solace and understanding. As you open your heart, you begin to listen attentively to its whispers, fears, and longings.

You sit together, cross-legged on a soft, plush rug, and engage in heartfelt conversations. You ask questions like, "What did you dream of becoming?" or "What made your heart leap with joy?" In this tender dialogue, you learn about the wonders and dreams that once ignited your spirit.

Slowly but surely, you embark on a journey of rediscovering the activities and experiences that brought your inner child immense delight. You revisit forgotten hobbies, such as painting, dancing, or playing make-believe. You allow yourself to be silly, to laugh wholeheartedly, and to embrace the sheer delight of being fully present in the moment. In this sacred space, you also acknowledge and address the pain that your inner child carries—the hurts, disappointments, or unmet needs. You offer a compassionate presence, wiping away tears and providing the comfort and reassurance that may have been absent in the past.

As the days go by, you notice a remarkable transformation unfolding. Your inner child begins to trust and believe in the love and care you provide, and a newfound sense of joy and freedom emerges within you. The shackles of self-doubt and self-criticism loosen, making way for self-compassion and self-acceptance.

Reparenting your inner child matters because it allows you to heal the wounds of the past and reclaim your sense of wholeness; it is a way of rewriting the narrative of your past, not by changing the events themselves but by altering the emotional impact they continue to have on your life. When you reparent your inner child, you consciously create new experiences of love, safety, and support. You become the caregiver, the protector, and the source of absolute acceptance that your younger self needed during moments of distress. By tending to the needs of your inner child, you cultivate a deep and profound connection with yourself—one that is rooted in love, understanding, and unconditional support.

As you step out of the enchanted cottage, you carry the essence of this transformative experience with you. Your relationship with your inner child becomes an ongoing journey—a commitment to nurturing and protecting the most vulnerable parts of yourself.

Through reparenting, you have the opportunity to:

- **Acknowledge the Pain.** Acknowledge the wounds your inner child carries without judgment, validating the emotions and experiences that were previously ignored or minimized.

- **Provide Nurturing.** Offer the love, security, and encouragement that may have been lacking in your formative years.

- **Set Healthy Boundaries.** Teach your inner child how to create and maintain boundaries, giving yourself the freedom to grow without fear of repeating past patterns.

- **Restore a Sense of Worth.** Remind your inner child of their inherent value and worth, even if those massages were not received from caregivers or others during childhood.

In doing so, you not only heal and grow but also create a ripple effect on your relationships and interactions with others. By embracing your own vulnerability and tending to your inner child, you show up in the world with greater authenticity, empathy, and compassion.

Exercise: A Magical Adventure of Inner Child Rediscovery

In this exercise, we are going to reconnect with our inner child and provide the nurturing and love it deserves. Prepare for an immersive experience meant to awaken your sense of wonder and joy.

1. Find a quiet and comfortable space where you can fully immerse yourself in this exercise. Close your eyes, take a deep breath, and envision the enchanted cottage within your heart—the place where your inner child resides.

2. Imagine stepping through the threshold of the cottage and en-

tering a lush garden teeming with vibrant flowers, singing birds, and fluttering butterflies. Feel the soft grass beneath your feet and the warm sunlight on your skin.

3. Ahead of you, a winding path appears, leading to a mysterious door. You approach the door with anticipation, knowing that behind it lies an extraordinary adventure. Open the door and step into a magical world that reflects the essence of your inner child.

4. Allow your imagination to run wild. What does this magical world look like? Are there fantastical creatures, sparkling streams, or towering castles? Let your inner child guide you as you explore this wondrous realm.

5. As you journey through this magical world, pay attention to the things that catch your eye. What activities, toys, or experiences bring an instant smile to your face? Take the time to engage in those activities—whether it's swinging on a swing, building sandcastles, or chasing fireflies.

6. Along your adventure, you may encounter challenges or obstacles that represent the wounds or fears of your inner child. Approach them with compassion and curiosity. Ask yourself, "What can I do to comfort and support my inner child in this situation?" Trust your intuition and offer the love and guidance that your inner child needs.

7. As you near the end of your magical adventure, find a peaceful spot—a cozy nook, a babbling brook, or a quiet meadow. Sit down, inviting your inner child to join you. Engage in a heartfelt conversation, listening attentively to its hopes, dreams, and fears. Offer comfort, understanding, and unconditional love.

8. When you feel ready, slowly bring your awareness back to the present moment. Take a deep breath, feeling the connection between your inner child and your present self. Open your eyes and carry the joy, wisdom, and love you have cultivated throughout your day.

Reparenting your inner child is not a quick fix, but it's a powerful practice for long-term emotional healing. As you nurture your inner child, you restore your connection to innocence, joy, and a deep sense of belonging. Over time, you'll find that the pain of past trauma becomes less overwhelming, and in its place, you will feel a growing sense of peace and self-compassion. By reparenting your inner child, you break free from the chains of your past and step into a more liberated, authentic version of yourself.

The beauty of this practice lies in its simplicity—by offering your inner child the love and care they deserve, you cultivate a more loving, compassionate, and resilient adult self.

Understanding the Impact of Unforgiveness

Unforgiveness is often compared to carrying a heavy weight—a burden that grows more oppressive the longer we hold onto it. When we refuse to forgive, it's as though we are binding ourselves to the pain and hurt of the past, dragging it with us into each new moment. Unforgiveness doesn't just impact the person we refuse to forgive—it seeps into every corner of our lives, affecting our mental and emotional well-being, our physical health, and even our relationships.

At its core, unforgiveness is a defense mechanism. We hold onto resentment and anger as a way of protecting ourselves from further harm, thinking that if we stay vigilant, we can avoid being hurt again. But this self-protective stance has its own cost. Instead of healing the wound, unforgiveness keeps it open, festering, and leaves us stuck in a cycle of pain.

The effects of unforgiveness often manifest in our bodies, too. It can create chronic tension, stress, and even illness. Research has shown that holding onto anger and resentment can lead to a weakened immune system, higher blood pressure, and an increased risk of depression and anxiety. The emotional energy spent on harboring grudges also depletes us, robbing us of peace, joy, and fulfillment.

But perhaps the most significant damage done by unforgiveness is the way it keeps us from moving forward. We remain tethered to the past, replaying the hurt over and over again, trapped in an endless loop of pain. Forgiveness, on the other hand, is an act of liberation. It frees us from the chains of resentment and allows us to live fully in the present, no longer defined by our past wounds.

Unforgiveness is like a smoldering ember buried deep in the heart. Though unseen, it quietly seethes, sending out toxic tendrils that invade the mind, body, and spirit, slowly consuming the very soul it resides in. To truly grasp the devastating impact of unforgiveness, consider Emily's story.

The Poison of Unforgiveness: Emily's Story

Emily was once the embodiment of light—her laugh could lift the heaviest hearts, and her compassion seemed boundless. Friends and family often marveled at her ability to forgive the most painful slights, to let go with grace, and move forward with kindness. But life, as it often does, took a sudden, heartbreaking turn when she experienced a betrayal so profound, so personal, that her forgiving heart faltered.

Her best friend, Sarah, the person she trusted above all others, had done the unthinkable. Whispers and rumors, all dripping with lies, spread like wildfire through their small community, each word a dagger aimed at Emily's reputation. It was Sarah who had fanned the flames, spreading falsehoods that shattered Emily's trust and left her isolated. The shock of the betrayal struck her like a blow, but it was the bitterness that followed that truly began to destroy her.

At first, Emily tried to brush it off as she had done so many times before. But this time, the wound ran too deep. A darkness settled in her heart—an anger she couldn't shake, a resentment that felt like fire in her veins. She replayed the betrayal over and over, her thoughts circling back to Sarah's smiling face, now twisted with cruelty in her mind. Revenge became her constant companion, her waking thoughts poisoned by a desire to make Sarah suffer, to feel the pain she had inflicted.

As the months passed, Emily's inner turmoil began to manifest outwardly. The warmth that had once defined her slowly ebbed away. Her bright smile, once so quick and effortless, became a rare and hollow thing. Her face, once soft with joy, grew hard, etched with lines of tension and anger. Friends who once found comfort in her presence began to drift away, sensing the coldness that now surrounded her. In her quiet moments, Emily could feel the weight of her bitterness, like a heavy stone lodged deep in her chest, pressing harder with each passing day.

Physically, the toll was unmistakable. Her nights were restless, her mind too loud to let her sleep. Anxiety gnawed at her, her body always tense, always on edge. Her health began to falter—small aches and pains crept in, her body stiffened with stress, and her energy drained away as if her very life force was being siphoned off by the bitterness she clung to. Emily was no longer the vibrant woman she had been. She had become a ghost of herself, haunted by the past, trapped in a prison of her own making.

But perhaps the greatest tragedy was not what others could see—it was what Emily had lost within herself. Her unforgiveness became a barrier, a thick wall that kept her locked in the past, unable to heal, unable to grow. The anger she nursed became her identity, and in that, she lost the beauty of who she once was. Every time she looked in the mirror, she saw the pain staring back at her, a constant reminder of the betrayal she refused to release.

Then, one cold and quiet evening, as she sat alone with her thoughts, Emily reached a breaking point. She realized that her unforgiveness hadn't harmed Sarah—it had harmed her. The bitterness had stolen her joy, strained her relationships, and taken years off her life. It had burned through her heart like acid, leaving scars she could no longer ignore. In that moment of stark clarity, she knew something had to change.

Forgiveness, she realized, was not about letting Sarah off the hook. It wasn't about excusing the betrayal or pretending it never happened. It was about setting herself free. It was about reclaiming her own peace, her own spirit, her own life.

With trembling hands and a heavy heart, Emily made the decision to let go. She began to release the anger, slowly at first, as if peeling away layers of armor she had built around her heart. It was painful, and yet, with each step toward forgiveness, she felt a lightness she hadn't known in years. The bitterness that had coiled inside her for so long began to unwind, and in its place, she found a fragile but growing sense of peace.

As Emily walked this path of forgiveness, something remarkable began to happen. The lines on her face, once carved deep by resentment, softened. Her smile returned, tentative at first, but real. Her relationships, strained for so long by the toxic fog of bitterness, began to heal. Friends who had distanced themselves slowly came back, sensing the shift in her spirit. Most importantly, Emily found herself again—the vibrant, compassionate woman she had been before the betrayal. In forgiving Sarah, she had rediscovered her own freedom.

Emily's story is not one of simple resolution or easy answers. Forgiveness, she learned, is not a single act but an ongoing process, a choice made again and again to let go of the past and choose peace over pain. But her story is a testament to the transformative power of forgiveness. It is a reminder that holding onto anger and resentment only serves to chain us to the very pain we seek to escape.

Unforgiveness, like a smoldering ember, will eventually consume us if we let it. But forgiveness, like water poured on the flame, brings cool relief, a balm to the soul, and the chance to heal. In letting go, we set ourselves free.

Consequences of Holding onto Past Trauma and Resentment

Imagine life as a vast garden, where each experience we have—both good and bad—plants a seed. Some seeds bloom into beautiful, life-affirming flowers, while others, particularly the seeds of trauma and resentment, take root in ways that can strangle our joy. These painful memories grow like stubborn weeds, entangling themselves around our hearts and minds, constricting our ability to breathe freely and live fully.

When we hold on to the pain of past betrayals or injustices, it's as though we continually water these weeds of resentment. They begin to overshadow the other parts of our emotional garden, choking the vibrancy of new growth and robbing us of the mental and emotional space we need to thrive. The impact of this is far-reaching.

On a physical level, carrying unresolved trauma can manifest as chronic tension, fatigue, digestive issues, or even unexplained illnesses. These ailments are not simply coincidences; they are the body's way of storing and expressing what the heart and mind cannot release. Resentment and trauma can embed themselves into our very muscles, creating tension in our shoulders, neck, and chest—areas often associated with the burden of emotional weight.

Emotionally, the repercussions are profound. Like a river that overflows its banks, unhealed wounds from the past can spill into all areas of our lives, causing waves of anger, sadness, or fear that we can't easily control. Holding onto bitterness warps our perceptions, making it difficult to trust, love, or open ourselves to new experiences. Our relationships often suffer because we are preoccupied with guarding against future hurts, even when no danger is present.

Psychologically, this can create a cycle of obsessive rumination—reliving the pain, replaying old memories, and revisiting the betrayal. It stirs an internal dialogue steeped in "what ifs" and "if onlys," trapping us in the past and preventing us from fully engaging in the present. Anxiety, depression, and even a sense of hopelessness can arise, as our minds become more focused on survival and less on thriving.

But there is hope. Just as plants can wither or grow depending on how they are tended, we too have the power to uproot those seeds of pain and nourish the ground where healing and renewal can take place. Releasing past trauma is not about pretending it didn't happen or dismissing the hurt—it's about transforming it. By facing our pain, acknowledging it, and choosing forgiveness—not as a way to absolve others but as an act of self-compassion—we begin to pull out those weeds. Slowly but surely, we clear space for love, joy, and peace to take root once again.

In letting go of past trauma and resentment, we open ourselves to new possibilities—ones where emotional freedom, inner peace, and personal growth can flourish. Like a forest regrows after a wildfire, our inner landscape has the capacity for incredible regeneration, if only we tend to it with care.

Examining the Nature of Forgiveness and Dispelling Common Misconceptions

The human heart is a remarkable canvas painted with a myriad of emotions. Amidst all of this, forgiveness stands out as one of the most profound and powerful hues. It is not merely a word spoken, but an act that resonates deep within the soul, a symphony of acceptance and letting go.

One common misconception about forgiveness is that it is an act of mercy toward the one who has inflicted harm. However, in reality, forgiveness is a gift we give to ourselves. It is a way to liberate our hearts from the shackles of resentment and bitterness, a path toward inner peace and tranquility. It is not about forgetting the past, but about reframing it, not letting it dictate the course of our present and future.

Forgiveness can often be mistaken for weakness, seen as an act of surrender. This could not be further from the truth. There is a profound strength in forgiveness, in the capacity to rise above the understandably human impulse for retribution. It takes courage to choose understanding over anger, compassion over vengeance, and love over hate.

Another widespread fallacy is that forgiveness is instantaneous, a switch to flick when ready. The truth is, forgiveness is a journey, not a destination. It is a winding road filled with bumps and turns, requiring patience, resilience, and time. It is a process of healing, where the wounds of the past gradually lose their sting, transforming into scars that remind us not of our pain, but of our capacity to heal.

Commonly, forgiveness is seen as a prerequisite for reconciliation. However, they are not mutually inclusive. You can forgive without reconciling, and that is completely valid. Forgiveness is a personal choice, an inner dialogue that does not necessarily require a harmonious resolution with the wrongdoer.

In a world often torn apart by conflict and hatred, forgiveness is our bridge to unity, our gateway to understanding. It heightens our humanity, illuminates our empathy, and underscores our capacity for boundless love. And in the end, it is not just about forgiving others, but also about extending that same grace to ourselves. For, as Alexander Pope famously wrote, "To err is human, to forgive, divine."

The notes of forgiveness are often the sweetest. In embracing it as a process, we grant ourselves the time we need to heal, to rebuild trust, and to develop resilience. Every step forward serves as a testament to our strength and willingness to cultivate a state of emotional freedom. Through the process, we learn to live authentically, unburdened by the chains of anger and resentment, allowing us to soar freely toward self-discovery and personal fulfillment.

So, remember that forgiveness is not an instant destination, but rather a journey, both transformative and profound. Embrace the process. As you walk this path, allow patience to guide you, and may the gentle whispers of forgiveness's name pave the way for a life unencumbered by the chains of the past.

Letting Go of Resentment and Anger

Anger and resentment can become anchors that keep us tied to the past, dragging our emotions backward instead of allowing us to move forward. These emotions often hold us captive, tethered to the very trauma we are trying to heal from, causing us to replay the painful events in our minds. Each time we dwell on the details—reliving the betrayal, injustice, or hurt—we allow these emotions to re-injure us, over and over again. This cycle of revisiting the pain can become exhausting, draining us of the energy we need to heal and grow.

At their core, anger and resentment tend to create a sense of victimhood, where we perceive ourselves as powerless and unjustly treated. While it's perfectly human to feel these emotions in the aftermath of trauma, staying in this emotional state for too long can limit our ability to take ownership of our healing. It can lead to identifying so strongly with being a victim that we stop seeing ourselves as the hero of our own story—capable of overcoming adversity and finding new strength in the process.

Resentment and anger don't just impact our inner world; they seep into our relationships as well. They can create a barrier between us and the people who care about us, leading to conflict, arguments, and emotional distance. In pushing others away, we inadvertently isolate ourselves in our pain. This isolation deepens the emotional wounds, creating a cycle of bitterness that becomes increasingly hard to escape.

When we hold onto resentment, we limit our ability to cultivate a deeper understanding of our experiences. We close off the possibility of forgiveness—both for ourselves and others—and without forgiveness, we miss out on the opportunity for personal growth and closure. Resentment, like a toxin, can seep into our souls, poisoning our ability to see beyond the pain and into the realm of healing.

But here's the transformative truth: Learning to let go of resentment and anger is not about erasing the hurt or pretending the trauma never happened. Instead, it's about releasing the emotional hold it has over you. It's about reclaiming your power and your peace of mind. By choosing to let go, we open ourselves to healing in ways we never thought possible.

In Zen Buddhism, non-attachment is a core principle that offers a pathway to inner peace. When we release our attachment to anger and resentment, we free ourselves from the suffering they bring. The key is not to deny or suppress these emotions, but to acknowledge them, understand their origins, and consciously choose to let them go. By practicing non-attachment, we create space within ourselves for new growth, compassion, and clarity. Let's look at how to apply this concept in our daily lives.

Zen Buddhism and Non-Attachment

Imagine a serene pond nestled deep within an ancient forest. The surface of the water is perfectly still, reflecting the towering trees, the soft clouds drifting above, and the distant, silent mountains. This pond mirrors the essence of Zen Buddhism: a practice rooted in deep stillness, awareness, and the pursuit of seeing life exactly as it is, free from distortion or desire. In this tranquility, we glimpse the core of Zen—where clarity is born not from striving or effort but from the quiet practice of simply being.

Zen is not a conventional religion bound by doctrine or dogma. It is a way of living—a philosophy that invites us to pause, breathe, and look deeply into the nature of our existence. Its teachings urge us to strip away the illusions created by our attachments, fears, and desires, revealing the profound truth that lies beneath: everything is impermanent, and the only constant is change.

At the heart of Zen lies the concept of non-attachment, a principle often misunderstood. Non-attachment is not indifference. It is not about distancing ourselves from emotions or the world. Instead, it is a liberating practice of embracing life without clinging to it. It's like the breeze that rustles through the leaves of a tree—touching, moving, and flowing, without ever holding on.

Non-attachment allows us to feel deeply while remaining free. It gives us permission to experience joy, love, and connection without the fear of losing them or the need to control their outcomes. When we learn to release our grip on how we think life should be, we open ourselves to the vastness of how life actually is, with all its unpredictable beauty and complexity.

Consider, for a moment, holding a delicate bird in your hands. Clasp it too tightly, and you will harm it. Hold it too loosely, and it will fly away. But if you find the balance—cradling it with care, gentleness, and respect—the bird may rest in your hand, not out of force but out of trust. This balance embodies the art of non-attachment: the wisdom to hold life's experiences, relationships, and even its pain, with open hands rather than clenched fists.

In Zen, life is viewed as a continuous flow, like the seasons that come and go, or the cherry blossoms that bloom in their radiant beauty only to fall and wither in a matter of days. We are reminded that everything is transient—our joys, our sorrows, our possessions, and even our identities. But rather than seeing this impermanence as something to fear, Zen teaches us to find freedom in it. By accepting the inevitability of change, we can appreciate each moment more fully, without grasping for permanence where it does not exist.

This practice of non-attachment doesn't mean we detach ourselves from the world or withdraw into isolation. On the contrary, it allows us to engage with life more authentically. We learn to love without conditions, to give without expecting anything in return, and to live without being weighed down by the fear of loss. Zen shows us that everything in life is interconnected—every action, every thought, every emotion is part of the larger fabric of existence.

In practicing non-attachment, we step out of the limited view that life must be a certain way for us to be happy. Instead, we open ourselves to the endless possibilities that life presents. We learn to dance with the flow of existence, moving with it rather than against it, finding grace in every step, no matter how uncertain the path ahead may seem.

Zen Buddhism and non-attachment offer us a path not only to inner peace but to a profound freedom. By releasing our attachments to outcomes, desires, and even our sense of control, we free ourselves from suffering and make room for the wonder of simply being present in this fleeting, beautiful world.

Interactive Element

The Letting Go Ritual

This exercise helps readers release the emotional baggage of resentment and anger. It incorporates both mindfulness and non-attachment techniques from Zen Buddhism.

1. **Prepare a Quiet Space.** Sit somewhere peaceful. Have a pen and paper ready for the exercise, as well as a safe way to dispose of the paper afterward (like a fireproof bowl or shredder).

2. **Identify the Resentment.** Begin by writing down the specific event or person that has caused you anger or resentment. Be honest with your emotions—allow yourself to fully express the pain, frustration, or sadness you've been holding onto.

3. **Acknowledge Your Emotions.** Reflect on the emotions that arise as you write. Allow yourself to feel them fully, but without judgment. In Zen, this process of non-attachment doesn't mean ignoring your feelings but recognizing them without letting them control you.

4. **Visualize the Burden.** After writing everything out, close your eyes. Visualize your resentment or anger as a heavy weight you're carrying—perhaps in the form of a stone or boulder. See yourself holding this burden. Feel its weight, its texture, and its significance. As you do, recognize the pain it represents and the power it holds over you.

5. **Release the Burden.** In your mind's eye, imagine setting the weight down. Picture yourself walking away from it, feeling lighter, freer, and more at peace. Breathe deeply and imagine each exhale as a release of the negative emotions you've been carrying. Allow yourself to bask in this newfound freedom.

6. **Physically Release.** Now take the paper you wrote on and dispose of it. You can burn it safely or tear it into tiny pieces, symbolizing the act of letting go. As you do so, repeat to yourself: *I release you. I free myself from this burden.*

7. **End with Gratitude.** Take a few moments to reflect on how it feels to release the resentment. Offer gratitude for the lesson the experience taught you, and for your own strength in letting go.

The Power of Gratitude: A Pathway to Inner Healing

Gratitude is more than just an emotional response to the good in our lives—it's a powerful tool for transforming pain and opening the door to healing. When we practice gratitude, we actively shift our focus away from trauma and resentment, creating space for joy, self-compassion, and inner peace. This exercise is designed to help you engage with gratitude as a healing force, inviting positive energy into your life as you release the burdens of the past.

Gratitude Meditation for Releasing Trauma

1. **Prepare Your Space.**

   - Find a calm, quiet space where you won't be disturbed for the next 10-15 minutes.

   - Sit comfortably, either on the floor or in a chair, with your spine straight and your hands resting gently on your lap.

   - Close your eyes and take several deep breaths, allowing your body to relax and your mind to settle.

2. **Begin with Awareness.**

   - Shift your awareness to the present moment. Feel the rise and fall of your breath. Allow yourself to be here, in this moment, free from the distractions of the past or worries of the future.

3. **Invite Gratitude.**

   - Bring to mind three things or people in your life that you feel grateful for. Focus on one at a time, imagining these people or experiences vividly. Visualize each in rich detail—how it feels, what it looks like, or any sensory connection you have.

- Example: Perhaps you think of a close friend who has supported you through hard times. Picture their face, hear their laughter, and feel the warmth of their care.

4. **Deepen the Experience.**

- As you focus on each gratitude item, immerse yourself in the positive emotions it brings. Allow your heart to expand with feelings of appreciation, comfort, and peace. The key is to feel the gratitude in your body. Notice how your breath slows, your muscles relax, and your chest feels lighter.

- Connect these sensations to your healing journey. Each moment of gratitude is an act of self-compassion and release—an opportunity to let go of past hurts and embrace the love and joy that exist in your life right now.

5. **Reflect on Healing.**

- For each gratitude item, reflect on how it contributes to your healing. Ask yourself:

  - *How has this person or experience supported me in letting go of past pain?*

  - *What lessons have I learned from this that help me grow stronger?*

- Allow yourself to feel that this moment of gratitude is also a moment of release. Each breath of appreciation moves you further away from old wounds and closer to a future filled with peace.

6. **Express Gratitude.**

    - When you are ready, silently or aloud, express your gratitude for these moments or people. Speak to them as though they are present, thanking them for the role they have played in your healing. If you wish, place your hand over your heart as you do this, physically connecting to the gratitude within you.

7. **Close the Practice.**

    - Take a final deep breath and, as you exhale, imagine yourself releasing any remaining anger, pain, or resentment that lingers within. Visualize yourself free and light, as if the weight of the past has lifted from your shoulders.

    - When you're ready, open your eyes. Feel the sense of calm and gratitude within, and take a moment to acknowledge the power you hold in your healing journey.

Why Gratitude Matters in Healing Trauma

Gratitude shifts our perspective from what has been lost to what is still here, from the pains of the past to the gifts of the present. It serves as a powerful antidote to resentment and anger, softening the hard edges of trauma and opening us to the possibilities of love and forgiveness. By practicing gratitude, you nurture your inner child, honor your emotional journey, and remind yourself that healing is possible with each mindful breath.

Practice Daily: Remember, consistency matters and is key. As you continue to practice gratitude, you may find that healing happens in small, gentle moments. The more we focus on the good in our lives, the more we create an internal environment where peace and joy can flourish. Incorporating gratitude as a daily practice can help sustain the emotional resilience needed to let go of the past and embrace a brighter future.

As we heal the wounds of our past, we step into the future with newfound clarity and strength. But healing is not a one-time event—it's a continuous process that requires awareness and intention. As we move forward, it's crucial to remain mindful of the patterns and behaviors that may still hold us back or pull us into old cycles. In the final chapter, we'll dive deeper into how we can recognize and break free from these self-sabotaging tendencies, ensuring that our journey toward wholeness remains steady and transformative.

As we heal the wounds of our past, we step into the future with newfound clarity and strength. But healing is not just about understanding our pain—it's about weaving that understanding into the fabric of our daily lives. True transformation happens when self-awareness becomes self-embodiment, when the lessons we've learned shape the way we move through the world. In the final chapter, we'll explore how to integrate this healing fully, ensuring that our growth is not just something we reflect on but something we live—with intention, with presence, and with an open heart.

Chapter Eight

Integration and Embodiment

The Compass to Continued Healing

We don't become healers. We came as healers. We don't become storytellers. We came as carriers of the stories we and our ancestors lived. We don't become artists. We came as artists. We don't become writers... dancers... musicians... helpers... peacemakers. We came as such. When we forget, we exile our true selves. When we remember, we return home. –Clarissa Pinkola Estés

This quote is a beautiful reminder that healing is not about becoming someone new—it is about remembering who you have always been—remembering who you were before the world told you who to be. The journey of inner child healing is not just about uncovering wounds, but about reclaiming the parts of yourself that have always been whole.

In this chapter, we shift our focus from healing as an act of discovery to healing as an act of embodiment. What happens after the breakthroughs, the deep emotional work, and the self-reflection? How do we live our healing journey every day—not as something separate from us, but as the very fabric of our being? Healing is a return, a homecoming, and this chapter will guide you in fully integrating everything you've learned so that it becomes second nature—woven into your thoughts, choices, and daily life.

This chapter is about integration—the sacred process of embodying everything you have learned. Think of healing as a seed you have planted deep within your soul. Awareness is the water, intention is the sunlight, and integration is the process of allowing it to grow strong enough to weather any storm. Without integration, healing remains theoretical, something understood but not fully embodied. True transformation happens when knowledge becomes practice, when insight shifts into action, when self-awareness moves beyond reflection and begins to shape the way you show up in the world.

Like a gravitational force, you may still feel the pull of old patterns, the whisper of self-doubt, the urge to retreat into the familiar. That is okay. Healing is not about erasing the past but about learning how to walk forward with all the parts of yourself, even the wounded ones, and choosing to respond in new ways. It is about developing the self-awareness to recognize when you are slipping into old wounds and the self-compassion to guide yourself back to center.

In this chapter, we explore how to maintain your healing through conscious self-awareness, embodied practices, and deep inner trust. You will learn how to remain present with yourself, nurture your emotional resilience, and continue growing into the person you were always meant to be. Healing is not just about what happens in quiet moments of introspection—it is about how you move through life, how you love, how you rise after setbacks, how you choose yourself over and over again.

This is the work of integration. This is where your healing becomes your way of being.

Recognizing When Old Patterns Resurface

Healing is not a straight path—it curves, doubles back, and sometimes leads us through familiar terrain before guiding us somewhere new. You may have spent months, even years, unraveling the patterns of your past, only to find yourself standing in their shadow once again. This is not failure. This is not proof that you have not healed. It is simply an invitation to deepen your awareness, to recognize where old wounds still whisper, and to meet them with a wiser, more compassionate gaze.

Old patterns do not always announce themselves with blaring sirens. Sometimes, they return as a whisper, a fleeting discomfort, a hesitation that tightens in your chest before you even realize why. Maybe you find yourself reacting defensively in an argument, as if bracing for an attack that isn't coming. Maybe you withdraw when a loved one offers intimacy, caught in an invisible tug-of-war between wanting connection and fearing it. Or perhaps you say "yes" when your heart is screaming "no," slipping back into people-pleasing before you even realize what's happened.

Recognizing these moments is an act of self-honesty. It requires you to pause, to step outside the automatic response, and ask: *Where have I felt this before? What am I protecting myself from? Is this a response to the present moment, or am I reacting from an old wound?*

The beauty of recognizing resurfaced patterns is that it allows you to shift from self-judgment to self-inquiry. Your triggers are not just obstacles;

they are messengers. When something stirs an emotional reaction within you—whether it be anger, fear, shame, or sadness—it is often pointing toward something unresolved.

Rather than berating yourself for falling back into old ways, see these moments as opportunities for deeper healing. Instead of saying, *I thought I was past this,* try saying, *This is another layer I am ready to explore.* Healing is a spiral, not a finish line. Each time a pattern resurfaces, it does so to offer you a chance to meet it differently—with more wisdom, more self-compassion, and more intentionality.

Keep an eye out for some signs that an old pattern is resurfacing:

- **Reactivity Over Response.** Your emotions feel heightened, disproportionate to the situation, or automatic rather than intentional.

- **Repeating Cycles in Relationships.** You find yourself in familiar relational dynamics—choosing emotionally unavailable partners, attracting controlling friendships, or struggling with the same conflicts.

- **Physical Sensations.** Your body remembers what your mind may have tried to forget. Pay attention to tightness in the chest, a sinking stomach, or tension in the jaw when certain situations arise.

- **Inner Narratives That Don't Serve You.** Thoughts like *I'm not good enough, No one truly cares,* or *I have to handle this alone* resurface, dragging you back into outdated beliefs.

Recognizing these signs is a profound act of self-love. It means you are paying attention. It means you are honoring your inner child's voice rather than silencing it. With this awareness, you can begin choosing differently.

Breaking Free from Cycles That No Longer Serve You

There comes a moment in every healing journey when awareness alone is no longer enough. You see the patterns. You recognize the triggers. You know the steps of the dance you've been performing for years—the one where you shrink, chase, avoid, overextend, or self-sabotage. And yet, the pull of the familiar can be deceptively strong. Even when we know something no longer serves us, stepping outside of it can feel like stepping into the unknown.

But freedom begins with a choice. A choice to no longer follow the well-worn path of the past. A choice to stand at the crossroads and take the road less traveled—the one where self-abandonment is no longer the cost of love, where you no longer mistake survival strategies for your identity, where you learn that growth, though uncomfortable, is the ultimate act of self-honoring.

Patterns do not break themselves. They are disrupted through deliberate, conscious action. Every time you catch yourself slipping into an old behavior—seeking external validation instead of looking inward, reacting with defensiveness instead of curiosity, silencing your needs instead of voicing them—you are standing at the precipice of change.

Ask yourself: *If I were someone who had already healed from this, what choice would I make right now?*

This simple question creates space. Space between impulse and action. Space between the past and the present. And in that space, you give yourself permission to respond differently.

One of the greatest barriers to breaking free from unhealthy cycles is the illusion of comfort. Familiarity feels safe, even when it isn't. The toxic relationship, the avoidance of intimacy, the need to prove your worth through overachieving—these may not make you happy, but they are known. And the nervous system craves what is known.

But growth requires discomfort. It requires learning to sit with the unease of choosing something new before it feels natural. When you say no to the friend who constantly takes but never gives, when you hold your boundary even when guilt tugs at you, when you let yourself receive love without earning it—you will feel off-balance at first. That is not a sign to go back. It is a sign you are stepping into something new.

Consider these steps to help you break the cycles that no longer serve you:

- **Name the Pattern.** A cycle cannot be broken if it remains unnamed. Write it down. Say it aloud. Bring it into the light. *I have a pattern of overgiving and feeling resentful. I have a pattern of fearing abandonment and clinging to relationships that are not good for me.*

- **Track Your Triggers.** Pay attention to when and where this pattern shows up most. What people, situations, or emotions tend to activate it? Awareness is the first step to conscious intervention.

- **Pause Before Reacting.** When you feel yourself slipping into an old behavior, take a deep breath. Count to five. Interrupt the automatic response. Then, ask yourself: *What would my healed self do?*

- **Introduce Small Shifts.** Change does not have to be drastic to be powerful. If you've always kept quiet about your needs, start by voicing small preferences. If you tend to avoid vulnerability, try sharing just one more layer of truth.

- **Rewrite the Inner Narrative.** Every pattern is rooted in a belief. If you continually overextend yourself, you may believe *I must be useful to be loved*. If you push love away, you may believe *I am safer alone*. Challenge these stories. Reframe them. *I am worthy without proving myself. I am safe in connection.*

- **Practice Until It Feels Natural.** The first few times you do something new, it will feel wrong. Your brain will resist. Your nervous system will protest. Keep going. Over time, the unfamiliar becomes second nature.

When you choose differently, everything shifts. The friendships that relied on your silence may fade, but deeper connections will emerge. The self-doubt that once ruled you will begin to soften, making space for self-trust. The version of you that lived in survival mode will slowly dissolve, revealing a self that moves with intention, clarity, and confidence.

This is the work of breaking free. It is uncomfortable. It is uncertain. But it is also liberation. And you are ready.

Cultivating Self-Trust and Inner Guidance

Breaking old cycles is only part of the journey; the next step is learning to trust yourself enough to navigate life without falling back into familiar wounds. Self-trust is not something we are born lacking—it is something that was taught out of us through inconsistency, invalidation, or betrayal in our formative years. If you were often told that your feelings were "too much," your needs were "inconvenient," or your instincts were "wrong," you may have learned to silence your inner voice in favor of external validation.

But healing is about reclaiming that voice. It is about tuning into your inner guidance—the deep, quiet knowing that exists beneath fear, conditioning, and past wounds.

Self-trust is not restored overnight. It is built in small, intentional moments—each time you listen to yourself and honor what you hear. The more you choose yourself, the louder your inner guidance becomes. The process looks something like this:

- **Create Space for Stillness.** The world is loud. The opinions of others can easily drown out our own. Carve out moments of silence—whether through meditation, nature walks, or simply sitting with your thoughts—to hear your own voice more clearly.

- **Validate Your Emotions.** Trust grows when we acknowledge our feelings rather than dismiss them. If something makes you uncomfortable, listen. If something feels off, pay attention. Your body and intuition speak in whispers before they ever scream.

- **Make Small Decisions for Yourself.** If trusting yourself feels overwhelming, start with the small things. Choose what you want to eat instead of what you think you should eat. Pick a book or movie based purely on what excites you, not what others recommend. Each time you make a choice based on your inner knowing, you strengthen the muscle of self-trust.

- **Follow Through on Commitments to Yourself.** Every time you break a promise to yourself, your subconscious learns that you are unreliable. Start with manageable commitments—drinking a glass of water in the morning, journaling for five minutes, stretching before bed. Show yourself that you can count on you.

- **Reflect on Past Times You Were Right.** Look back on moments when you had a gut feeling about something and it turned out to be accurate. Did you sense that a friendship wasn't genuine? Did you know deep down that a job or relationship wasn't right for you? Reminding yourself of these moments reinforces the idea that your intuition is worth trusting.

Distinguishing Fear from Intuition

One of the most challenging aspects of cultivating self-trust is learning to distinguish between intuition and fear. Fear is loud, chaotic, and urgent—it shouts at you to run, to fix, to control. Intuition, on the other hand, is quiet and steady. It does not panic. It simply knows.

Here's how to tell the difference:

- **Fear is Reactive; Intuition is Grounded.** Fear triggers immediate anxiety, urging you to act impulsively. Intuition, even when it warns you, carries a sense of clarity and calm.

- **Fear is Rooted in Past Wounds; Intuition is Anchored in the Present.** Fear often echoes old traumas—*What if I get hurt again? What if they leave me?* Intuition responds to what is actually happening now, rather than past pain.

- **Fear Speaks in "What Ifs"; Intuition Speaks in Certainty.** Fear spins worst-case scenarios, leading you in circles. Intuition is simple, direct, and unwavering: *This is not right for me. This* *path feels aligned.*

When in doubt, take a breath. Drop into your body. Ask yourself: *Is this fear from an old wound, or is my intuition trying to protect me?*

When you learn to trust yourself, you stop seeking permission to live life on your own terms. You stop outsourcing decisions to others. You stop doubting your own emotions and instincts. You learn that you *already know*—that the answers you've been looking for have always existed within you.

Rebuilding self-trust is one of the most powerful gifts you can give yourself. Because once you trust yourself, you no longer need to chase certainty outside of you. You *are* the certainty. And that, more than anything, is what sets you free.

Nurturing Growth Through Conscious Daily Practices

Healing is not a one-time event—it is a lifelong commitment to self-awareness, self-compassion, and conscious action. Just as wounds do not form overnight, neither does deep transformation. Growth requires consistency, patience, and the willingness to show up for yourself every single day. It is not about perfection but about intention—small, mindful choices that slowly reshape the way you move through the world.

Morning Rituals to Set the Tone for Healing

The way we begin our day has a profound impact on our mindset. If we start in a rush, overwhelmed before we even step out of bed, we set ourselves up for disconnection. But if we begin with intentionality—grounding ourselves before engaging with the outside world—we create space for growth.

Try incorporating one of these simple practices into your morning routine:

- **Mindful Awakening.** Before reaching for your phone, place a hand on your heart, take a deep breath, and ask yourself, *How do I feel right now? What do I need today?* This small act of self-awareness helps you tune in before external distractions take over.

- **Gratitude Practice.** Keep a small notebook by your bed and write down three things you're grateful for each morning. Gratitude shifts your focus away from lack and toward abundance, helping you start the day with an open heart.

- **Setting an Intention.** Choose a word or phrase to carry with you throughout the day. *Today, I will be kind to myself. I will practice presence. I will set boundaries with confidence.* Setting an intention acts as a compass, guiding your actions and thoughts.

- **Grounding Movement.** Whether it's stretching, yoga, or simply standing outside and breathing in the fresh air, moving your body first thing in the morning helps you feel more present and connected.

Even five minutes of mindful morning practice can shift the energy of your entire day. The key is not how much you do, but how intentional you are in doing it.

Infusing Mindfulness into the Ordinary

Growth does not only happen in therapy sessions, journal pages, or meditation cushions—it happens in the small, ordinary moments of daily life. It happens in the way you pour your coffee, the way you take a deep breath before responding to frustration, the way you notice beauty in the simplest things.

Here are ways to practice mindfulness throughout your day:

- **Pause Before Reacting.** When you feel triggered, take a breath before responding. Ask yourself, *Am I reacting from an old wound, or from my present self?*

- **Turn Daily Tasks into Rituals.** Instead of rushing through chores, bring presence to them. Feel the warmth of the water as you wash dishes, listen to the rhythm of your footsteps as you walk, savor the flavors of your food as you eat.

- **Use Reminders to Check In.** Set an alarm on your phone or place a sticky note where you'll see it with a simple prompt: *Breathe. Be here now. How am I feeling?*

- **Engage in Deep Listening.** When in conversation, give your full, undivided attention to that person, while setting aside your own judgements, thoughts, and responses. Truly listen—not just to their words, but to their tone, their emotion, and their body language.

- **Find Moments of Stillness.** Whether it's sitting in silence for a few minutes, staring up at the sky, or listening to the sounds around you, carve out moments to simply *be*.

Mindfulness is not about adding more to your to-do list; it is about bringing awareness to what you are already doing.

Evening Practices to Reflect and Reset

Just as mornings set the tone for the day, evenings provide an opportunity to reflect, process, and release. Winding down with intention helps us close the day with gratitude and prepares us to rest with a sense of peace.

Consider adding one of these practices to your nightly routine:

- **Journaling.** Write down a few thoughts about your day. What emotions came up? What are you proud of yourself for? What is something you learned?

- **Releasing Tension.** Take a few minutes to stretch or do deep breathing exercises before bed to release any tension your body may be holding onto.

- **Emotional Check-In.** Before sleeping, place a hand over your heart and ask yourself, *How do I feel? What do I need to let go of before tomorrow?*

- **Gratitude Reflection.** Mentally list three things that brought you joy today, no matter how small. Channeling the emotion of gratitude before you go to sleep can do wonders for relaxing your nervous system as it shifts the mind toward appreciation, fostering a sense of contentment.

By bookending your day with mindful awareness, you cultivate a continuous connection to yourself—ensuring that healing is not just something you think about, but something you live.

You will not always get it right. Some days, you will forget to be mindful. You will react instead of pausing. You will fall back into old patterns. But healing is not about never slipping—it is about noticing when you do and choosing to return to yourself with compassion.

Healing is found in the return—the moments when you catch yourself slipping into old patterns and gently choose a new way forward, realigning with the person you are becoming.

With every mindful moment, every act of self-awareness, and every choice to show up for yourself, you reinforce a new way of being—one where healing is not just an abstract concept, but a lived, embodied experience.

The Power of Daily Check-Ins

Just as a garden requires consistent tending, so too does the inner landscape of your heart and mind. Without regular care, the weeds of old wounds and unconscious patterns can creep back in, tangling themselves into the progress you've made.

This is where daily check-ins become a powerful tool for transformation. They are moments of intentional pause, an opportunity to ground yourself in the present and assess the state of your emotions, thoughts, and energy. A check-in does not need to be elaborate; it is not a test you must pass or a duty to perform perfectly. It is simply an act of self-listening, a willingness to turn toward yourself with curiosity rather than judgment.

Begin with a breath. Close your eyes, inhale deeply, and allow yourself to settle into your body. Ask yourself:

- *What emotions are moving through me right now?*

- *Is there tension or ease in my body? Where am I holding energy?*

- *What thoughts have been occupying my mind today? Are they rooted in love or fear?*

- *Have I acted in alignment with my values, or have I slipped into old habits?*

- *What is one small act of care I can offer myself today?*

Sometimes, the answers will be clear. Other times, they may feel murky, just out of reach. That's okay. The goal here is not to force clarity but to create space for self-awareness. When we build the habit of checking in, we become more attuned to the subtle shifts in our inner world, recognizing unhealthy patterns before they spiral into problematic, unconscious behaviors.

Daily check-ins are a practice of devotion to yourself. They remind you that healing is not about being perfect, but about being present. They give you permission to be both a masterpiece and a work in progress—to hold space for the person you are and the person you are becoming, all at once.

Embracing Growth Without Perfection

Personal growth is often romanticized as a graceful ascent—a steady climb toward a wiser, more enlightened self. But in reality, growth is messy. It is filled with stops and starts, breakthroughs and backslides, moments of clarity followed by moments of doubt. The path is not straight, nor is it always well-lit. Some days, progress feels effortless; on others, it feels like wading through thick fog, unsure of which way to turn.

This is why embracing growth requires releasing the illusion of perfection. Healing does not demand flawlessness. It does not require that you never fall back into old habits or have moments of struggle. Instead, it asks for your willingness to return—to notice when you've veered off course and to gently guide yourself back, again and again.

Think of the moon. It does not shine at full brilliance every night. Some nights, it is barely a sliver in the sky, and yet, it is no less whole. Your healing is the same. You will not always feel radiant, strong, or deeply connected to your progress. Some days, you may feel like you have regressed. But just as the moon waxes and wanes, you are always moving through cycles of growth, even in moments of seeming darkness.

Self-compassion is what allows you to continue forward. Instead of shaming yourself when you falter, can you offer yourself the same kindness you would a close friend? When you stumble, can you see it not as failure, but as proof that you are still learning, still human, still growing?

The true measure of healing is not in never struggling again—it is in how quickly you catch yourself, how gently you self-correct, and how much love you offer yourself in the process.

Staying Committed to Your Healing in the Long Run

Healing is more than just a phase—it is a lifelong relationship with yourself. In the beginning, your growth may feel exhilarating, each breakthrough a confirmation that you're on the right path. But what happens when the momentum slows? When life gets busy, stress piles up, and old patterns resurface? This is where true commitment begins—not in the grand moments of clarity, but in the quiet decision to keep showing up for yourself, even when it feels difficult.

Imagine tending to a vast, untamed garden. At first, the work is obvious—pulling the weeds, breaking the hardened earth, planting new seeds. Each day brings visible progress, and the transformation is exciting. But as time passes, the changes become subtler. Some days, all you can do is water the soil and trust that the roots are growing beneath the surface. There will be dry spells when nothing seems to flourish, and monsoon seasons when storms threaten to undo all you've worked for. But healing, like tending a garden, is an act of patience, of faith, of returning—again and again—to nurture what is growing, even when you cannot yet see the blooms.

Remember these words when your momentum falters, when your healing journey feels suspended in the quiet limbo between what was and what has yet to be:

- **Redefine What "Progress" Looks Like.** Growth isn't always measurable. Some days, healing looks like self-reflection and breakthroughs. Other days, it looks like simply getting out of bed and doing your best. Let go of the need to constantly feel like you're making progress—sometimes, the most profound changes happen beneath the surface.

- **Anchor Yourself with Practices that Evolve with You.** The tools that help you today may not be the same ones you need a year from now. Be open to changing your approach. Maybe journaling worked for you before, but now movement or creative expression feels more aligned. Stay flexible in your healing, allowing your methods to shift as you grow.

- **Know When to Take a Step Back.** Healing isn't about constantly digging into your past or forcing yourself to process emotions every single day. Sometimes, the best thing you can do is step away, live your life, and trust that healing is happening in the background. Honor your need for rest, for play, and for moments of simply being.

- **Return to Your "Why."** When the journey feels long or exhausting, reconnect with why you started in the first place. What kind of life are you building for yourself? What patterns are you breaking for future generations? What version of yourself are you trying to become? Let your "why" guide you through the moments of doubt.

The garden of your healing does not require you to toil over it every moment of every day. Some days, tending to it means digging deep, turning over the soil of your past. Other days, it means resting in the shade, trusting that the work you've already done is enough. And still, the seeds you've planted will grow—slowly, steadily, in their own time.

Interactive Element

Personal growth and healing is not just about what we understand—it's about what we practice. Integration is the bridge between knowing and becoming. These exercises will help you consciously embody your healing in everyday life, deepening your self-awareness, strengthening your emotional resilience, and anchoring your personal growth in the present moment.

The Integration Journal: A Week of Embodiment

For the next seven days, set aside 10–15 minutes each evening to reflect on how you embodied your healing throughout the day. Use the following prompts to explore your journey:

- **Awareness Check-In.** *What moments stood out to me today? Did I notice myself falling into old thought patterns or emotional reactions?*

- **Compassion in Action.** *How did I show up for myself today? Did I practice self-kindness, self-trust, or self-respect in any way?*

- **Triggers & Growth Opportunities.** *Was there a situation that challenged me today? How did I handle it differently than I might have in the past?*

- **Small Wins.** *What is one small but meaningful way I honored my healing journey today?*

- **Looking Ahead.** *What is one way I can embody my healing more deeply tomorrow?*

Optional Expansion: If you enjoy creative expression, consider incorporating doodles, poetry, or symbolic imagery in your journal. Allow it to become a living, breathing reflection of your personal transformation.

Why this works: Journaling helps anchor your healing in real-time, giving you a tangible record of your growth and reinforcing positive change in your subconscious.

The Embodiment Mirror: Speaking to Your Healed Self

This practice may feel unfamiliar at first, but eye contact with yourself is a powerful act of self-acceptance. Stand in front of a mirror, take a few deep breaths, and look yourself in the eyes. At first, just observe—without judgment—what emotions arise. Do you feel resistance? Tenderness? Discomfort?

Then, speak to yourself as if you are your own loving mentor, guiding the version of you who is still learning, healing, and growing. Say things like:

- *I see how far you've come, and I am so proud of you.*
- *You no longer live in survival mode—you are safe, worthy, and whole.*
- *It's okay to make mistakes. Growth isn't about perfection; it's about showing up.*
- *Keep choosing yourself. Keep listening to your heart. Keep going.*

If certain affirmations feel uncomfortable, lean into *why*. Those areas of resistance often point to the wounds that need the most love.

Why this works: Self-recognition is essential to healing. When you validate yourself, you are rewiring the subconscious belief that worthiness must come from external sources. Over time, this practice strengthens self-trust and emotional security.

The Daily Integration Practice: Embodying Healing in Action

The true measure of healing is how we show up for ourselves in ordinary moments. For the next week, choose one of the following healing commitments to practice daily.

Option 1: Mindful Mornings—Setting the Tone for Healing

- Begin each day without immediately reaching for your phone.
- Instead, take three deep breaths and set an intention:
    - *Today, I choose to be present with myself.*
    - *Today, I honor my emotions without judgment and welcome them with compassion.*
    - *I choose to move through the day with grace and self-trust, knowing that I am enough as I am.*
    - *Just for today, I will focus on being mindful of my internal dialogue.*
- Stretch, journal, or simply place a hand on your heart and check in: *How am I feeling this morning?*

Why this works: How we start our mornings shapes the energy we carry throughout the day. A mindful morning creates an anchor of self-awareness before external distractions take over.

Option 2: Self-Compassion Check-Ins—Transforming Inner Criticism

- Every time you catch a negative thought about yourself, pause and ask: *Would I speak to a child or a dear friend this way?*

- Gently reframe the thought:
    - *Instead of I'm not good enough,* try *I am learning and growing every day.*
    - *Instead of I always mess things up,* try *Every mistake teaches me something valuable.*

Why this works: Self-compassion builds emotional resilience and interrupts old patterns of self-criticism.

Option 3: Present-Moment Awareness—The Art of Simply Being

- Choose an ordinary activity to do with full presence—drinking tea, brushing your hair, walking outside.

- Engage all five senses: *How does the tea taste? How does the air feel on your skin?*

- When your mind drifts, gently bring it back to the present moment.

Why this works: Awareness transforms even mundane moments into opportunities for connection and grounding.

INTEGRATION AND EMBODIMENT

Option 4: Nurturing Relationships—Breaking Old Patterns

- Before reacting in conversations, pause and ask: *Am I responding from my wounded self or my healed self?*

- If a loved one upsets you, take a breath before speaking. Choose curiosity over defensiveness: *What might they be feeling right now?*

- Practice expressing needs clearly instead of expecting others to guess.

Why this works: Many of our old wounds stem from relationships. Healing must also happen through relationships—by choosing healthier ways to connect.

Remember, healing is not something you complete. It is something you live.

It is in the conversations you have with yourself, the way you hold space for your emotions, and the way you choose to respond rather than react. It is in how you treat yourself on difficult days and the small, quiet choices you make each day to nurture your growth.

Which of these practices resonated with you the most? How will you integrate healing into your daily life?

Final Thoughts

Healing takes courage, and that is a little something that all of us have. It's the spark in us that drives us to rise each morning, to face the challenges that the day brings, and to keep pushing forward, even when the world seems to weigh heavy on our shoulders. It's that ember of resolve that glows within us, often unnoticed until we need it most.

Think of a vast landscape, with mountains and valleys, rivers and forests. This is the terrain of your soul, a mirror of the life you have lived. There are places where the sun always shines, filled with the memories of joy and love. There are also shadowy valleys where past hurts and traumas reside, places we often avoid for fear of the pain they hold.

The journey to heal your inner child is a trek across this terrain, a brave expedition to those dark valleys. It's a voyage that demands courage, but one that holds the promise of transformation. You'll need to scale the steep cliffs of past wounds, trek through the dense forests of self-doubt, and navigate the swift rivers of deeply buried emotions. Yet, with every step, you lighten your load, shedding the weight of past burdens and making room for new growth.

Your inner child waits for you in these valleys. They are the part of you that was hurt, the part that felt neglected, misunderstood, or unloved. They are also the part of you that holds the keys to your healing. They carry the wisdom of your pain and the lessons of your past. Embrace them, listen to them, and you'll find that they have much to teach you about who you are and who you can become.

As you journey, remember that healing is not a destination but a continual process. There will be times when the road is rough, when the weather is harsh, and when you want to turn back. But courage does not mean the absence of fear or pain. It means choosing to move forward despite them.

Picture your courage as a small flame that you carry with you on your journey. The wind may howl, the rain may pour, but your flame continues to burn. It illuminates your path, warms you in the cold nights, and serves as a beacon when you've lost your way. And as you heal, your flame grows brighter, stronger, casting long shadows behind you and lighting the way ahead.

On this journey, you are not alone. Imagine a host of fellow travelers, each on their own journey of healing. They traverse their own landscapes, carry their own flames. They understand your struggle, for it mirrors their own. They are your support, your community, your tribe. Together, you are a constellation of healing lights, each flame a testament to the courage it takes to face your past, embrace your pain, and heal your inner child.

The journey to heal your inner child is a profound voyage of self-discovery and transformation. It's a testament to the strength and resilience that resides within each of us. It's a journey that requires courage, but as you travel, you'll find that you have more courage than you ever knew—for within you is a flame of resolve, a beacon of hope, and an unquenchable spirit of healing. Remember, your inner child, your past, and your pain do not define you—but your courage to heal does.

Thank You & A Special Request

Dear Reader,

If you've made it to this page, I want to pause and say thank you—not just for reading, but for allowing me to walk alongside you on this journey of healing. Writing this book was a deeply personal experience, and knowing that it found its way into your hands means more than I can express.

If this book touched you, challenged you, or supported you in any way, I humbly ask for a small favor: **please leave a review.**

Your review does more than help me as an indie author—it helps others who are searching for guidance, just like you. When you share your thoughts, you make it easier for someone else to take that first step toward inner healing.

Even a few heartfelt words can make all the difference. Thank you for being part of this mission to spread healing, self-love, and transformation.

With immense gratitude,

Barbara Oshenska

References

Ackerman, C. (2016, December 13). *The pursuit of happiness: Using the power of positive emotions*. PositivePsychology.com. https://positivepsychology.com/benefits-of-positive-emotions/

Aletheia. (2024, June 1). *25 signs you have a wounded inner child (and how to heal)* LonerWolf. https://lonerwolf.com/feeling-safe-inner-child/

Amen Clinic. (n.d.). *6 ways childhood trauma impacts adult relationships*. https://www.amenclinics.com/blog/6-ways-childhood-trauma-impacts-adult-relationships/

Beck, J. S. (2011). *Cognitive behavior therapy: Basics and beyond (2nd ed.)*. Guilford Press.

de Becker, G. (2000). *The Gift of Fear: Survival Signals That Protect Us from Violence*. Bloomsbury Publishing PLC.

BetterHelp Editorial Team. (2024a, October 9). *How does childhood trauma affect adulthood and Emotional Well-Being?* Betterhelp. https://www.betterhelp.com/advice/childhood/how-does-childhood-trauma-affect-adulthood/

BetterHelp Editorial Team. (2024, October 28). *4 Ways that adverse childhood experiences affect adults*. Better-Help. https://www.betterhelp.com/advice/childhood/4-ways-that-adverse-childhood-experiences-affect-adults/

Bowlby, J. (1988). *A Secure Base: Clinical Applications of Attachment Theory*. Routledge.

Boyes, A. (n.d.). *30 types of self-sabotage (and what to do about it)*. Psychology Today. https://www.psychologytoday.com/za/blog/in-practice/201805/30-types-of-self-sabotage-and-what-to-do-about-it

Brach, T. (2003). *Radical acceptance: Embracing Your Life with the Heart of a Buddha*. Bantam.

Brain First. (n.d.). *Somatic awareness: The science of connecting mind and body*. https://www.brainfirsttraininginstitute.com/blog/somatic-awareness-the-science-of-connecting-mind-and-body

Brown, B. (2010). *The Gifts of Imperfection: Let Go of Who You Think You're Supposed to Be and Embrace Who You Are*. Hazelden.

Brown, B. (2012). *Daring Greatly: How the Courage to Be Vulnerable Transforms the Way We Live, Love, Parent, and Lead*. Penguin Random House

Brown, B. (2017). *Braving the Wilderness: The Quest for True Belonging and the Courage to Stand Alone*. New York: Random House.

Brown, K. W., & Ryan, R. M. (2003). *The benefits of being present: Mindfulness and its role in psychological well-being*. Journal of Personality and Social Psychology, 84(4), 822–848. https://doi.org/10.1037/0022-3514.84.4.822

Campbell, K. (2017, September 7). *How to identify your emotional triggers and what to* Tiny Buddha. https://tinybuddha.com/blog/how-to-identify-your-emotional-triggers-what-to-do-about-them/

Celestine, N., Ph.D. (2021, December 16). *What is zen therapy? The influence of buddhism in psychology*. PositivePsychology.com. http://www.antibullycampaign.org/index-652.html

REFERENCES

Cherry, K., MSEd. (2024b, March 6). *20 defense mechanisms we use to protect ourselves*. Verywell Mind. https://www.verywellmind.com/defense-mechanisms-2795960

Children's Bureau. (2018, September 25). *Why the first 5 years of child development are so important*. https://www.all4kids.org/news/blog/why-the-first-5-years-of-child-development-are-so-important/

Chödrön, P. (2001). *The Wisdom of No Escape and the Path of Loving-Kindness*. Shambhala.

Chowdhury, M. R. (2019, August 13). *Emotional regulation: 6 key skills to regulate emotions*. Positive Psychology. https://positivepsychology.com/emotion-regulation/

Cmurray. (2019, April 16). *Healthy vs. Unhealthy Boundaries – Healthy Relationships Initiative*. https://healthyrelationshipsinitiative.org/healthy-vs-unhealthy-boundaries/

Counseling, C. (2022, October 17). *Unpacking your past relationships: Advice from a relationship counselor*. Catalyss Counseling. https://www.catalysscounseling.com/post/unpacking-your-past-relationships-advice-from-a-relationship-counselor

CTRI. (2017, May 4). *Trauma: The brain-body-mind connection - crisis & trauma resource institute*. Ctrinstitute.com. https://ctrinstitute.com/blog/trauma-brain-body-mind-connection/

Dale, C. (1999). *The Subtle Body: An Encyclopedia of Your Energetic Anatomy*. Sounds True.

Darcy, A. (2019, June 4). *The real reason your self worth is low - and how to fix it*. Harley Therapy™ Blog. https://www.harleytherapy.co.uk/counselling/low-self-worth.htm

Davis, K. (n.d.). *5 Ways your childhood affects your romantic relationship*. Dr. Kristin Davin, Psy.D. https://reflectionsfromacrossthecouch.com/blog/5-ways-how-your-childhood-affects-your-romantic-relationships

Davis, S. (2020, July 13). *The wounded inner child*. CPTSD Foundation. https://cptsdfoundation.org/2020/07/13/the-wounded-inner-child/

Deci, E. L., & Ryan, R. M. (2000). The "What" and "Why" of goal pursuits: human needs and the Self-Determination of behavior. Psychological Inquiry, 11(4), 227–268. https://doi.org/10.1207/s15327965pli1104_01

Duval, S., & Wicklund, R.A. (1972). *A theory of objective self-awareness*. New York: Academic Press.

Earnshaw, E. (2019, July 20). *6 Types of boundaries you deserve to have (and how to maintain them)*. MindBodyGreen. https://www.mindbodygreen.com/articles/six-types-of-boundaries-and-what-healthy-boundaries-look-like-for-each

Ellis, A. (2001). *Feeling Better, Getting Better, Staying Better: Profound Self-Help Therapy for Your Emotions*. Impact Publishers.

Enright, R. D., & Fitzgibbons, R. P. (2000). *Helping clients forgive: An empirical guide for resolving anger and restoring hope*. American Psychological Association. https://doi.org/10.1037/10381-000

Erikson, E. H. (1968). *Identity, Youth, and Crisis*. Norton & Company.

Estrada, J. (2022, December 10). *How healed is your inner child? These are 8 strong signs. Well+Good*. https://www.wellandgood.com/signs-youre-healing-your-inner-child/

Eurich, T. (2023, April 6). *What self-awareness really is (and how to cultivate It)*. Harvard Business Review. https://hbr.org/2018/01/what-self-awareness-really-is-and-how-to-cultivate-it

Family Tree. (2016, July 12). *3 Tips for recalling your childhood memories*. Family Tree Magazine.

Gaiam. (2019). *Deepak chopra's 7-step exercise to release emotional turbulence*. Gaiam. https://www.gaiam.com/blogs/discover/deepak-chopras-7-step-exercise-to-release-emotional-turbulence

Gilbert, P. (2010). *Compassion Focused Therapy: Distinctive Features*. Routledge.

Goleman, D. (1995). *Emotional Intelligence: Why It Can Matter More Than IQ*. Bantam Books

GoodTherapy Editor Team. (2019, September 6). *Helplessness / victimhood therapy, helplessness / victimhood therapist*. GoodTherapy. https://www.goodtherapy.org/learn-about-therapy/issues/helplessness

Greenberg, M., PhD. (2019, August 13). *How traumas create negative patterns in relationships*. Psychology Today. https://www.psychologytoday.com/intl/blog/the-mindful-self-express/201908/how-traumas-create-negative-patterns-in-relationships

Jannyca. (2023, February 10). *Yoga's koshas: The 5 layers of self-awareness*. YogaUOnline. https://yogauonline.com/yoga-basics/koshas-5-layers-of-self-awareness/

JHV. (n.d.). *Balancing inner child, outward adult most important of struggles*. Jhvonline.com. https://jhvonline.com/balancing-inner-child-outward-adult-most-important-of-struggles-p23299-153.htm

Johns Hopkins Medicine. (2019). *Forgiveness: Your health depends on it*. Johns Hopkins Medicine. https://www.hopkinsmedicine.org/health/wellness-and-prevention/forgiveness-your-health-depends-on-it

Judith, Anodea. (1987). *Wheels of Life: A User's Guide to the Chakra System*. Llewellyn Publications.

Kabat-Zinn, J. (1990). *Full Catastrophe Living: Using the Wisdom of Your Body and Mind to Face Stress, Pain, and Illness*. New York: Delacorte.

Kabat-Zinn, J. (1994). *Wherever You Go, There You Are: Mindfulness Meditation in Everyday Life*. New York: Hyperion.

Kabat-Zinn, J. (2018). Meditation *is not what you think: Mindfulness and why it is so important*. Hachette Books.

Kosslyn, S. M., & Moulton, S. T. (2009). *Mental imagery and implicit memory*. In K. D. Markman, W. M. P. Klein, & J. A. Suhr (Eds.), *Handbook of imagination and mental simulation* (pp. 35–51). Psychology Press.

Kyeong, S., Kim, J., Kim, D. et al. (2017). *Effects of gratitude meditation on neural network functional connectivity and brain-heart coupling*. Scientific Reports, 7, 5058.

Laine, K. (2022, September 6). *7 ways chakra healing can help you cope with past traumas*. YouAligned™. https://youaligned.com/mindfulness/chakra-healing-past-trauma/

Lawler, K. A., et al. (2003). *A Change of Heart: Cardiovascular Correlates of Forgiveness in Response to Interpersonal Conflict*. Journal of Behavioral Medicine, 26(5), 373-393. https://doi.org/10.1023/A:1025771716686

Leachman, A., & Leachman, A. (2023, July 19). *The rejection wound.* Clear Your Head Trash. https://clearyourheadtrash.com/blog/the-rejection-wound/

Leachman, A., & Leachman, A. (2023a, July 19). *The injustice wound.* Clear Your Head Trash. https://clearyourheadtrash.com/htc-tips/the-injustice-wound/

Leachman, A., & Leachman, A. (2023a, July 19). *The humiliation wound.* Clear Your Head Trash. https://clearyourheadtrash.com/articles/the-humiliation-wound/

Leahy, R. L. (2017). *Cognitive therapy techniques: A practitioner's guide (2nd ed.).* Guilford Press.

Lets Pause. (2021, May 14). *How to use breathwork to release stuck emotions & energy in the body.* Pause Breathwork. https://www.pausebreathwork.com/how-to-use-breathwork-to-release-stuck-emotions-energy-in-the-body-2/

Levine, Peter A. (1997). *Waking the Tiger: Healing Trauma.* North Atlantic Books.

Linder, J. (2019, April 18). *How mindfulness can reshape negative thought patterns.* Psychology Today. https://www.psychologytoday.com/us/blog/mindfulness-insights/201904/how-mindfulness-can-reshape-negative-thought-patterns

Linehan, M. M. (2014). *DBT® skills training manual.* Guilford Publications.

Lipton, B. H. (2005). *The Biology of Belief: Unleashing the Power of Consciousness, Matter & Miracles.* Mountain of Love/Elite Books.

Mate, G. (2003). *When the Body Says No: Understanding the Stress-Disease Connection*. Vintage Canada.

McIlroy, T. (2024, September 26). *The stages of emotional development in early childhood*. Empowered Parents. https://empoweredparents.co/emotional-development-stages/

Meinke, H. (2019, December 30). *Understanding the stages of emotional development in children*. Rasmussen University. https://www.rasmussen.edu/degrees/education/blog/stages-of-emotional-development/

Myss, Caroline. (1996). *Anatomy of the Spirit: The Seven Stages of Power and Healing*. Harmony Books.

Nakken, C. (2009). *The Addictive Personality: Understanding the Addictive Process and Compulsive Behavior*. Simon and Schuster.

Neenan, M., & Dryden, W. (2010). *Cognitive Therapy: 100 Key Points and Techniques*. Routledge.

Neff, K. (2011). *Self-Compassion: The Proven Power of Being Kind to Yourself*. William Morrow.

NIH News. (n.d.). *The real purpose behind your negative emotions*. The happiness doctor. https://www.thehappinessdoctor.com/blog/negative-emotions-purpose

NSPCC. (2020). *Children's stories*. NSPCC. https://www.nspcc.org.uk/what-is-child-abuse/childrens-stories/

Palmer, J. (2019, October 9). *Social and emotional development in early learning settings*. NCSL. https://www.ncsl.org/human-services/social-and-emotional-development-in-early-learning-settings

Pennebaker, J. W., & Chung, C. K. (2007). *Expressive writing, emotional upheavals, and health.* Foundations of health psychology, 263-284.

Porges, S. W. (2011). *The Polyvagal Theory: Neurophysiological Foundations of Emotions, Attachment, Communication, and Self-Regulation.* W.W. Norton & Company.

Positive Emotions and Your Health. (2018, November). *Positive emotions and your health.* NIH News in Health. https://newsinhealth.nih.gov/2015/08/positive-emotions-your-health

Post, G. (2017, October 26). *Walk in their little shoes: Understanding your child's point of view.* Children's Literacy Foundation. https://clifonline.org/walk-in-their-little-shoes-understanding-your-childs-point-of-view/

Pryce, A. (2019, December 24). *The wounded child who's scared and running your life.* Tiny Buddha. https://tinybuddha.com/blog/the-wounded-child-whos-scared-and-running-your-life/

Rossman, M. (2000). *Guided Imagery for Self-Healing.* New World Library.

Rothschild, B. (2000). *The Body Remembers: The Psychophysiology of Trauma and Trauma Treatment.* W. W. Norton & Company.

Rubin, D. C. (2014). *Memory in Oral Traditions: The Cognitive Psychology of Epic, Ballads, and Counting-out Rhymes.* Oxford University Press.

Salzberg, S. (1995). *Lovingkindness: The Revolutionary Art of Happiness.* Shambhala.

Schwartz, J. M., & Begley, S. (2002). *The Mind and the Brain: Neuroplasticity and the Power of Mental Force.* Harper Perennial.

Shapiro, S. L., Oman, D., Thoresen, C. E., Plante, T. G., & Flinders, T. (2008). *Cultivating mindfulness: effects on well-being.* Journal of Clinical Psychology, 64(7), 840–862. https://doi.org/10.1002/jclp.20491

Siegel, D. J. (2010). *Mindsight: The New Science of Personal Transformation.* Bantam.

Siegel, D. J. (2012). *The Developing Mind: How Relationships and the Brain Interact to Shape Who We Are.* New York: Guilford Press.

Singer, M. A. (2007). *The Untethered Soul: The Journey Beyond Yourself.* New Harbinger Publications.

Souders, B. (2019, July 4). *What is forgiveness and what are the benefits?* PositivePsychology.com. https://positivepsychology.com/forgiveness-benefits/

Stålberg, A., Sandberg, A., Söderbäck, M., & Larsson, T. (2016). *The child's perspective as a guiding principle: Young children as co-designers in the design of an interactive application meant to facilitate participation in healthcare situations.* Journal of Biomedical Informatics, 61, 149–158. https://doi.org/10.1016/j.jbi.2016.03.024

Sutin, A. R., & Robins, R. W. (2008). *When the "I" looks at the "me": Autobiographical memory, visual perspective, and the self.* Consciousness and Cognition: An International Journal, 17(4), 1386–1397. https://doi.org/10.1016/j.concog.2008.09.001

Team, M. (2020, October 21). *The facts (+ tips) about healing trauma through meditation.* Mindworks Meditation. https://mindworks.org/blog/healing-trauma-through-meditation/

The Newman Group, Inc. (2023, September 25). *Use mindfulness to increase your self-awareness and effectiveness*. Presenting Yourself and More. https://www.presenting-yourself.com/mindfulness-post/

Therapy Directory. (n.d.). *The chakras and the emotions*. https://www.therapy-directory.org.uk/memberarticles/the-chakras-and-the-emotions

Thewellness. (2016, March 27). *Story and testimonials - inner child work & healing from within*. Wellness Space. https://wellness-space.net/story-and-testimonials-inner-child-work-healing-from-within/

Tolle, E. (2004). *The Power of Now: A Guide to Spiritual Enlightenment*. New World Library.

Toussaint, L.L., Owen, A.D. & Cheadle, A. (2012). *Forgive to Live: Forgiveness, Health, and Longevity*. Journal of Behavioral Medicine, 35(4), 375–386. https://doi.org/10.1007/s10865-011-9362-4

Trieu, T. (2020, December 31). *5 signs you may need to heal your inner child & how to start*. Mindbodygreen. https://www.mindbodygreen.com/articles/inner-child-work

University of Rochester Medical Center. (2019). *Journaling for mental health*. Rochester.edu. https://www.urmc.rochester.edu/encyclopedia/content.aspx?ContentID=4552&ContentTypeID=1

Van Der Kolk, Bessel. (2015). *The Body Keeps the Score: Brain, Mind, and Body in the Healing of Trauma*. Penguin Books.

Wade, D. (2022, January 26). *Can you change core beliefs?* Psych Central. https://psychcentral.com/health/core-beliefs-examples

Winfrey, O. (2021, July 25). *Oprah says this one act can change the way you move through the world.* Oprah Daily. https://www.oprahdaily.com/life/a37117486/oprah-forgiveness/

Worthington, E. L., & Scherer, M. (2004). *Forgiveness Is an Emotion-Focused Coping Strategy That Can Reduce Health Risks and Promote Health Resilience: Theory, Review, and Hypotheses.* Psychology & Health, 19(3), 385-405. https://doi.org/10.1080/0887044042000196674

Writer, S. (2019, November 7). *How to heal your inner child in seven steps | solara mental health.* Solaramentalhealth.com.

Young, G. (n.d.). *Symbology of the child – gigi young.* Gigiyoung.com. https://gigiyoung.com/symbology-of-the-child/

Young, J. E., Klosko, J. S., & Weishaar, M. E. (2003). *Schema therapy: A practitioner's guide.* Guilford Press.

Zukav, G. (2014). *The Seat of the Soul: 25th Anniversary Edition with a Study Guide.* Simon and Schuster.

About the Author

Barbara Oshenska is a writer, scientist, and self-proclaimed **pedantic lunatic** (her words, not ours). With a background in forensic science and a master's degree to prove it, she has spent years analyzing scientific data, but her greatest investigation has always been the human experience—unraveling the mysteries of healing, self-awareness, and the untamed power of the soul.

A dedicated **CrossFit athlete for over a decade**, Barbara has been immersed in health, fitness, and holistic wellness since the early 2000s. She believes in the deep connection between mind, body, and spirit—how strength isn't just physical, but something built through resilience, self-discovery, and the willingness to face life's challenges head-on.

When she's not in the lab, writing or training, Barbara can usually be found **wandering the wilderness**, whether on a short trail or a multi-day backpacking trek. She believes there's nothing quite like the whisper of the trees, the call of distant mountains, and the grounding presence of the earth beneath her feet to bring clarity and connection.

If you enjoyed this book, she'd love to hear from you—preferably in the form of a glowing five-star review, but she'll accept an interpretive dance if that's more your style.

www.ingramcontent.com/pod-product-compliance
Lightning Source LLC
Chambersburg PA
CBHW050853160426
43194CB00011B/2144